AFTERWORD

AfterWord

CONJURING THE LITERARY DEAD

Edited by Dale Salwak

UNIVERSITY OF IOWA PRESS IOWA CITY

University of Iowa Press, Iowa City 52242
Copyright © 2011 by the University of Iowa Press
www.uiowapress.org
Printed in the United States of America

Design by Omega Clay

The University of Iowa Press is a member of Green Press
Initiative and is committed to preserving natural resources.

Printed on acid-free paper

Library of Congress Cataloging-in-Publication Data
Afterword: conjuring the literary dead / edited by Dale
Salwak.
p.   cm.
Includes bibliographical references and index.
ISBN-13: 978-1-58729-989-6 (pbk.)
ISBN-10: 1-58729-989-5 (pbk.)
1. Imaginary conversations.   2. Authors, English—Inter-
views.   3. Authors, American—Interviews.   4. Authors—
Interviews.   I. Salwak, Dale.
PR107.A47 2011   2010046503
820.9—dc22

CONTENTS

Part Four *Consolidation*

The Crucible of the Imagination

DALE SALWAK AND LAURA NAGY

"It is well known," Joseph Conrad wrote in his author's note to *Heart of Darkness*, "that curious men go prying into all sorts of places (where they have no business) and come out of them with all kinds of spoil." He is referring with characteristic irony to his narrator Marlow, the intrepid seer who is about to recount the dark tale of his journey into the unknown reaches of the human soul. While the nature of the "spoil" Marlow bears back from his encounter with Kurtz may be equivocal, the journey and its perils symbolize just how far humans will go to follow an inborn inquisitiveness that knows few bounds. Some years earlier, Conrad had noted in his preface to *The Nigger of the "Narcissus"* that great art "speaks to the sense of mystery surrounding our lives"; it affirms a "latent feeling of fellowship with all creation" that "binds men to each other, which binds together all humanity—the dead to the living and the living to the unborn."

Indeed, the nature of that life-and-death bond has always been a source of fascination and conjecture, an eternal question mark. On a rational level, we understand what mortality means, what the shutting down of the body brings, and we endure and eventually become accustomed to the physical separation from the ones we have lost. Yet the dead endure indelibly in our minds; even when they are gone from our lives, they are vivid in our memories, only a breath or a thought or a reminder away. Long after their departure, we may conjure their image to ensure their presence at times of need, happiness, and sorrow; throughout our lives, they bear silent witness to our ongoing struggles and joys.

But what if we could break down the wall of silence that separates us from the dead and give them voice? We suspect—or want to believe—that they know more than they said in life, more than they had the opportunity to say, more than we had the insight, maturity, or prescience to ask for. What if we had another chance to communicate with them, not for companionship or succor, but for answers that are otherwise unobtainable? What if we were somehow granted just an AfterWord?

"There have been very few human societies in which the dead are thought to vanish completely once they are dead," Margaret Atwood observes in the essay that follows this introduction and that serves as an entry point—a crossing over, as it were—to this theme. "Sometimes there's a taboo against mentioning them openly, but this doesn't mean they're gone: the absence from conversation of a known quantity is a very strong presence, as the Victorians realized about sex." Her personal exploration of the concept leads Atwood to identify a common human desire "to go to the land of the dead, to bring back to the living someone who has gone there." This impulse, she asserts, remains strikingly deep even in our own seemingly callous age, when just the existence of an afterlife, let alone speaking to or hearing from those inhabiting it, is hardly otherwise credible to many people.

Nevertheless, quite apart from issues surrounding spirituality or religious belief, communication with the dead remains an intriguing notion, and one avenue by which humans have historically approached intriguing notions is by creating stories about them. As Atwood points out, a long literary tradition involving dialogues with the dead extends from Homer and Virgil to the Bible and Beowulf, from Gilgamesh to medieval morality plays, from Dante and Shakespeare to James and Lawrence. This is a way to get in touch with the dead, not through séances or prayer, but through the imagination. Atwood contends, "not just some, but *all* writing of the narrative kind, and perhaps all writing, is motivated, deep down, by a fear of and a fascination with mortality—by a desire to make the risky trip to the Underworld, and to bring something or someone back from the dead." There is no denying that in countless stories spanning many centuries and societies, the dead have cautioned, comforted, confessed, and cajoled. In some ways, looking to the dead for answers is a component of what Dante, that underworld explorer extraordinaire, saw as the quintessential human quest for the divine in all its forms. If, as Dante believed, the impulse to look for meaning beyond the mundane is so compelling that it "moves the sun and the other stars," surely it can propel our imaginations from this world to envision other, unseen ones.

Following in that tradition, this book postulates how living authors might speak with their predecessors, under what circumstances, and what conversations might transpire in a community of writers unbounded by the limitations of time and death. It is the product of an abiding curiosity about how voices from the past stay with us and how we yearn to connect with them. As many quests do, this one began with a single question that evolved into several rather simple, interrelated ones: "If you could meet one deceased literary figure, who would that be, what would you ask, what would you say, what would they say, and why?" This prompt was presented to seventeen writers who have spent much of their lives and careers thinking and writing about English and American literature. These people (along with two others whose essays had been previously published) were selected because of their distinguished records as scholars and writers; all have focused on a particular literary luminary at some time in their writing life, and all represent varying types and degrees of involvement with their subjects. Some are biographers, some are literary historians and critics, some are journalists, some are novelists, some are literati in their own right. All are able to draw from their decades of experience in studying writers, writing, and, in a more theoretical sense, The Writer.

Each contributor received the same prompt, and all had free rein to select their own queries and the personage to whom these would be posed. Not surprisingly, all chose to address someone from their area of specialty. Interestingly, none of the essays summoned authors writing before the early eighteenth century; no Dante, Chaucer, Shakespeare, or Milton passes across this stage. Perhaps this makes sense when viewed in light of social and literary history. Both poesy and fiction evolved radically during the 1700s, and the new definition of "literature" included works both more secular and less bound by rigid conventions than those of earlier eras. As Ian Watt has observed in *The Rise of the Novel*, the "increasingly prosperous and numerous social groups concerned with commerce and manufacture," that burgeoning middle class that arose during the century, "altered the centre of gravity of the reading public," creating a "new literary balance of power" that "tended to favour ease of entertainment at the expense of obedience to traditional critical standards." Relieved from the political and economic limitations of the patronage system, authors found prosperity not in felicity of phrase for the few, but in production of works that attracted the widest possible audiences. Literature, as we say these days, became market-driven. Concomitantly, the perception—frequently well-founded in reality—of author as solitary cleric or scholar laboring far removed from the real world began shifting to author as literary persona. This transformation would reach full flower with the Romantics and extends into our own postmodern age of megamedia and multimedia publication. Distinguished Shakespearean scholar Peter Saccio sees the late eighteenth century as a watershed, "the time that authors came to be taken as personalities"; from then on, "we record their table talk, we interview them, we believe it's essential to understand their personal lives in order to fully understand their work. Authorship was different in Shakespeare's time, and Shakespeare was the most elusive of them all. He never emerges from behind his characters."

Whether or not that veil influenced subject selection, chronologically this volume's earliest figures are from the early eighteenth century; contributors were not otherwise intimidated by history or reputation. Most proved unconcerned with relating the circumstances of their subject's life, since numerous biographies and collections of letters, memoirs, and journals have already documented both significant life histories and more mundane or peripheral facts. Rather, in an attempt to get past what Victoria Glendinning has called the "lies and silences" in the public record, the contributors homed in on questions that have seldom been asked and incidents that have often been suppressed. In a sense, then, this was an invitation to come face-to-face with a literary personage in a new way, and the task compelled some contributors to test, expand upon, or even question what they know. The recurrent impulse to ask the dead about their sex lives, for example, arises because this perhaps vital information was rarely disclosed when they were alive.

The result is an inquiry into the lives, minds, and art of a variety of deceased English and American authors who continue to have great appeal, despite the often radical differences between their worlds and ours. Why do we still care what Henry James, Jane Austen, Samuel Beckett, and the others in these essays might have to say for themselves? Certainly their life stories and the themes and politics rooted in their personal experiences are deeply and intrinsically interesting. But these artists are also attractive for more purely literary reasons. Perhaps it is the extraordinary breadth of their intellect and the range of emotions they explored that still draw us to their novels, poems, and plays. Perhaps it is the cultural richness of the respective milieus they portrayed in their works. Perhaps it is the sheer beauty and command of their language, or the universality of their themes, or the depth of their insights. Perhaps it is simple human curiosity, a desire to catch glimpses that make others seem more "real" to us, and more human.

Whatever the attraction, readers remain haunted by the presence of these writers, and each essay provides what Shelley called a "bridge thrown over the stream of time." In these pages, Edith Wharton frets about the financial woes of "poor dear Henry." A clearly puzzled and slightly peevish William Faulkner exclaims, "I've never understood why it is supposed that characters in novels speak for their authors." George Orwell surmises that the various wraiths trailing in and out of his hospital room are the product of an imagination that "is unable to make the leap beyond the self—another way of saying, I suppose, that I must be something of an egotist, maybe even a sublime one." Samuel Beckett ponders the paradox of how angst can be simultaneously his tormentor and his inspiration, supposing he is "doomed to spend the rest of [his] days digging up the detritus of [his] life and vomiting it out over and over again." Samuel Johnson excoriates Jonathan Swift's "pessimism—far more extreme than mine—and his nasty satire on the human race." And so it goes.

Yet, enlightening and entertaining as these conversations are, the essays speak at a much deeper level. As the completed pieces arrived in the mailbox and a composite slowly grew, it became clear that another theme was taking form: while the book began as an inquiry into the connection between the living and the dead, it became an exploration of the relationship between author and text, between reality and imagination. It is no coincidence that three of the contributors to this volume evoke Henry James, the patriarch of American literary theory who so famously and frequently wrote about the art and the craft of storytelling. James believed that invention—the "art" that flows from sheer inspiration—is a necessary component of good fiction, but so, too, is "craft," the conscious shaping that occurs as an author makes choices about how to form and frame a work. Art and artifice must combine within what James called "the great stewpot or crucible of the imagination, of the observant and recording and interpreting mind" if a work is to relay anything approaching essential truth. "Life," he said, is "all inclusion and confusion," but well-crafted art is "all discrimination and selection." The writer's task is to channel the inherent tension between reason and fancy into a coherent, dynamic whole, to make the choices that life does not, the choices that impose, albeit inconspicuously, order onto chaos. As Shelley described it in "A Defense of Poetry," his 1821 essay about the essence of creativity, "reason is to the imagination as the instrument to the agent, as the body to the spirit, as the shadow to the substance." And later in the current volume, Robert Frost instructs Jay Parini that fiction is "a shaped thing. *Fictio.* That's Latin. It means shaping."

Thus, while the subject authors, the questions, and the posited answers are in themselves revealing, what may be even more remarkable here are the constructs by which they are conveyed. The task required contributors to create a conceit; they needed to invent an apparatus by which to give their subject a voice. That is, these inquiries began by asking, "What can the dead tell us?" but in the end they broached an even broader question: "How does a writer envision worlds, and transmute those visions into words?"

These questions are not by any means new ones. Writers as far back as the early Greeks have pondered it. In *Poetics*, Aristotle theorized that verbal representations of reality contain discrete elements: *logos*, the "argument" or content; and *mythos*, the way that content is selected, arranged, and presented. Separate, these are only pieces; intertwined, they are the lifeblood of a narrative whole. Contemporary literary critics still acknowledge this dichotomy, although they have defined it in somewhat different terms. David H. Richter, analyzing the components of narrative literature, separates "the what from the how, the story that is told from the way that story is told." Seymour Chatman, in *Story and Discourse*, his seminal book on narrative theory, writes, "Story is the content of the narrative expression, while discourse is the form of that expression."

In Chatman's terms, then, each essay here can be viewed as both story and discourse. The "what" of these pieces ranges from Joseph Conrad's views on Polish independence to Oscar Wilde's last days at the seedy Hôtel d'Alsace in Paris to Edmund Gosse's literary associations in Victorian London. The initial prompt elicited questions in contributors' minds, and the answers take the form of unique material, a compendium of "what" from a starting point of "what if?" On the other hand, the "how"—the discursive stance contributors chose to relate that content—seemed to take one of three rather distinct approaches, and these forms became the organizational scheme of this book. We are calling these modes of discourse *visitation*, *evocation*, and *consolidation*. Each describes a way of engaging and expressing the "what," and the mode of discourse itself—the "how"—that reveals much about its creator.

The most common mode of discourse was visitation, the construction of a conceit that allowed contributors to travel backwards in time to encounter their subjects in their own eras and native locales. Some interviewers are bidden; some request meetings; some rather mysteriously simply show up. Whatever the route of transfer, these visits to the subject author place readers in a milieu alien to them but familiar to the object of the visit; the sounds, smells, and ambiance of the bygone era give these pieces a peculiar realism that, in turn, infuses them with great power. When we accompany Jeffrey Meyers to the Bolt Court lodgings of Samuel Johnson, we are plunged into the maelstrom that is London in 1784: "The street outside smelled of horse manure and garbage; the house inside reeked of a damp mixture of cabbage and cheese from the kitchen, charred logs and dead ash in the grate, and the sweaty bodies of those sitting round the table. The plaster walls were stained, and smeary windows filtered the pale light." Dr. Johnson is "grotesquely pale" and rather disheveled but nonetheless commanding. In a very different visitation, Nora Crook describes a much more tranquil scene as she is transported "in reverie into a sultry evening during the last days of August 1821 and into the saloon that ran the length of the upstairs floor of Casa Prini in the small resort of Bagni di Pisa." Here, Percy and Mary Shelley are enjoying the ceremonial evening lighting of the rooms in their Tuscan palazzo. A different visit takes Cynthia Ozick to Lamb House, Rye, Sussex, or "rather, its precise duplicate in the Other World," to interview Henry James. On the other hand, William Chace takes advantage of an unidentified but nonetheless "extraordinary technological breakthrough" that carries him to 1927 and a restaurant terrace overlooking the Gulf of Tigullio, where he dines and talks with an émigré Ezra Pound.

Why meet these people on their turf and in their time? Alive again in their milieu, they can speak with ease and candor. Perhaps visualizing the subject author in his or her own setting provided an entrée, a setting that facilitated re-creation of the subject's voice and thoughts. Interestingly, instead of narrating his visitation to his subject's era, Peter Firchow turned to a genre that allowed him even more license for dramatization, for placing readers in the action, as it were. He adopts the fourth-wall convention of the dramatist, creating a play in one act in which George Orwell, hospitalized with what proves to be his final illness, nonetheless cheerfully puffs on purloined cigarettes and sips surreptitious rum as he greets visitors like Lionel Trilling and, oddly, Tony Blair.

Although a large number of contributors chose to "visit" their authors by going back to them, an almost equal number engaged their subjects by a sort of evocation. They created an imaginative reincarnation that drew the authors forward from their own time and set them down into a contemporary situation. The effect of displacing an author into the present is very different from visiting him or her in the past; there is something jarring but intriguing about the retrospective power this provides the interviewees. Not only are they speaking from beyond the grave, but they may have the added perspective of history beyond their allotted years on Earth. Edith Wharton, for example, admits that "it's a relief to be taken seriously as a writer" by modern literary critics and suggests to the interviewer, "If you run into Pearl Buck, please let her know that the Nobel Prize should have gone to me." H. G. Wells, who has connected his famous time machine to a telephone for a little beyond-the-grave bookstore surfing, has discovered Paul Delany's 2008 publication of *George Gissing: A Life*. Wells rings up Delany from the year 1901 to broker a meeting between the biographer and Gissing, his ill and struggling friend: "The safest place for him at present is the future," Wells tells Delany. On the other hand, Brian Aldiss's meeting with Thomas Hardy is more serendipitous; strolling "along a dusty Wessex lane," Aldiss has a chance encounter with Hardy, who's sitting on a stool and sketching a village church. Hardy's conversation turns to Charles Darwin and how the evolutionist's rationalistic vision freed us from "all that hocus-pocus" imposed by Christianity; the comment leads Aldiss to a meditation on attempts "to express a new awareness of humanity's predicament" in Hardy's poetry and prose. Joseph Conrad greets Alan Sillitoe at the ramp leading to the old seaman's "luxuriously fitted out" coal barge docked along the Thames, where the drink is whisky and the conversation takes a slightly edgy turn. Such "evoked" dialogues allow the subject to retain his or her identity but at the same time be transplanted to the twenty-first century, where they are "living" within but not necessarily changed by the postmodern world. For these contributors, it was more important to bring their subjects here than to visualize them "there," that is, in their own era.

A third group of essays took a mode of discourse that was more focused on the consolidation of ideas than on the imagined appearance of the subject author in a specific setting either past or present. As Webster's dictionary defines it, to consolidate is to bring together separate parts into a single whole, to solidify and strengthen, to unite or combine. The "consolidating" contributors chose to amalgamate facts, ideas, and quotations from the subject's life, to conflate many answers already expressed by the subject or others into "the" answer to a new question. Rather than engage in a direct imaginative confrontation with their subjects, these contributors framed an intellectual encounter that was expressed in more objective, even analytical terms.

A certain detachment arises from this approach to suggest intriguing implications about the nexus of writer and subject. Certainly, choosing *not* to use some kind of fictional meeting with the literary figure is interesting; by definition, the prompt provided license to go outside the bounds of time and place, to ignore the "reality" of death as terminus to communication. Yet several contributors felt compelled to stay within those bounds, to defer from a face-to-face "confrontation" with a fictional persona, instead turning to their subject's own words or information about the subject from other sources.

Thus these more traditional literary essays make new raiment of old cloth, weaving supposition and interpretation into a fabric that has a distinctive texture and sheen. For example, Catherine Aird lists questions she *would have* asked Rudyard Kipling, "if by some happy chance" she had been able to make her way "into the Punjab Club in Lahore in northwest India," but relies on Kipling's autobiographical, fictional, and poetic writings for the answers. Alan W. Friedman calls upon biographies, correspondence, and Samuel Beckett's own plays, characters, and commentaries to try to illuminate the period in the writer's life from 1940 to 1945 and answer his key question: "How did the war experience enable and inspire this obscure and unsuccessful author to launch the career that, in 1969, culminated in his being awarded the Nobel Prize?" Colin Dexter turns the whole assignment on its head by listing the questions he would *not* ask A. E. Housman, and then rather delightfully provides his own answers.

And so the psychic distance that stems from avoiding direct address has a purpose, too. Writing of Beckett, Friedman observes that his "silences were never devoid of substance," but the idea applies here, too. The literary figures seem to speak by their absence. One wonders, for example, if Margaret Drabble is thinking solely about Arnold Bennett when she ponders "how he came to have such faith in his own talent." Does her desire "to know which were the periods of his life that were most strongly marked by self-doubt" suggest a common thread in the development of The Writer? When Drabble muses that "maybe he had moments, in the small hours, when his worldly success seemed like a mirage, when he saw his reputation slipping away from him as a new generation of writers rose to challenge him," is she really describing a more universal fear of the senescence that inevitably weakens the power of the artist?

Regardless of the means they chose to achieve the end, these contributors were guided by a love for literature and a hunger for truth. Of course, the thought experiment was fanciful and somewhat unconventional. Margaret Atwood grants that exploring the connection between the dead and the living is "a little peculiar," but, she goes on, "writing itself is a little peculiar." Carl Rollyson, in his encounter with William Faulkner, urges the reader to "forget whether you like this sort of hypothetical narrative and concentrate on what it speaks to: our desire to be at another place in another time in order to witness, if not to change, an important moment in history." Another contributor, Eugene Goodheart, echoes that sentiment in his book *Culture and the Radical Conscience*, writing that "the authority of the imagination has its basis in the belief that it can transform the world or even realize it." Granting these writers the authority of their imaginations led them to a new rendering of the world, which is what art ultimately does. Oscar Wilde, speaking through a character in "The Decay of Lying," an 1889 mock dialogue on aesthetics, declared art to be "a veil, rather than a mirror. She has flowers that no forests know of, birds that no woodland possesses. She makes and unmakes many worlds, and can draw the moon from heaven with a scarlet thread."

In the end, then, this book is as much about creating art as it is about seeking knowledge. To make and unmake the world, these writers—subjects and interlocutors alike—pushed beyond literary and social conventions, beyond aesthetic assumptions, beyond realistic mindsets, beyond death itself. As Flaubert once observed, "No horizon perceived by human eyes is ever the shore, because beyond that horizon lies another, and so on for ever." Pursuing that horizon can lead to the very edge of our comfort zone; there, perhaps breathless and teetering, we confront a dissonance that can be at once discomfiting and transformative. Pushing this edge in life and in art is at the center of the spirited, if imaginary, exchange between Jane Austen and Eugene Goodheart in this volume. Austen acknowledges that her signature character, Emma, "misfires, as do all artists or artist types who want to rearrange the world to suit their ideal conception of it." But never mind the misfires, Austen asserts: "All her mistakes are part of the design" of the story, and "there would be no story to tell without error. When everything at the end comes together in 'perfect happiness,' the story is over. 'Perfect happiness' is what the storyteller wants to put off as long as possible. . . . Storytelling, indeed living, is the making and unmaking of error."

Yet, as Austen points out, "something is gained in the process." The quest for truth may begin in untruth, indeed, may necessarily arise out of mistake or misconception or misapprehension; had Dante not become lost in that dark wood, he would never have encountered Virgil. But the journey itself is where illumination lies. As it was for Dante, literature can be an ongoing conversation between modern readers and the past—a ghost story for the living. Each contributor here is a Virgil, the voice of reason and insight and experience that guides us, as pilgrims, into uncharted territory. If we follow our guides, we may travel perhaps a little bewildered, but we may also learn to call upon the past to direct us through the present. During Nora Crook's interlude at the Italian palazzo, Mary Shelley tells her, "We are spirits, you know—we inhabit your century as well as our own." These spirits still have stories to tell. How fortunate we are to encounter here all these authors—the dead ones through the imaginations of the living, and the living through their own devices—to get so much beyond just an AfterWord.

PART ONE

CROSSING OVER

Descent

Negotiating with the Dead

MARGARET ATWOOD

When I was a young person reading whatever I could get my hands on, I came across some old books of my father's, in a series called Everyman's Library. The endpapers of that date were a sort of William Morris design, with leaves and flowers and a lady in graceful medieval draperies carrying a scroll and a branch with three apples or other spherical fruit on it. Interwoven among the shrubbery there was a motto: "Everyman I will go with thee and be thy guide. In thy most need to go by thy side." This was very reassuring to me. The books were declaring that they were my pals; they promised to accompany me on my travels; and they would not only offer me some helpful hints, they'd be right there by my side whenever I really needed them. It's always nice to have someone you can depend on.

Imagine my consternation when—some years later, and enrolled in a university course that required me to fill my gaps, Middle English among them—I discovered the source of this cuddly quotation. It was a medieval play called *Everyman*, in which Everyman is not on some pleasant country stroll but on his way to the grave. All Everyman's friends have deserted him, including Fellowship, who wanders off in search of a stiff drink as soon as he hears the proposed destination. The only loyal one is Good Deeds, who isn't up to the job of saving Everyman from the consequences of himself, being too feeble. However, Good Deeds has a sister called Knowledge, and it is Knowledge who offers to be the helpful guide on Everyman's ramble to the tomb, and who speaks the words I have just quoted.

The relationship between me and these books, then, was not as cozy as I'd once thought. In the light of their newly discovered context, the three round fruits toted by the Pre-Raphaelite lady looked positively sinister: I was acquainted by then with Robert Graves's book *The White Goddess*, and I felt I could recognize the food of the dead.

I remain rather amazed at the long-ago editors of this series, and their choice of design and epigraph. What possible help did they think *Pride and Prejudice* and *Mopsa the Fairy* were going to be to me on my leisurely hike to the crematorium?—though when you come to think of it, I suppose we're all on the same train trip, and it's a one-way ticket, so you might as well have something good to read on the way. And some lunch too—that must be where the fruit comes in.

The title of this essay is "Negotiating with the Dead," and its hypothesis is that not just some, but *all* writing of the narrative kind, and perhaps all writing, is motivated, deep down, by a fear of and a fascination with mortality—by a desire to make the risky trip to the Underworld, and to bring something or someone back from the dead.

You may find the subject a little peculiar. It is a little peculiar. Writing itself is a little peculiar.

This hypothesis was suggested to me by several things. The first of them was a throwaway sentence in Dudley Young's book, *Origins of the Sacred*, to the effect that the Minoan civilization which once flourished on Crete left remarkably few written texts, and this was possible because the Minoans weren't overly afraid of mortality—writing itself being, above all, a reaction to the fear of death. Despite all the remarks about enduring fame and leaving a name behind them that are strewn about in the letters and poems of writers, I had not thought much about writing per se as being a reaction to the fear of death—but once you've got hold of an idea, the proofs of it tend to proliferate.

Here are a few of the citations drawn almost at random from the heaps of printed material piled on my study floor. "They're all dead now," begins Ann-Marie MacDonald's novel *Fall on Your Knees*. "That [her brothers] Thomas and Timothy were killed before she was born was another part of the reason Ruth Cole became a writer," says John Irving in his novel *A Widow for One Year*. And from Chekhov:

> When a man in a melancholy mood is left tête-à-tête with the sea, or any landscape which seems to him grandiose, there is always, for some reason, mixed with melancholy, a conviction that he will live and die in obscurity, and he reflectively snatches up a pencil and hastens to write his name on the first thing that comes handy.

There are many other examples of this connection—not necessarily a fear of death, as in *Timor mortis conturbat me*, but a definite concern with it—an intimation of transience, of evanescence, and thus of mortality, coupled with the urge to indite. But let us take the connection as given, or as given in enough instances to establish a working premise, and ask ourselves: why should it be writing, over and beyond any other art or medium, that should be linked so closely with anxiety about one's own personal, final extinction?

Surely that's partly because of the nature of writing—its apparent permanence, and the fact that it survives its own performance —unlike, for instance, a dance recital. If the act of writing charts the process of thought, it's a process that leaves a trail, like a series of fossilized footprints. Other art forms can last and last—painting, sculpture, music—but they do not survive as *voice*. And as I've said, writing is writing down, and what is written down is a score for voice, and what the voice most often does—even in the majority of short lyric poems—is tell, if not a story, at least a mini-story. Something unfurls, something reveals itself. The crooked is made straight, or, the age being what it is, possibly more crooked; at any rate there's a path. There's a beginning, there's an end, not necessarily in that order; but however you tell it, there's a plot. The voice moves through time, from one event to another, or from one perception to another, and things change, whether in the mind alone or in the outside world. Events take place, in relation to other events. That's what time is. It's one damn thing after another, and the important word in that sentence is *after*.

Narration—storytelling—is the relation of events unfolding through time. You can't hold a mirror up to Nature and have it be a story unless there's a metronome ticking somewhere. As Leon Edel has noted, if it's a novel, there's bound to be a clock in it. He was the biographer of Henry James, one of the most time-conscious novelists that ever was, and so he ought to know. And once you've got clocks, you've got death and dead people, because time, as we know, runs on, and then it runs out, and dead people are situated outside of time, whereas living people are still immersed in it.

But dead people persist in the minds of the living. There have been very few human societies in which the dead are thought to vanish completely once they are dead. Sometimes there's a taboo against mentioning them openly, but this doesn't mean they're gone: the absence from conversation of a known quantity is a very strong presence, as the Victorians realized about sex. Most societies assign these dead souls to an abode, and sometimes to several abodes: if the soul after death is assumed to be divisible, or if there's more than one kind of soul, as among the ancient Egyptians, then each part or soul must have its own territory.

Societies also have a way of devising rules and procedures— "superstitions," they're now called—for ensuring that the dead stay in their place and the living in theirs, and that communication between the two spheres will take place only when we want it to. Having the dead return when not expected can be a hair-raising experience, especially if they are feeling slighted and needy, or worse, angry. "Remember me," as the ghost of Hamlet's father commands, is not the first such heavy injunction to be laid on the living by the dead, nor will it be the last. The unrequested arrival of a dead person is seldom good news, and may indeed be distinctly alarming. "Tomorrow in the battle think of me," says the ghost of murdered Clarence to Richard III. But to Richmond, Richard's adversary, the same ghost says, "Good angels guard thy battle! Live, and flourish," for although the dead have negative powers, they have positive and protective ones as well. Consider Cinderella's dead mother, purveyor of ball gowns and glass slippers.

A lot of the superstitions, or rules and procedures, governing life-death traffic involve food, because the dead are assumed to be hungry and unsatisfied. In Mexico, the Day of the Dead is, among other things, a feast day for dead people. In addition to the sugar skulls eaten by children, and the jolly tin assemblages depicting skeletons having a whale of a time doing all the things the living do—dressing up, playing music or cards, dancing and drinking—the family will prepare a special meal for its dead people, with all their favorite foods, and perhaps even a basin and towel so they can wash their invisible hands. In some communities the meal is eaten by the family itself, right on the grave; in others, a trail is made—of marigold petals, usually—from the grave to the house, so the dead person will be able to find his way to the meal, and also make his way back to his proper domicile after it. The dead are considered to be still part of the community, but they are not permanent residents. Even the most beloved one is only a guest, to be treated with honor, consideration, and a bite to eat, in return for which the dead person is expected to behave as a good guest should, and go home when the party's over.

These are not by any means extinct practices, and similar ones—or vestiges of them—are widespread. I was talking about these matters a while ago with someone from Greece. He described a custom whereby a certain kind of bread is baked—it's round in shape, as the food of the dead often is—and on the day set aside for the dead, you are supposed to take this bread object to the ancestral tomb, and then persuade as many passing strangers as you can to take a nibble of it. The more strangers you corral, the better your luck will be in the coming year. Perhaps the strangers are the stand-ins for the dead, and giving them this special food is meant to propitiate them and ensure their support. Similarly, in Japan and China and many other cultures the ancestors must be given their share, at least symbolically. If they feel they've been respected, they'll help you. If not—well, it's always best to be on the safe side.

Then there's our own Halloween, a remnant of the pre-Christian Celtic night of the dead—primarily, now, a North American phenomenon. The spirits are abroad, and you need protection, so you make a pumpkin with a goblin face and a light inside it, to act as the guardian of your threshold. The dead are represented by children wearing masks and costumes—it used to be ghosts, witches, and goblins, but today it's just as likely to be Elvis Presley, Superman, or Mickey Mouse, whom we have apparently now claimed as ancestral spirits. These come to your door and demand food. "Trick or treat" is one of the verbal formulae—which means that unless the spirits get the food, you'll get the mischief. Again, giving food to the dead is supposed to propitiate them and bring luck to the living, even if that luck consists only in the freedom from being annoyed.

We lived in an old house in rural Ontario during the 1970s, and this house was haunted—so the local people said, and so some visiting the house experienced while we were there—and we asked the lore-conscious woman from the farm across the road what to do. "Leave food out overnight," she said. "Make them a meal. Then they'll know you accept them, and you won't be bothered." We felt kind of silly, but we did it, and it worked. Or, as the German poet Rilke puts it in a slightly different way, in his *Sonnets to Orpheus*, "Don't leave bread or milk on the table / At night: that attracts the dead."

It does make you thoughtful about Santa Claus and his milk and cookies on Christmas Eve, especially when you know that in Sicily the presents for the kiddies are brought on All Souls' Eve, not by a man in a red suit, but by the dead grandparents. Why should we be surprised? Santa Claus himself is from the Other Place, disguise it as we may by calling it the North Pole; and anyone from the Other Place—whatever we may name that other place—Heaven, Hell, Fairyland, the Underworld—will bring luck to us, or else keep us free from harm, only if given something in return—at the very least, our prayers and gratitude.

What else might the dead want? Various things, depending on the circumstances. Hamlet's father, for instance, wants revenge, nor is his desire unique: Abel's blood cried out from the ground after the first murder, thus giving us the first example of talking blood, though not the last. Other body products that have been known to vocalize include bones and hair, as in folk songs—consider the extremely widespread "Twa Sisters of Binnorie"—and folktales such as "The Singing Bone," the bone in question being a murdered girl's leg-bone that becomes a flute.

Modern stories about forensic pathologists, such as Patricia Corn-well's thriller-heroine Kay Scarpetta, or forensic doctor–anthro-pologists such as the protagonist of Michael Ondaatje's novel *Anil's Ghost*, are firmly of this tradition—such an old and persistent one because it's so elemental, interbound as it is with the desire for jus-tice and the longing for revenge. When the blind old man in the Ondaatje novel "reads" a skull with his fingers, it's a recap of a very ancient scene. The premise is that dead bodies can talk if you know how to listen to them, and they *want* to talk, and they want us to sit down beside them and hear their sad stories. Like Hamlet laying a death-scene narrative injunction on his friend Horatio—"in this harsh world draw thy breath in pain / To tell my story"—they want to be recounted. They don't want to be voiceless; they don't want to be pushed aside, obliterated. They want us to know. The harp or other musical instrument made from the dead girl's hair in the "Twa Sisters" ballad speaks for them all when it denounces the murderer by singing, "Woe to my sister, false Ellyn." As Shakespeare said—or rather, as Macbeth says—"Blood will have blood."

But revenge and justice are not the only desires of the visitants from other worlds. Sometimes, as in many ballad apparitions—*my love she came all dressed in white*, and any other ex-inamoratas likely to materialize wistfully at your bedside before cockcrow—their desires are erotic, and they want you to go with them. Sometimes there's a demon-lover element. Sometimes there's a contractual one—you've sold your soul, and the creditor has come to collect. If we could sum up what all of them want, in one word—a word that encompasses life, sacrifice, food, and death—that word would be *blood*. And this is what the dead most often want, and it is why the food of the dead is often, though not always, round, and also red. Heart-shaped, more or less, and blood-colored, like Persephone's pomegranate.

Here is Odysseus, making the necessary sacrifice to attract the spirits of the dead, in Book XI of the *Odyssey*:

> When I had finished my prayers and invocations to the communities of
> the dead, I took the sheep and cut their throats over the trench so that
> the dark blood poured in. And now the souls of the dead came swarm-

ing up. . . . From this multitude of souls, as they fluttered to and fro by the trench, there came an eerie clamor. Panic drained the blood from my cheeks.

As well it might. Odysseus sits beside the trench with drawn sword in hand, to keep any of the souls from drinking the blood until he gets what he wants, because he's there to do a negotiation, to make a trade. Of what he wants in return, more shortly.

The dead, then, are fond of blood. Animal blood will do, or for very special occasions, human blood. It's often the same thing gods want, not to mention vampires. So do think twice about Valentine's Day. I always do—I had a boyfriend once who sent me—in a plastic bag, so it wouldn't drip—a real cow's heart with a real arrow stuck through it. As you may divine, he knew I was interested in poetry.

One of the first request-by-the-dead poems I was ever exposed to was the most famous poem ever written by a Canadian: we all had to memorize it in school. It isn't usually thought of as a negotiate-with-the-dead poem—more as a pious commemoration verse; and so it duly made its appearance every year on Remembrance Day, at the eleventh hour of the eleventh day of the eleventh month. The eleventh month is November, and my birthday is situated in it, which used to displease me because there wasn't anything you could put on the birthday cake, not like May with its flowers or February with its hearts; but then I found out that, astrologically speaking, November was the month governed by Scorpio, sign of death, sex, and regeneration. (This still wasn't much help with the birthday cakes.)

Why all three of these things together? What does death have to do with sex and regeneration? That's a whole footnote to itself; in fact, it may be a whole book to itself, the name of which might possibly be Frazer's *The Golden Bough*; but meanwhile, here's the poem—"In Flanders Fields," by John McCrae:

In Flanders fields the poppies blow
Between the crosses, row on row,
  That mark our place; and in the sky
  The larks, still bravely singing, fly
Scarce heard amid the guns below.

We are the Dead. Short days ago
We lived, felt dawn, saw sunset glow,
   Loved and were loved, and now we lie,
      In Flanders fields.

Take up our quarrel with the foe:
To you from failing hands we throw
   The torch; be yours to hold it high.
   If ye break faith with us who die
We shall not sleep, though poppies grow
   In Flanders fields.

Note how the living are embedded in time, between dawns and sunsets, and how the Dead, capital D, are embedded out of time. Note the deal proposed by the Dead. Note the threat of retaliation if the terms are not respected: we'd better do as requested, because we wouldn't want any sleepless dead prowling around. You may think there's no food in this poem, apart from the poppies—round and red, like the food of the dead—but note what the Dead want. Yes, it's traditional: they want blood. They want the blood of the living, or at least they want the blood put at risk in behalf of their own cause.

At the time of its first publication, this poem was thought to be about the sustaining of belligerence toward enemy aliens during World War I. However, that is now over eighty years ago, and if this were all the poem ever said, it would long ago have run out of energy. But something powerful remains, because it embodies a very old and very strong pattern. The dead make demands, says the poem, and you can't just dismiss either the dead or the demands: you'd be wise to take both of them seriously.

Calling up the dead, and dealing with them across the threshold —because there always is a threshold, between our world and their world, and that's what those hex signs are doing on the old barns in Pennsylvania, and that's why you draw a circle around yourself if conjuring up the dead, and I suppose that's why Odysseus sat with drawn sword, because the spirits, in many traditions, can't pass metal—invoking these spirits, then, is one thing. At least you have

some control over the situation. Even when the dead arrive unin-
vited, as in the Hamlet's-father and defunct-true-love scenarios, as
a rule you know that if you can just last out until daybreak, they'll
be gone. But there's something quite a lot riskier: instead of dealing with the dead on your own territory—middle merry-earth—you
can cross over into theirs. You can go on a journey from this world to
that. You can go down into the land of the dead, and then you can
get out again, back to the land of the living. But only if you're lucky.
As the Sibyl of Cumae tells Aeneas before they begin such a journey,
in Book VI of the *Aeneid,*

> . . . the way to Avernus is easy;
> Night and day lie open the gates of death's dark kingdom:
> But to retrace your steps, to find the way back to daylight—
> That is the task, the hard thing.

In other words, this is a very tricky business—you might get stuck
down there—and it's also quite a test of your fortitude, which is
probably why so many heroes and heroines in the Western tradition, and in many other traditions as well, have undertaken it. Why
do these heroes do it? Why take the chance? Because the dead have
some very precious and desirable things under their control, down
there in their perilous realm, and among these are some things you
yourself may want or need.

What sort of things? To summarize: (1) riches; (2) knowledge; (3)
the chance to battle an evil monster; (4) the loved and the lost. This
list is not all-inclusive, but it includes the main aims of such journeys. You can gain more than one thing at a time, of course. You
can get riches plus the loved and the lost, or knowledge plus the fight
with the monster, or any other combination.

For "riches," I'll just mention fairy gold, that substance with the
unfortunate habit of turning to coal in the morning; and also the
riches controlled by the Chinese ancestors, for whom you burn red
paper money in return for the real money you want them to bring
you. Then there are the sacrifices made so that the dead will ensure
a bountiful harvest: "Give us this day our daily bread," that simple
request in the Lord's Prayer, is a very modest version of an invoca-

tion to the Other World in the hope of material welfare. Wealth of every kind flows from the invisible world to the visible one, and the trance journeys made by the shamans of hunting societies in search of the locations of desired animals are based on this belief: the dead control the harvests, and they can tell you where the caribou are to be found. The realm of the dead is a cavern of wonders, an Aladdin's treasure trove. Like the abode of Epic, the very weird opera monster in *The Phantom of the Opera*, it's rich and strange; like the subterranean world of the not unrelated Grimms' fairy tale "The Twelve Dancing Princesses," down there the trees bear jewels for fruit. And like the treasure chambers of Bluebeard, another Plutonic monster, the gold and jewels must be handled with great care, for death itself may have touched them.

The second thing I mentioned was knowledge. Because they are outside time, the dead know both the past and the future. "Why have you called me up?" says the ghost of the prophet Samuel to King Saul, through the medium of the Witch of Endor. King Saul has done this thing—a thing he himself has forbidden—because he wants to know what the coming battle has in store for him. (Nothing good, as it turns out.) Similarly, it's for knowledge of the future that Odysseus seeks out the ghost of the double-sexed seer Tiresias, and such knowledge is also the motive of Aeneas, who goes to the realm of the dead with the aid of the Sibyl of Cumae in order to learn all about the glorious future of his own descendants. (Macbeth wants the same thing, but it backfired; through the three Sibyls, now downgraded to nasty old witches, he learns all about the glorious future of somebody else's descendants.)

Knowledge and riches can be connected, of course—knowledge can be knowledge about how to get hold of the riches. One of the first modern short stories I ever read was D. H. Lawrence's classic "The Rocking-Horse Winner," which has haunted me ever since. It's a complex story, but in relation to our subject it goes as follows. A beautiful woman has no luck with money, and does not really love her little boy. This little boy longs for some luck, so he can acquire the riches his mother desires; the implication is that by doing so he might also get some love from her. He has clairvoyant powers, and takes to riding his rocking-horse to put himself into a trance. When things go well, his horse takes him to "where there is luck," and he is able to learn the names of the winners in upcoming races. By this means he becomes rich, but he still doesn't get love. That the place "where there is luck" is also the land of the dead becomes clear at the end of the story: the boy gets to the place, all right, but this time he isn't able to make the journey back, and he dies. Such a fate is always a possibility for journeyers to the Other World.

The third item I mentioned was a battle with a monster. Among the shamans, the battle was usually a battle with a spirit, and if you won, the spirit would become your familiar, and if you lost, you'd become possessed by it. Or it could be a fight with the spirits of the dead for control of the harvest. In myths that get into literature, things are usually narrowed down to one or two monsters per hero. There's Theseus and his labyrinth and Minotaur, of course, and Beowulf and his dark tarn and his Grendel's Mother. And there's Bilbo Baggins and his underground riddle contest in Tolkien's *The Hobbit*, not to mention Gandalf and the Balrog in *Lord of the Rings*. And there's Christ, who during the three days between Good Friday and Easter Sunday goes down to Hell and defies the Devil, and rescues a group of good people who have been kept down there because until Christ's advent there hasn't been a redeemer to redeem them.

The fourth thing I mentioned was the quest for a lost beloved; this is an important motif when we're talking about writers and what drives them on. At first the vanished one may have been male: one of the most ancient seekers is the Egyptian goddess Isis, who sorrowfully gathers together the scattered body parts of her slain husband Osiris, and by doing so restores him to life.

The Greek goddess Demeter pulls off a similar feat. She loses her daughter Persephone to Hades, the King of the Underworld; but she has a lot of bargaining power—she's the vegetation goddess, and she decrees that nothing will bear fruit again until the lost one is restored. Hades agrees to give Persephone back, on condition that she has eaten nothing while below ground. Unfortunately the girl has taken seven seeds from a pomegranate—one of those round, red foods of the dead. The prohibition against eating the food of the dead is enormously ancient—

> They will offer water from the river,
> Do not take the water of death.
> They will give you grain from the fields
> Of the dead, do not take that seed

says the Mesopotamian poem about the goddess Inanna's journey to Hell.

In the Persephone story, as in the one about Inanna, her husband Dumuzi, and his sister Geshtinanna, a compromise is reached—part of the year in the Underworld, part above ground—and that's why we have winter.

Orpheus the musician and poet went in search of his dead wife Eurydice, and managed a successful negotiation with the rulers of the Underworld: he charmed them with his songs, and they agreed that he could have Eurydice back, just so long as he didn't look at her while leading her up to the land of the living. But he couldn't hold to his resolution, and so Eurydice went fluttering back to the dark halls. You should not eat the food of the dead, but also you should not question their take-home gifts too closely.

To go to the land of the dead, to bring back to the land of the living someone who has gone there—it's a very deep human desire, and thought also to be very deeply forbidden. But life of a sort can be bestowed by writing. Jorge Luis Borges, in his "Nine Dantesque Essays," puts forward an interesting theory: that the entire *Divine Comedy*, all three sections of it—the *Inferno*, the *Purgatorio*, and the *Paradiso*—this whole vast and intricate structure was composed by Dante so he could get a glimpse of the dead Beatrice, and bring her back to life in his poem. It is because he is writing about her, and only because he is writing about her, that Beatrice is able to exist again, in the mind of writer and reader. As Borges says,

> We must keep one incontrovertible fact in mind, a single, humble fact: the scene was imagined by Dante. For us, it is very real; for him, it was less so. (The reality, for him, was that first life and then death had taken

Beatrice from him.) Forever absent from Beatrice, alone and perhaps humiliated, he imagined the scene in order to imagine that he was with her.

Borges then comments on the "fleetingness of her glance and smile," and the "eternal turning away of the face." How like the story of Orpheus this is—the poet, armed only with his poetry, enters the realm of the dead, traverses the Inferno, reaches the Elysian Fields or their equivalent, and finds the beloved again, only to lose her once more, this time for ever. As Dido turns away from Aeneas, as Eurydice turns away from Orpheus, thus Beatrice turns away from Dante. Never mind that it's toward God, never mind that she's happy—the essential thing *for him* is that she is lost. But regained again. But lost again. The end of the *Paradiso* is a happy ending only if we squint very hard.

And so it is with all happy endings of all books, when you come to think about it. You can't go home again, said Thomas Wolfe; but you can, sort of, when you write about it. But then you reach the last page. A book is another country. You enter it, but then you must leave: like the Underworld, you can't live there.

Virgil is usually assumed to be the first writer to have given us a full account of the Underworld in his function *as writer*. Note his short introduction in Book VI of the *Aeneid*:

> You gods who rule the kingdom of souls! You soundless shades!
> Chaos, and Phlegethon! O mute wide leagues of Nightland!
> Grant me to tell what I have heard! With your assent,
> May I reveal what lies deep in the gloom of the Underworld!

Grant me to tell. May I reveal. These are the prayers of a writer, and you'd almost think he'd been there himself. This is perhaps why Dante chooses the poet Virgil to be his guide in the *Inferno*: in visiting a strange location, it's always best to go with someone who's been there before, and—most important of all on a sightseeing tour of Hell—who might also know how to get you out again.

Rilke, in his *Sonnets to Orpheus*, makes the underworld journey simply a precondition of being a poet. The journey must be undertaken, it is necessary. The poet—for whom Orpheus is the exemplary model—is the one who can bring the knowledge held by the Underworld back to the land of the living, and who can then give us, the readers, the benefit of this knowledge. "Is he of this world? No, he gets / his large nature from both realms," says Rilke of the Orpheus poet in Sonnet 6 (Part I). In Sonnet 9 (Part I), he spells this out at more length:

> You have to have been among the shades,
> turning your lyre there too,
> if you want vision enough to know
> how to make lasting praise.
>
> You have to sit down and eat
> with the dead, sharing their poppies,
> if you want enough memory to keep
> the one most delicate note . . .
>
> And the world has to be twofold
> before any voice can be
> eternal and mild.

This poet doesn't just visit the Other World. He partakes of it. He is double-natured, and can thus both eat the food of the dead and return to tell the tale.

I said that Virgil is usually assumed to be the first *writer* to make the underworld trip—that is, he makes the imaginary trip for the purpose of relating it. It, and all the other stories he gets told down there; and it's by the inmates of the *Inferno*, not in the *Purgatorio* or the *Paradiso*, that Dante is told the most stories, and also the best ones. It's somewhat daunting to reflect that Hell is—possibly—the place where you are stuck in your own personal narrative forever, and Heaven is—possibly—the place where you can ditch it, and take up wisdom instead.

I would now like to propose a much earlier prototype for the subterranean adventurer as writer—the Mesopotamian hero Gilgamesh. Since the epic poem that contains him was not deciphered until the nineteenth century, he can hardly have been a direct influence on either Virgil or Dante; he is even more of a test case, then, for Dudley Young's thesis about the essential connection between the urge to write things down and the fear of death.

In the first part of his story, Gilgamesh—a king who is half-divine—is concerned mostly to make a name for himself, a name that will outlast him. He has a companion, a tamed wild-man called Enkidu, and together they accomplish heroic feats. But they insult the goddess Ishtar—a sex-and-death goddess, as it turns out—and thus Enkidu must die. He has to go down to the extremely unpleasant Underworld of that time, where you ate mud and were covered with frowsy bird feathers.

Gilgamesh is deeply distressed: he can't get Enkidu back, and in addition he is now afraid of death. So he sets out to find the secret of eternal life, from the one mortal man who has never died. The way leads over the wilderness and through the middle of a dark mountain, and then through a garden where the trees bear jewels for fruit, and then over the water of death. He finds Utnapishtim, the immortal man, who tells him the story of the flood and then gives Gilgamesh the key to eternal life; but Gilgamesh loses it, and then he has to come all the way back to his own kingdom again. Here is the end of his journey: "He was wise, he saw mysteries and knew secret things, he brought us a tale of the days before the flood. He went a long journey, was weary, worn out with labor, and returning engraved on a stone the whole story."

I was holding forth about this a while ago at a dinner for a bunch of writers. "Gilgamesh was the first writer," I said. "He wants the secret of life and death, he goes through hell, he comes back, but he hasn't got immortality, all he's got is two stories—the one about his trip, and the other, extra one about the flood. So the only thing he really brings back with him is a couple of stories. Then he's really, really tired, and then he writes the whole thing down on a stone."

"Yeah, that's what it is," said the writers. "You go, you get the story, you're whacked out, you come back and write it all down on a stone. Or it feels like a stone by the sixth draft," they added.

"Go where?" I said.

"To where the story is," they said.

Where is the story? The story is in the dark. That is why inspiration is thought of as coming in flashes. Going into a narrative—into the narrative process—is a dark road. You can't see your way ahead. Poets know this too; they too travel the dark roads. The well of inspiration is a hole that leads downwards.

"Reach me a gentian, give me a torch!" says D. H. Lawrence, that most chthonic of writers, in his poem "Bavarian Gentians":

> Let me guide myself with the blue, forked torch of this flower
> down the darker and darker stairs, where blue is darkened on blueness
> and even where Persephone goes . . .

Yes, but why does the poet himself want to go down those dark stairs? It isn't a question he answers in the poem, but I'd guess it's not because he wants to die. Rather it's because he's a poet, and he must make such a descent in order to do what he does. He must partake of both realms, as Rilke claimed.

The Underworld guards the secrets. It's got the skeletons in the closet, and any other skeletons you might wish to get your hands on. It's got the stories, or quite a few of them. "There is something down there and you want it told," as poet Gwendolyn MacEwen says. The swimmer among the jeweled dead—double-gendered, like the seer Tiresias—in Adrienne Rich's poem "Diving into the Wreck" has a similar motive:

> There is a ladder.
> The ladder is always there . . .
> We know what it is for,
> we who have used it . . . I go down.
>
> I came to explore the wreck.
> The words are purposes.
> The words are maps.
> I came to see the damage that was done
> and the treasures that prevail . . .
>
> . . . the thing I came for:
> the wreck and not the story of the wreck
> the thing itself and not the myth

The Québecoise poet Anne Hébert also wrote an astonishing poem along these lines. It's called "The Tomb of Kings." In it, a dreaming child—a girl, "amazed, barely born"—goes down into a tomb, through an underground labyrinth, carrying her heart on her fist in the form of a blind falcon. Down there she finds the dead kings; she also finds their stories, "a few patiently-wrought tragedies" that now appear as jeweled works of art. An exchange takes place—a vampiristic ritual in which the dead drink the living, and try to kill her. She shakes the dead away and frees herself; but as a result of whatever it is that has gone on, her heart—the blind bird—shows signs of being able to see.

The dead get blood; as I said earlier, they are assumed to be hungry and thirsty. In return, the poet gets clairvoyance, and the completion of her identity as a poet. It's an old arrangement.

All writers learn from the dead. As long as you continue to write, you continue to explore the work of writers who have preceded you; you also feel judged and held to account by them. But you don't learn only from writers—you can learn from ancestors in all their forms. Because the dead control the past, they control the stories, and also certain kinds of truth—what Wilfred Owen, in his descent-to-the-Underworld poem, "Strange Meeting," calls the "truth untold"—so if you are going to indulge in narration, you'll have to deal, sooner or later, with those from previous layers of time. Even if that time is only yesterday, it isn't now. It isn't the *now* in which you are writing.

All writers must go from *now* to *once upon a time*; all must go from here to there; all must descend to where the stories are kept; all must take care not to be captured and held immobile by the past. And all must commit acts of larceny, or else of reclamation, depending on how you look at it. The dead may guard the treasure, but it's useless treasure unless it can be brought back into the land of the living and allowed to enter time once more—which means to enter the realm of the audience, the realm of the readers, the realm of change.

We could go on to make explicit what has been implicit. We could talk about inspiration, or about trances and dream visions, or about charms and invocations—all of them linked with poetic traditions of long standing; then we could go one step further, and talk—as many have—about the shamanistic role of the writer. This may of course be a metaphor, but, if so, it does seem to be one that has held a central significance for writers over a very long period of time.

Such subjects can get murky or pretentious with astonishing rapidity, but I'll try to lend some respectability to the proceedings by leaving you with the words of a real scholar. This is from the Italian social historian Carlo Ginzburg's book *Ecstasies: Deciphering the Witches' Sabbath*:

> Indubitable . . . is the deep resemblance that binds the myths that later merged in the witches' Sabbath. All of them work a common theme: going into the beyond, returning from the beyond. This elementary narrative nucleus has accompanied humanity for thousands of years. The countless variations introduced by utterly different societies, based on hunting, on pasture and on agriculture, have not modified its basic structure. Why this permanence? The answer is possibly very simple. To narrate means to speak here and now with an authority that derives from having been (literally or metaphorically) there and then. In participation in the world of the living and of the dead, in the sphere of the visible and of the invisible, we have already recognized a distinctive trait of the human species. What we have tried to analyze here is not one narrative among many, but the matrix of all possible narratives.

As the best authorities have it, easy to go there, but hard to come back; and then you must write it all down on a stone. Finally, if you are lucky and if the right reader comes along, the stone will speak. It alone will remain in the world to tell the story.

I will give the last word to the poet Ovid, who has the Sibyl of Cumae speak, not only for herself, but also—we suspect—for him, and for the hopes and fates of all writers:

> But still, the fates will leave me my voice,
> and by my voice I shall be known.

PART TWO

VISITATION

Sometimes Counsel Take, and Sometimes Tea

Samuel Johnson at Home

JEFFREY MEYERS

I turned off Fleet Street into the quiet, pocket-sized Bolt Court where Mr. Samuel Johnson had lived, and suddenly found myself in the year 1784. It was noon on a Sunday, and the tall, narrow house, tucked into a corner and laced by an iron railing, stood still and silent in the faint summer sunshine. I hoped he had already risen from his bed. I went up the stone steps and banged the thick knocker. A moment later I heard the heavy chain drop and saw the door swing open. A sulky Jamaican face detached itself from the dark interior. "Frank Barber," I said, and he broke into a charming smile of welcome.

Mr. Johnson was indeed at home, taking tea with his companions in the parlor. The street outside smelled of horse manure and garbage; the house inside reeked of a damp mixture of cabbage and cheese from the kitchen, charred logs and dead ash in the grate, and the sweaty bodies of those sitting round the table. The plaster walls were stained, and smeary windows filtered the pale light. I followed Frank across the creaky bare floorboards, suddenly aware of how clean I was, how crisp in my neat jacket and sharply creased pants.

I had some idea of Johnson's appearance from Joshua Reynolds's meditative and heroic portraits, but seeing him in the flesh was a shock. In the gloom the seventy-five-year-old man was grotesquely pale, with his rocky face all bumps and indentations, his parchment skin still scarred with scrofula, his huge arms resting on the table next to the bread and bacon. Tall and stout, with a commanding air, he slowly rose to greet me, his mountainous belly foremost. His brown suit looked threadbare, his wig shriveled; his collar and knee breeches were loose, his stockings wrinkled. As he inspected my face, his defective eyes had a terrifying glare. My greeting seemed to set off an anxious train of thought. He started convulsively, his face a riot of tics. When he spoke, his mouth opened and shut as if chewing a piece of meat. He twirled his fingers and twisted his hands and heaved his vast body forwards and backwards like a sailor in a storm at sea.

Johnson introduced me to the other people at his table, the silent Dr. Levet, who nodded soberly as he poured another cup of tea, and the blind gentlewoman Anna Williams. "A cup of tea for our guest!" Johnson commanded. She tetchily turned in my direction, felt for a cup, stuck her grubby index finger inside it, and poured till she felt the hot liquid. I thanked her, privately deciding not to drink it. Two other women, one a sluttish creature in a soiled pink skirt and bodice, the other a sober widow in dark wool, hovered about, snapping at one another. Johnson gestured in their direction. "May I introduce Poll Carmichael and Mrs. Desmoulins?"

Poll smirked, and familiarly plucked my sleeve, while the widow scowled in her direction. "Leave us now, ladies," he roared, and they went downstairs to carry on their bickering. From below I could hear someone singing a coarse ballad and guessed that must be Bet Flint, the other ex-prostitute Johnson had sheltered. Her song abruptly ceased, there was a thumping noise, and a black cat sprang up the stairs, into the room, and onto his master's lap. "Dear Hodge," he said, stroking the pet's tail. "You'll be safer up here. And you and I, sir," he said, turning to me, "had better ascend." He signaled to me to follow him up the rickety staircase, pausing only to listen to the racket below and yell down in passing: "At her again, Poll! Never flinch, Poll!"

Johnson walked like Frankenstein's monster, with a heavy shuffling movement. Following behind, I noticed he wore his shapeless buckled shoes on the wrong feet. "Don't you find these domestic quarrels annoying?" I ventured. Panting from asthma and stopping on the first landing to catch his breath, he assured me that he relished them. "Miss Williams," he said, "does not love Bet Flint—but Bet Flint makes herself very easy about that."

In the top-floor study, Johnson balanced his bulk on a crippled three-legged chair, placing the fourth quarter into a gouge in the wall. I winced at the sight of his papers scattered about, his valuable books, their spines bent back, the pages stained with food, thrown facedown on the floor. In the corner I spotted a loose box of slips left over from the *Dictionary*. I perched on an ancient chair, breathing in the dust as the contentious voices rose from below, and respectfully broached the subject of my visit. Mr. Johnson's fame was so great, I said, especially in America, that I wanted to write his biography and portray him as he really was.

"Ah!" he said, "that explains it. Your odd clothes and your peculiar speech. And I notice you wear your own hair—such of it that remains. I am willing to love all mankind, *except an American*."

"It's true I come from America, but indeed I cannot help it. I hope you're not going to hold me responsible for the Revolution. That was well before my time."

"A sad business, the loss of our colonies. I applaud you, sir, for bringing a modicum of culture to that benighted land. As you know, I myself have toiled in the vineyards of biography. It is the most delightful and useful kind of writing. It irresistibly enchains the heart and gives exemplary instruction to all mankind."

Instruction wasn't entirely what I had in mind. I wanted to know about the incidents Boswell suppressed or was unaware of. Though Johnson seemed well disposed toward me, I was afraid I might provoke his notorious temper. I was determined to endure any insult till I found out what I wanted to know. But my first problem was to stop him from interviewing *me*.

"And how, pray, do you intend to profit from your book? Grub Street is so infested with scribblers. Are you a man of means?"

"No sir," I said, "I've made my precarious living as a writer and teacher. I've heard that your academy at Edial was perhaps the most unsuccessful school in the history of education."

"A wretched life, teaching, I made no money at it. I presume you make good use of the whip? There is no other way of getting boys to learn. As for writing—I hope you keep your publishers in their place. When they insist and exploit, knock them down. Get a stout stick, sir, and shake it in their faces. You have chosen two difficult professions."

"Your life has been hard, I know. In fact, a writer has called you 'the most tragic of all our major literary figures.'"

"All human life is tragic, and my life no more so than any other. It's true I'm half-blind and half-deaf, and I've had to fight my way through life, against disease, depression, and poverty. But," he added, smiling, "you have read *Rasselas*? Then you know that overcoming obstacles is the greatest joy in life. My pension allows me to support my poor companions in this house. Death has claimed many of those I loved, but I still have my friends in the Club, even Bozzy when he descends from Scotland."

"Boswell compared you to a Roman gladiator in the Colosseum. Why were you so violent?"

"I had the reputation of being so," he said pensively. "At Oxford I was miserably poor and mad with rage, and I opposed all power and authority. My only weapons in life were my learning and my wit, which were woefully lacking there. I despised the place and I left."

"What about your temper, that time in the theater, when you threw into the pit the man who'd taken your seat? What happened to the poor folk down where he landed?"

"My intention has always been to chastise vice. The dog got what he deserved, and the rough fellows in the pit could handle him."

"What about your violent threats against your father?"

"Surely not, what can you mean?"

"After your father had printed your college translation of Alexander Pope's *Messiah* into Latin verse, you told a friend that had it not been your father you would have cut his throat. What made you so angry?"

"My father was a decent, learned man but unfortunate in business. I was an ugly, shambling creature and he was ashamed of me. But he liked to exhibit my knowledge. He published the poem without my consent, and he wanted to push me forward in Lichfield and Oxford. It was an angry threat, and I regret it now."

"You said you inherited a vile melancholy from your father," I said, trying to persuade him to talk about his mental illness.

"I meant by that a morbid disposition of body and mind, a depression that bordered on insanity. Misery, and greater misery. Such pain you could not possibly imagine. I once stared at the town clock for hours, unable to tell the time. From this dismal malady I was never perfectly relieved. But what prompts you to ask about this? Do you want to send me mad, sir?"

Thinking to shift the topic to something more pleasant, I asked if his religion was a source of comfort: "I believe you were reading William Law's *Serious Call to a Holy Life* just before you dropped out of Oxford."

"I had no religious belief until I was twenty years old. I picked up that book, expecting to find it dull, and discovered Law was quite an overmatch for me. He made moral demands on me, and hellfire and damnation darted from every page. Thank God I had a spark of piety left. He made me aware of my sinfulness and the neglect of my devotions."

"Did Christianity light your darkness and alleviate your misery?"

"I have tried to prepare for the final Judgment, but my sins have at times overwhelmed me," he said, sadly and, I thought, evasively.

"Come, sir," I said, with a smile that may have seemed patronizing, "I can't share your sense of sin. You must have heard of Thomas Jefferson and his Declaration of Independence. We Americans believe it's our right to pursue happiness. Suppose you'd never answered Law's call to become a fervent Christian, what then? You might have cheerfully indulged, like your rakish friends, Hervey and Beauclerk, in all life's pleasures."

"Outrageous puppy!" He leaned back, teetering on his chair, and reached for his stick. Sharply rapping it on the floor, he blew out his cheeks and stared at me with flashing eyes.

"You dare to suppose that men can be independent? Pah! Such foolishness, such *American* self-delusion! Fidelity to the crown maintains the *stability* of society. What do you think will become of a nation where every man thinks he is the equal of another? Except, of course," with a sneer, "those poor slaves who are forced to till your soil?"

"And who trades in slaves?" I asked, angry myself.

"Yes, it is a disgrace and a curse, and can bring no good to either of us. As for Jefferson and his Declaration, he claims the freedom any true Englishman already has, in the name of a boundless optimism."

"Jefferson is a man of the Enlightenment," I said, which was truly a red rag to a bull.

"Americans love to think that progress is not merely possible, but inevitable. Such an idea is in error. What did you do to the loyalists after your war of so-called independence was won? You slaughtered them, every one. Is this what enlightened people do? Wretched man! If your nation consists of such paltry hedonists as yourself, I tremble for your fate! Fear of God keeps the passions in check, and without it you court damnation."

He was infuriated, so I hastily drew attention to his greatest poem, a work of sustained pessimism that had always troubled me. "I wanted to ask you about *The Vanity of Human Wishes*, the first work published under your own name. You suggest that all human endeavor is vain and destined to disappointment. If that is so, wouldn't it then be wise to give up all ambition and do nothing?"

"My poem is a fine one, if I may say so, and that is not nothing, that is not in vain! Literature is not in vain, poetry and drama are not in vain. War, slavery, pillage, cruelty, conquest—all that is in vain, sir! Have you read my pamphlet on the late war in Falkland's Islands? *That* is the fate of ordinary men, to fight wars to please the powerful, to die or be maimed on foreign shores. I also wrote about the abominable treatment of our French prisoners taken in the Seven Years' War, left to starve and die of cold. You Americans are so enlightened, you would, I'm quite certain, *never* do such things! You are so proud to have thrown off the tyrant's yoke, but history will show that you will do the same, or *worse*." This last remark he pronounced with great self-satisfaction, grinding his stick into the floor as if he were twisting it into *me*.

"But," I said, determined not to let him off the hook, "you urge us to trust in Christian belief. Yet you find in religion not peace and happiness, but wretchedness and despair."

He turned to look at me with a solemn expression. "I have beliefs and I have feelings. I do all I can to reconcile them, as all men must, and I do not always succeed."

"You call me a hedonist, Mr. Johnson," I said, "but surely you must admit that pleasure is an important part of life. Your most famous pupil, the actor David Garrick, once asked you to name the greatest pleasures in life. Instead of mentioning religious devotion, intellectual conversation, foreign travel, or literary creation, you shocked him by declaring that the first pleasure was 'fucking and the second drinking.'"

"Did I actually say that? At that time I may well have longed for what I could not have. But what business is it of yours?"

"I need to ask you in order to write my book."

With a savage glare he vehemently announced, "I would advise no man to write a book who is not likely to propagate understanding."

Ignoring this, I pressed on boldly. "At the start of your marriage, it seems, your wife pleaded with you to come to bed; at the end, she excluded you from her bedroom. Do you regret marrying a woman so much older than yourself?"

"My poor dear Tetty. At first, the difference was not obvious; later on, it was all too apparent. In failing health toward the end of her life and unfortunately addicted to cordials, her passions subsided more rapidly than mine. But you must remember, sir, her little fortune gave me a start in life, even if I lost most of it. And what other woman would have loved me?"

"Elizabeth Desmoulins told Boswell that sometimes, when Tetty was asleep in the next room, Elizabeth would join you in your bed. Did you kiss her? Did you fondle her?" I braced myself, expecting an explosion at any moment.

Taken aback, he responded with unexpected calm. "I did nothing that went beyond the limits of decency. I struggled with the demons of sensuality and I overcame them. I did not proceed to the *magnum opus*."

"I gather you enjoyed women's company and respected their intelligence. Do you consider women the equal of men?"

"I do not see how women can be equal to men when they are occupied with childbearing. My friend Hester Thrale had twelve children and eight of them died. She was a clever woman with a fine head for business. I have known many bright and lively women, and though I admire intellectual ladies, I find a woman without amorous heat a dull companion."

"Your friend and biographer Sir John Hawkins says that Richard Savage tempted you to consort with prostitutes in London when your wife remained in Lichfield. Did you do so, in fact?"

"Mind your business, sir! You have a salacious mind and vex me with such persistent questions. Hawky was a most unclubbable man, and I suspect you may be, too," he added, grumpily.

"Some say all writing is partly autobiographical. When you wrote about Falstaff and Prince Hal in your notes to *Henry IV, Part I*, did you have one of your friends in mind?"

"I quote from memory but, I think, accurately: 'Yet the man thus corrupt, thus despicable, makes himself necessary to the prince, by the most pleasing of all qualities, perpetual gaiety, by an unfailing power of exciting laughter.' Now let me reflect a moment. What drunkard and sometime buffoon played Falstaff to my Prince Hal? Yes," he said, laughing, "perhaps I did have Bozzy in mind when I wrote that!"

"You seemed to count rakes and killers among your close friends. Savage was, by his own account, a liar, parasite, and murderer. Jonathan Swift, like yourself, was a Tory and Church of England man who maintained the honor of the clergy. Yet you loved Savage and attacked Swift. Why is that?"

"I could not bear Swift's pessimism—far more extreme than mine—and his nasty satire on the human race. I don't need Swift to tell me we are smitten with pride. He did nothing to elevate, and all he could to denigrate, mankind. Savage had charm and we suffered poverty together—that was a great bond. He was angrier and more desperate than I, and I took vicarious pleasure in his sins. He may have been a fraud and was certainly a troublemaker, yet I loved him."

"You once said that a second marriage was a triumph of hope over experience. But after Tetty died, you tried to find a second wife. Your love letters to Miss Hill Boothby were very moving." I thought for a moment I had gone too far. But Johnson rolled with the punches.

"*Where* did you read my private letters? Have you no shame?"

"In the Harvard library."

"The founder of that college, I believe, was placed in the pillory and then transported to America for indecent behavior." I pressed on, once again ignoring the insult.

"I was surprised to see that you hoped to win her maidenly heart by offering homely advice about constipation and suggesting remedies for lubricity of the bowels."

"She was no romantic. Hill Boothby had a *bottom* of good sense," he observed, at which I could not repress a smile. Then Johnson dug himself into a deeper hole. "Where's the merriment? I say the woman was *fundamentally* sensible."

We were interrupted by a creaking on the stair outside, and Mrs. Desmoulins pushed open the door with a tea tray. She set it down on the table and poured a cup for Johnson. He took it eagerly, joyfully slurping and remarking that all this biography was a thirsty business. Instead of offering one to me, she gave me a nasty look, and I wondered how long she might have been listening at the door. When she left I tried to steer the conversation into more troubled waters.

"After completing your edition of Shakespeare you had, if I may say so, a second mental breakdown. What do you think precipitated that tragic event?"

Twitching and trembling more than ever, for the recollection was clearly painful, Johnson began to explain: "When my work was done, I felt a great void in my life. I was gloomy and distracted, tormented with perplexities by day and with terrors by night. But then my guardian angel appeared: Hester Thrale. She understood, as no one else did, that my very fear of madness drove me mad. She was lively and animated. I was a guest in her home every week for nearly twenty years and she did everything in her power to please me."

"And yet you broke off your friendship?"

Johnson's face was creased with grief. He wrung his hands, and I waited for him to recover.

"I wanted to ask you about a Latin entry in your diary of March 1771: '*De pedicis et manicis insana cogitatio*,' which means, if I translate correctly, 'mad thought of fetters and handcuffs.' What was going on?"

"Hester agreed that when my madness came on I would submit to chains and handcuffs and have my door padlocked for safety. Fortunately, things never went quite that far."

"But didn't Hester use these chains and the whip she mentioned in her diary?"

"They were penitential. I was tormented by sin and guilt, and she whipped me. I adored that woman. My only happiness was to be in chains, on my knees, kissing her little foot."

"You were upset when the widowed Hester revealed her intention to marry the Italian singer Gabriele Piozzi. But why did you quarrel over it? Didn't she have the right, after an unhappy marriage, to choose the man she truly loved?"

"No, sir," he said indignantly. "My reaction was not entirely selfish. There were other, far more serious considerations: her country and children, her religion and reputation. Piozzi was simply unsuitable."

"Do you regret your behavior now?"

"It was a tremendous blow when our friendship ended in bitterness. I tried to mollify her, but it was too late. She is gone to Italy. I shall never see her again."

"Mr. Johnson," I said, "you have achieved so much, and had so many friends, so many fine talks, so many evenings of laughter and argument. Do you have any regrets about things you didn't do? Are you sorry to have foregone other pleasures in life?"

"How you do go on, sir, about happiness, joys, pleasure! Don't you Americans care about anything else? As Prince Hal observed, 'If all the world were playing holidays, to sport would be as tedious as to work.' Life is grim, life is earnest, it is not for man's pleasure." He paused a moment to drain his tea, and I got up to pour him another cup.

"It is true," he went on, "I do have some regrets. I was precipitate in my recent dealings with Hester Piozzi. I disobeyed my father and neglected my mother. When we are young we do not understand that death cuts us off from those we love and that we cannot recapture lost opportunities.

"My father used to set up a book stall on market days. One day he was unwell and asked me to take his place. I was lazy and thought tending a stall beneath my dignity, so I refused. My father died a few weeks later. Three years ago I returned to that market and stood for two hours in the rain to do penance, but nothing could extinguish my guilt. Pride was our original sin, and the source of all other sins."

"You've been accused of being uncivil, even rude."

"On the contrary, sir, I am exceedingly well bred. I am rude only when insufferably vexed. I cannot bear mindless foolishness."

"I've heard you'd do anything to win an argument. That just to show your powers, you even defended the Spanish Inquisition."

"Well, the Catholics were right to correct false doctrine, though they may have gone a bit too far."

I could not let Johnson get away with justifying everything he'd ever said or done, no matter how inconsistent. He was so rational, so progressive in some ways, yet so primitive in his dire pessimism, which nothing seemed to shake, and in his superstitious dread of death.

"Mr. Johnson, why should you fear death if you have done your best to live a good life? I am inclined to be optimistic about the future of man. As to life after death, I agree with your contemporary, the Scottish philosopher David Hume, who said he was no more disturbed to think he should *not be* after this life, than that he *had not been* before he began to exist. Once dead, he was not afraid to lie in dark obstruction and to rot."

Johnson looked at me sorrowfully, shaking his head. "If he really believes this, he must be mad. Your views are those of a healthy, untroubled man. I must urge you to alter them before it is too late.

How will you face sickness or death without the help of God? How can you reconcile the evil of the world with such foolish optimism? Or perhaps you are merely provoking me."

"No indeed, sir. My purpose is to understand your life: *tout comprendre c'est tout pardonner.*"

"Your French accent, if I may say so, is as appalling as your manners," he countered, testily. Then his expression softened a little, and he added, "Don't be uneasy. I've come to like you very well. When, may I ask, do you plan to return to the wilderness?"

"In two days time, from Southampton," I said, hinting that I would leave by sea as they did in his time.

"You know how much I like a leisurely ramble. I propose to accompany you to the coast and see you out of England."

And so he did, and was vastly entertaining along the way. As my vessel left its berth and put out to sea, I kept my eye on him for a considerable time. He remained rolling his majestic frame like a sailor, till at last I perceived him walking back toward the town. His grubby clothes and urban grime made him kin to the exhausted homeless man who lay in a nearby doorway. Charity, first and last, was uppermost in his mind. He bent over and placed a coin in the hand of the sleeping man.

The Aziola and the Moth

The Shelleys at the Bagni di Pisa

NORA CROOK

I glided in reverie into a sultry evening during the last days of August 1821 and into the saloon that ran the length of the upstairs floor of Casa Prini in the small resort of Bagni di Pisa. It was the second summer that the Shelleys had rented the house for their *villegiatura*. The windows were open to admit any through breeze that might stir. At one end they looked out on a little garden, set with orange and lemon trees, fronting the torpid Canale di Ripafratta. A frail craft made of laths scarcely quivered on its surface; gnats lackadaisically danced in the last sunbeams of the day. Lining the canal were stunted willows, and beyond them parched meadows where the *cicala* had fallen silent. The windows at the opposite end looked out onto the piazza. A year before, squealing pigs brought there for sale at the Festa had drowned out the poet's reading of his "Ode to Naples," leading to an hour of merriment that resulted in his satire *Swellfoot the Tyrant*. Behind the townlet rose the marble hill of San Giuliano, overgrown with myrtle bushes. The slightly shabby but still fine room, with its high ceiling, plaster moldings, and tiled floor, was furnished in simple Tuscan style: a walnut refectory dining table; a large wood-burning stove, now of course unlit; chairs with worn but handsome tapestry seats and backs; a French chaise longue, relic of the period when Bonaparte had made Tuscany part of France; and a round table of bronze and *verde antica* on which were placed books, a chess set, a Grecian-style vase, and a palm-leaf fan from India.

There sat the Shelleys, by themselves for the first time in several weeks. Their friends, the Williamses, who lived at Pugnano, farther along the canal, were not calling on them that evening. Mary Shelley was dressed in a pink-and-white striped cotton gown. Her face was pale, her eyes were hazel-gray, her light gold hair was done up in a simple knot. Percy Shelley wore an ill-fitting jacket and trousers, with an open-necked shirt. Contemporaries described him as stooped and short-sighted; I could not judge of this, but his brown hair was flecked with gray. He had recently returned from a visit to Byron at Ravenna, where he had persuaded the noble poet and his mistress to move to Pisa, the family of the latter having been recently expelled from Ravenna for their support of Carbonarism; they would be arriving in about a month. The responsibility of finding a palazzo worthy of Byron and his entourage had devolved on his shoulders. He had seen little Allegra, daughter of Byron and Mary Shelley's stepsister, Claire Clairmont, in her convent but had failed to get Byron to agree to allow her to visit her mother. Shelley's *tendresse* for Claire was as strong as ever; he had chosen to spend his twenty-ninth birthday on 4 August in a tête-à-tête with her. To Mary Shelley's great relief, no doubt, Claire had just returned to Livorno to take sea baths for a scrofulous gland.

Mary Shelley, seated at the walnut table, a lap-desk in front of her, quill pen in hand, was neatly copying from a heavily corrected manuscript into a blank notebook, each page numbered in advance. Shelley, I knew, was between major poems, having finished *Adonais*; *Hellas* was taking shape in his mind. He lounged, watching the sky fade to an amethystine glow, glancing occasionally in irritation at a copy of Byron's *Marino Faliero*.

"Listen, Mary," he suddenly exclaimed. "I hear the little owl, the Aziola. Do you remember?"

"Yes. Last year, at Livorno, before I began *Castruccio*. And the fireflies."

"You heard it first. Do you know, when you asked me if I had heard the Aziola I half-misheard it as *Apollonia*, that tedious woman who moped that she was dying of love for Henry Reveley. How elated I was to realize that Aziola was a bird, not a human being."

"Poor girl, how we teased Henry about her." She sighed. I knew that she was also remembering that period as a dreadful time when Paolo, their servant, blackmailed Shelley, threatening to say that a child born at Naples in the winter of 1818 was the offspring of himself and Claire. In the 1930s, I remembered, Newman Ivey White had discovered that there *was* a Naples child, a baby girl; Shelley had been registered as the father, and Mary Shelley registered (impossibly) as the mother, apparently without her knowledge. White suggested that Shelley had adopted an orphan in order to comfort Mary for the death of baby Clara the previous September. But why, I had often wondered, would he have done this, when the two of them could have conceived another child—and did so, only two months after the supposed adoption? Paolo had somehow been silenced, but his allegations had eventually reached the ears of Byron, who had told Shelley of them during his visit to Ravenna. Horrified, Shelley had begged Mary to write a letter to be shown to Byron, "refuting the charge in case you believe & know & can prove that it is false." She had done so immediately, swearing by the life of her one surviving child, little Percy, that Claire had had no child at Naples. But she did not mention that a child had been born there. The aftermath of this recent commotion had left behind an unease that seemed to hover in the dusk with the faint scent of myrtle.

"I have loved the sad cry of the Aziola ever since." Shelley continued, "How wonderful are birds—they sound the deepest note of suffering, without suffering themselves. They have no self-pity."

A servant entered with candles as the light faded. "*Felicissima sera, Signora*," she said. "The bambino Percy sleeps. He has tired himself out trying to catch bees all day."

"*Felicissima sera*, Caterina."

"Signora, do you hear the little owl?" asked Caterina. "She is sad because her *sposo* and her children have left her." Caterina lit the large oil lamps and withdrew.

"How I love this ceremonious bringing in of the lights, Tuscan courtesy that is neither servility nor insolence," Mary Shelley remarked, "and the poetical fancifulness of the people. How dare the Austrians say that this intelligent race is unfit for independence?" She added, after a pause, "Did my letter persuade Lord Byron that everything alleged against you was false?"

"Who the devil is that?" asked Shelley abruptly, looking in my direction. The lamp had revealed my presence. I saw now that his eyes were large and of a deep, piercing blue.

"A gleam from a remoter world," I replied, emerging from the shadows, hoping that the idea would charm them. "A visitant from the twenty-first century. An editor of your works."

"Ah—so there *is* a tedious woman here after all," said Mary Shelley dryly. "A *seccatura*. I feared it. We are spirits, you know—we inhabit your century as well as our own. We know everything that has happened on earth since our animated clay dwelt there—I fancy that there is little that you can tell us." She fixed me with a gaze as piercing as her husband's.

"But may I not stay for a short while and enjoy Lucianic intercourse with the illustrious dead?"

"You know Lucian? His *Dialogues of the Dead*?"

"Only in translation," I admitted.

"A delightful author," she said. "Well—stay. But do not ask us to prophesy. Your futurity is as dark to us as it is to you."

Even this tart welcome was a relief: in 1984 I had had a visionary run-in with Shelley. At the time I was collaborating on my first book. Its argument was that much of Shelley's so-called hypochondria and the recurrent imagery in his poetry of nightshade, white-haired youths, and poisoned wells could be explained by his having contracted a venereal disease in youth, or fearing that he had. Thornton Hunt, son of one of Shelley's intimates, Leigh Hunt, had claimed to know that this was so. I had spent evenings in Cambridge University Library poring over old medical journals, gathering details of gummas and hydroceles, of dosing with nitric acid and other justly forgotten treatments for the *lues venerea*. These dreary activities infected my dreams. In one such dream I had met Shelley somewhere in limbo. He had allowed me to ask him one question. I had blurted out unhesitatingly, "*Did* you have venereal disease?" Shelley gazed at me with ineffable contempt and replied, "You could have asked me anything, yet you choose the most trivial and impertinent question imaginable." "Oh, I'm so sorry," I cried, mortified. "Wait, please wait—I have another question—how would you have completed *The Triumph of Life*?" "You've already asked your question," said Shelley, vanishing, and I awoke.

But Shelley seemed to have forgotten our unlucky meeting, and Mary Shelley to know nothing of it. I talked to her first, apart, while her husband watched the stars come out, still glancing at *Marino Faliero*. I thought it proper to address her formally, in contemporary style, as "Mrs. Shelley." This may have been wise, since it turned out that despite claiming that they were perfectly informed of events since their deaths, they sometimes spoke inconsistently, as if they had no glimmering of what lay ahead of that day in August, or of changed manners since their era.

"Mrs. Shelley, are you making a copy of *Castruccio, Prince of Lucca* for the publisher?"

"My *Castruccio*! Yes—it will be better than *Frankenstein*—it is even more political and philosophical. I am inspired by the stirring events that are taking place in Italy—the risings in Naples and in Piedmont have been crushed, but I am confident that it will be for a time only. The heroines are more interesting than the insipid Elizabeth and Justine—but I keep wishing to introduce more episodes. Today I went walking on the mountain in the cool of the morning—and revisited a spot that the *contadini* call the *Buche delle Fate*. Do you know it? You see some dark apertures in an outcrop of rock—some no larger than rabbit burrows—quite tame and uninteresting. But if you throw a pebble down one of them, you hear nothing for what seems to be an interminable interval—and then a series of ever-fainter reboundings and echoes as your pebble strikes rock after rock in the abyss—down, down, down, for hundreds of feet. The natural philosophers say that there is a huge hollow. You might fancy that a Sybil dwells within—that she knows all the secrets of the hidden caverns of the mind. I should like to make my heroines visit the *Buche* together, but the three volumes are already long enough—I must save this idea for my next novel."

"Mrs. Shelley, I recognize that something of the sort did appear in your subsequent novel *The Last Man*, though very changed, and transposed to the Sybil's cave, near Naples. But I'm afraid that *Ca-*

struccio, under the name of *Valperga*, achieved only one edition in your lifetime and was never reprinted until the late twentieth century. Many now regard it as a remarkable and unjustly neglected novel. But posterity judges *Frankenstein* to be your best, your masterpiece."

"And compliments me by adapting my tale to entertainments in which my articulate Creature becomes a grunting idiot! And blames me for a distrust of science when I intended merely to warn against its misuse. Well, let Posterity, who is sometimes a goose, cackle as she will, provided she acknowledges the book as mine. Owing to the manner in which *Frankenstein* appeared, many thought Shelley had written it—they believed that no woman could have conceived such a hideous tale. There is nothing to which contemporaries are more prone than to discover that authors do not write their own works. It went into the world without my name lest it should attract either condescending reviews damning the 'fair authoress' with faint praise—or vituperations on my character as an unsexed hyena in petticoats. To this day I believe I did right, but I have suffered disbelief as a result."

"Mrs. Shelley, I am sorry to say that a few—a very few—still disbelieve. Others have wondered whether Shelley should not be called a minor author of *Frankenstein*."

She retorted like the daughter of Wollstonecraft and Godwin. "I have stated publicly that I 'did not owe the suggestion of one incident, nor scarcely of one train of feeling' to Shelley. Of course, I borrowed incidents from his history—long familiar to me through his own relating them—some lines of his poetry—a few of his favorite expostulations."

"Yes, and you acknowledge his urging you to turn it from a short story into a novel and his incitement to publish it. But it appears that he is responsible for over a tenth of the actual words of the work in its first edition. Most of your rough transcript of *Frankenstein* was rediscovered in the 1970s. It was found that Shelley had made extensive corrections to it, most of which you adopted."

"Well, *Posterity* no doubt requires this information—but Mr. Colburn, who asked me to write an introduction to a new, revised edition in 1831, did not. He wanted an account of *Frankenstein*'s origins and an assurance for my readers that I had made no material change to the plot—such as would have been the case had I revised it so as to allow Walton to kill the Creature and avenge Elizabeth. To write on that occasion that Shelley had corrected the text was not to the purpose.

"But I gladly now affirm that Shelley spread the luster of poetic sublimity over the final speeches of the Creature—he corrected the language where the story read as though narrated by a young woman of nineteen, instead of by men in their prime of life. The female characters he left virtually untouched—but he was responsible for suggesting a coloring to the character of Henry Clerval as he travels with Victor down the Rhine—he rightly urged that readers should recall Victor's affection for this gentle and romantic being after his absence from an entire volume—or else his impending and shocking murder would not *come home* to them. But it was still *I* who accepted Shelley's corrections."

"But were you free to reject them? He was older, more experienced, and you have confessed that his mind was then more cultivated than yours. You describe yourself as a *devout listener* to the conversations of Shelley and Byron at the Villa Diodati when Byron proposed the volume of ghost stories. Surely Shelley must often have over-persuaded you."

"I *was* free to reject them. It is true that in 1817, the year I finished *Frankenstein*, I was still in awe of my father—intimidated by Lord Byron to a degree (even Shelley did not care to provoke his anger)—but I was no bread-and-butter school-room miss—I had the willful and bold self-confidence of youth—I was a mother, a woman of the world—I played the shy dormouse on occasion but was far more vigorous in maintaining my opinions than I was to become later—after *he* died, and I became as cold moonshine—repenting that I had not made the most beautiful spirit that had ever inhabited a mortal body as happy as I should have done—or as he deserved."

"Cease to put Mary to the question," intervened Shelley, evidently hearing her voice quiver. "I could never have conceived nor carried out her *Frankenstein*, nor for that matter *Mathilda* or *Valperga*, fictions written during my lifetime and also with my encouragement.

My own novels (boyish trash that I snatched in horror from Hunt when he tried to peruse them in our library, and beginnings that I could never develop to a fitting conclusion) stand as a refutation to those who would assert otherwise. I could think of situations, but narrative was never my strength. Let us hear no more of my being a minor author of *Frankenstein*. I do not begrudge the fact that Mary at present enjoys a celebrity greater even than mine."

"To return to the subject of beautiful spirits, Mrs. Shelley, was your ideal portrait of your husband well-judged? It enabled the critic Matthew Arnold to describe him as an ineffectual angel. This was surely to make him seem to be in a sense a eunuch."

"*Il povero* Arnold," she mocked. "Quite an *enfant perdu*, I fear. But Shelley can speak for himself."

"You are confounding an angel with a monk," said Shelley earnestly. "Recollect the question of Milton's Adam in *Paradise Lost*, 'Can angels love?' Remember the cherub's glowing smile of remembered pleasure, and above all his reply that when two angelic beings interpenetrate, finding no obstacle of membrane, joint, or limb, 'total they mix, union of pure with pure desiring.' Who that has loved, has not desired to love like an angel? Who has not felt some disappointment with mortal love, even in its dearest form? That is the profound truth upon which Lucretius dilates in the fourth book of *On the Nature of Things*, and which Shakespeare places in the mouth of Troilus: 'This is the monstrosity in love, lady, that the will is infinite and the execution confined; that the desire is boundless, and the act a slave to limit.' Now that we are portions of the Immortal, Mary and I and other chosen spirits enjoy in reality that boundless and infinite delight which Milton merely imagined for his angels."

They smiled like cherubs. But I reflected that there must have been many human beings who have not wished in the least to love like Milton's angels. I wondered whether Mary Shelley really did enjoy interpenetration with "other chosen spirits" as much as Shelley implied she did (I remembered the story of how she wept because Shelley wanted her to sleep with his friend Hogg); but while I was seeking to frame my next question with delicacy, she suddenly arose, saying: "I must leave you for a moment—I think I heard Percy cry out. Perhaps he has disarranged the *zanzariera* and the mosquitoes are biting him."

"You must excuse Mary," said Shelley. "We have lost two beautiful children to the climate of Italy. The least whimper might herald some grave alarm."

"Then you blame only the *climate of Italy*, and not yourself at all, for the death of your little Clara?" said I, turning on him, his companion having neatly finessed my question. "She had a fever, yet you made Mrs. Shelley travel with her from Bagni di Lucca to Venice, across rough roads, in the hot summer of 1818. And why? To save yourself from embarrassment, to cover up the lie you told Lord Byron that your family were with you, a pretense adopted to obscure the fact that you had traveled alone with Miss Clairmont on purpose that she might see her child by his lordship. And what exactly went on at Naples in the winter of 1818? Was there, as your cousin Medwin said, a lady who followed you there? Was *she* the mother of the child registered as yours, and were you the father? Mrs. Shelley lacerates herself with memories of her own shortcomings; do you ever reflect on the misery that you caused to women? Let me mention—"

"O cease—cease," he interrupted, his voice reaching a cracked, high-pitched register in its anguish. "If you knew how much I have inwardly castigated myself for the results of my many well-meaning actions, you would weep bitter tears for me rather than endeavor to reawaken *my* maddening self-reproaches, or to goad me into revealing what I have sworn never to divulge.

"But" (collecting himself and continuing calmly), "to resume the question of my angelic nature. I have no quarrel with those, including Mary, who promulgated this idea of me. You are aware, I trust, that an angel is an *angelos*, a messenger. At times I believed that I was indeed possessed by an almost divine power, that I was the apocalyptic herald of some mighty change in society. Revenge and wrong continue to bring forth their kind, yet I do not think that I have been ineffectual. I appeal to my biographer Richard Holmes's description of myself as a 'capable figure.'"

"Holmes's words are '*crueller and more capable* figure.'"

"Then let this suffice: can you maintain that the present situation in the civilized world, whereby those who live according to what used quaintly to be called 'in sin' are no longer driven from decent society and calumniated as depraved monsters, where atheists no longer see their legally abducted children shepherded to drink the poison dews of Christian superstition—can you maintain that this change is not in part due to my writings?"

"By the same argument, you also wrote a poem called *Laon and Cythna* in which sexual and religious oppression and tyrannical cruelty are metaphorically represented as *Islam*. Sophisticated readers knew and know that you were referring to *England* under a feigned name. But can you maintain that your poem did not contribute to Western cultural imperialism and the present evils that have ensued from it, which I need not expatiate on here?"

"I am all too aware of these evils, and pity those who are not inwardly tortured by contemplating them." There was a long silence. His face was now in shadow and I could not read it. "You insinuate that I have done harm while I maintain that I have been an unacknowledged legislator for good. I shall have to endure your skepticism."

I steered the conversation into less contentious waters. "You often were afraid that your poems would be forgotten; you must have been surprised to find yourself among the classic English poets."

"Yes, I had almost despaired of having any readers at the time of my death. Mary's part must not be overlooked. Her collection of my *Posthumous Poems* ensured that I remained in the public eye. My friend Leigh Hunt, too, and my cousin Tom Medwin, were indefatigable champions. I am also grateful to the early pirates—the Benbows and the Clarks and the Aschams—who reprinted and circulated my work during the two decades following my death, and the men and women of Britain and America who read them, in spite of all the abusive reviews could do."

"Did it not pain you that Mrs. Shelley suppressed your most radical pieces such as your witty and irreverent 'On the Devil and Devils' and mutilated your prose such as your discussion of the sexual morality of the Greeks?"

"But she preserved the manuscripts for future generations. The temper of the age, and the implacable malignity of my father, did not admit of their being published in my lifetime or hers. At the time I judged my publishers, the Hunts and Ollier, to be coldly prudent, but had they done as I urged, they would have hurt themselves by fines and imprisonment without benefiting me. Mary published as much as she thought that public opinion could stand. Had she lived longer, I believe that she would have published more. You will remember that I once wrote that even Christ had accommodated his words to the understandings of his listeners. This sagacious and amiable characteristic of Jesus I have always desired to emulate."

"But surely it was vexing to see her including among your *Posthumous Poems* the contents, as it were, of your wastepaper basket, discarded fragments that were never intended to be seen in cold print?"

"Why, when they appeared in *cold print*, as you style it, I realized that my mortal self had often been mistaken. I wrote two stanzas of a poem beginning 'Rose leaves, when the rose is dead,' but threw it aside as the mood of the morning evaporated. She found the fragment after my death and saw that the two stanzas, transposed, formed a little song beginning 'Music when soft voices die.' I consider that in this Mary showed the most exquisite taste and judgment. She disclosed to me my unconscious intent, and the stanzas became my most celebrated song for singing. Not that all her editing was equally happy. But her actions were sincerely intended to honor me, and she could not have done otherwise than she did. You see that I am a Necessitarian still."

"'Music when soft voices die' endeared you to a portion of the poetry-reading public that never tired of roses and soft voices, but it lowered your standing eventually. It was singled out by, among others, Dr. F. R. Leavis, who contributed so much to the decline in your reputation during the mid-twentieth century, especially in Britain, as exemplifying weaknesses in your work."

"I cannot nurse resentment against Dr. Leavis. He, and others of his generation, were obliged to admire my poems at school and were dosed sick with them. Admiration is not a voluntary passion.

What wonder if enforced admiration destroys both pleasure and itself? Do you think I could have loved Plato, or even relished Lewis's *The Monk*, if I had been made to study them at school? Dr. Leavis praised the *Mask of Anarchy* and *Peter Bell the Third*, neglected favorites of mine in his day, and commended *The Triumph of Life*. He wrote that my greatness was not in dispute and that I was a very intelligent man."

"A small correction. 'Shelley was *in some ways* a very intelligent man.'"

"Come," he replied, "we short-sighted mortals cannot be intelligent in *all* ways. Dr. Leavis, as I understand, was an atheist with republican leanings, a hater of the vulgarity of aristocracy, a pacifist who joined an Ambulance Unit, saving the lives of the wounded and succoring the dying during the First World War; he wore an open-necked shirt like mine. I find myself strangely drawn toward such a person."

He was provokingly disinclined to quarrel with the shade of Dr. Leavis. I remembered Peacock's testimony as to his equanimity in debate: "A personal discussion, however interesting to himself, was carried on with the same calmness as if it related to the most abstract question in metaphysics."

After a pause Shelley exclaimed: "And should I repine? My winged words continue to fly through the universe. My works, and even my rough notebooks, preserved with their apple pips, wine stains, grains of blotting sand, and even a miserable squashed fly, are published with learned annotations on both sides of the Atlantic, an attention formerly reserved for the classics, Dante, or Shakespeare. I deplore the fact that vast sums are paid for the most trifling scribble in my handwriting while people starve in Africa and Asia, but smile to think that my 'Ozymandias' is now more read than Lord Byron's *Prisoner of Chillon*."

Clearly, he was not so angelic as to have lost all his old sense of rivalry with Byron. At last I could put the question again to him that I had tried out abortively twenty-five years before: "You mentioned *The Triumph of Life* just now, your last work on a large scale, obviously written in part as a reaction to Byron's *Prophecy of Dante* and, like that poem, in *terza rima*. You left the manuscript incomplete and enigmatic when you sailed off on that first of July 1822, having written:

> "Then, what is Life?" I said . . . the cripple cast
> His eye upon the car which now had rolled
> Onward, as if that look must be the last
>
> And answered. . . . "Happy those for whom the fold
> Of

You broke off where the Chariot of Life is about to disappear from view. How would your poem have continued? What would Rousseau, the cripple, have said? That there is a way to escape bondage to the Chariot of Life? Or that the only escape is through death? Was hope about to arise from despair, as in 'Ode to the West Wind' and *The Mask of Anarchy*? Or was it to end like 'Ode to Liberty' or *Hellas*, in images of drowning, or collapse—or ambiguity?"

"I seem to remember that I suspended composition so as to shake off an almost irresistible impulse of the moment to terminate the poem then and there with: 'But what the cripple said—let it remain untold,' and so spare myself further wrestling with *terza rima*. But I had previously used this expedient to give a factitious ending to the fragment *Athanase*, and I disdained to repeat so paltry a device.

"What if I had resumed? *The Triumph of Life* begins at dawn; at one stage of composition my intention had been to trace the progress of a single day, as representative of the vicissitudes of human life. I intended to create a twilight moment so lovely that the dreamer whose narrative is the substance of the poem would involuntarily cry, 'Remain thou, thou art so beautiful!' upon which he would expire, and the poem would end. You will remember that the Faust of Goethe with wild solemnity promises his soul to Mephisto were he ever to address the passing moment thus.

"And yet, before Williams and I sailed that day for Livorno to meet Leigh Hunt and Lord Byron, my heart full of foreboding, methinks I intended that the poem should finish with the narrator waking from his dream to a thunderstorm and a shipwreck in broad daylight as he watches, aghast, from the safety of his promontory. So often does poetic inspiration prove true prophecy.

"But could I have seized paper and pen during the course of the fatal voyage *homeward*, a week later, before real thunderstorm and shipwreck overtook us—our journal *The Liberal* now in train, my bosom now bounding with hopes for the future, revived by seeing dear Hunt after four years, high-hearted Williams by my side, the hour enlivened by the sportiveness of that unfortunate sailor-boy, Charles Vivian, who perished with us,—I should have ended it with a paean to friendship and to poetry. Our feelings are a prey to circumstance, and each heart is its own oracle. In the words of the profoundest of dramas, *King Lear*, 'And that's true too.'"

He sat staring at a moth as Mary Shelley reentered.

"Percy is well," she said. "It was the cry of the Aziola."

"Mary, see that moth, drawn to the candle flame. Quick, extinguish it before it singes its wings."

She did so. Shelley picked up the Indian fan and waved the moth toward the window. It flew out and fluttered upward into the night air. The Shelleys watched it, their hands interlocked. As I faded from their world, I thought I heard him say: "There, Mary. When it is given its freedom, a moth . . ." She finished the sentence for him: ". . . will seek its bright particular star."

An (Unfortunate) Interview
with Henry James

CYNTHIA OZICK

The interview took place at Lamb House, Rye, Sussex—rather, its precise duplicate in the Other World. The house, red brick with numerous mullioned windows, fronts the street. One approaches it along the curve of a narrow flagstoned path. Four shallow steps lead up to a white door overhung by a cornice. The modest brass knocker is tapped, and a young man responds. He is Burgess Noakes, James's valet.

JAMES (*within*): Noakes? Is it our appointed visitor?

NOAKES: Yes, sir. It's the American lady from that magazine.

JAMES (*coming forward with a certain fussy anxiety*): A lady? I was rather expecting a gentleman. Forgive me, dear madam, do come in.—Noakes, the tea things, if you please.—Ah, my most admirable typewriter is just departing. Quite a morning's toil, Miss Bosanquet, was it not? We are getting on, we are getting on!

Miss Theodora Bosanquet, James's typist (writer's cramp has in recent years forced him to dictate), emerges from a room behind, pinning on her hat. She neatly rounds James's bicycle, precariously lodged against an umbrella stand in the central hall. She nods, smiles tiredly, and makes her way out with practiced efficiency.

JAMES (*seating himself before a finely tiled fireplace, and motioning for the visitor to join him there*): I must again beg your pardon. I discover myself increasingly perplexed by the ever-accelerating extrusions of advanced women—

INTERVIEWER (*interrupting*): You don't like us. You were opinionated enough about all that in *The Bostonians*.

JAMES (*taken aback by this feminist brashness, and glad to have Noakes deflect it with the arrival of a tray holding teacups and a variety of jel-*

lied pastries): Thank you, Noakes. The advent of cakes, the temptation to the sweet tooth, how it brings to the fore one's recent torments at the dentist's! One must perforce disclose one's most private crannies to this oral Torquemada—which I take to be the unhappy emblem of an age of interlocutory exposure. The ladies seem to swim in it! Especially the American ladies.

INTERVIEWER: I suppose that's what you were getting at in your portrait of Henrietta Stackpole, the peppy American journalist in *The Portrait of a Lady.*

JAMES: May I say, *mutatis mutandis*, that she might have been getting at me! In point of fact, dear madam, I have in mind rather my unfortunate engagement with your predecessor, an American lady journalist representing the *New York Herald*, with whom I sat, as it were, for an interview, during my American journey in 1904, my maiden voyage, so to speak, into a venture of this kind. This lady's forwardness, her hagiographical incessancy, was, in fine, redoubtable. She hastened to remark upon how I had so far, and so long, escaped the ministrations of uncanny inquirers such as herself, and undertook to portray my shrinking from her certainties as a species of diffident bewilderment. She declaimed it her right, as a free citizen of my native land, to put to me all manner of intimacies. I warned her, as I now warn you, madam, that one's craft, one's art, is in one's expression, not one's person. After you have heard Adelina Patti sing, why should you care to hear the small private voice of the woman?

INTERVIEWER: I gather that you intend to inhibit my line of questioning.

JAMES: Madam, I do not inhibit. I merely decline to exhibit.

INTERVIEWER: Is that why you've had the habit of burning things? When your ailing sister Alice died, her companion, Katharine Loring, had copies of Alice's diary printed up especially for you and your brother William. You burned your copy.

JAMES: Ah, the mask and armor of her fortitude, poor invalid!—and with such ironic amusement and interest in the presentation of it all. It would not, could not, do. My fraternally intimated morsels of London gossip, for the simple change and relief and diversion of it, came ultimately, and distressingly, to animate her pen. The wit of those lucubrations loomed, may I say, as a vulgar peril. So many names, personalities, hearsays, through me! I hardly wished to be seen as privately depreciating those to whom I was publicly civil.

INTERVIEWER: Yet in 1909 you might have been seen as doing exactly that. You made a bonfire in your garden of the thousands of letters sent you by your devoted correspondents, many of them your distinguished friends. And six years later, you threw still more papers into the fire: it took you a week to get the job done. Will you agree that you've been singularly merciless to your biographers?

JAMES: Put it that the forewarned victim subverts the future's cunning. I have been easier in my mind ever since, and my little conflagrations scarcely appear to have impeded posterity's massive interventions.

INTERVIEWER: Well, true, they haven't stopped us from speculating that you're gay and always have been.

JAMES: Indeed, there has been a frequency of jolly corners . . . delightful hours with Turgenev in Paris . . . the soliloquizing intimacy of one's London hearth in winter, or the socially convenient pleasures of the ever so felicitous Reform Club . . . going in to dinner with a gracious lady on one's arm in some grand country house . . . all rewardingly gay at times, to be sure; but neither have I been spared sojourns upon the bench of desolation. Despair, I own, dogged me in particular in the year 1895, when at the opening of my play, *Guy Domville*—

INTERVIEWER (*breaking in hurriedly*): I mean you've loved men.

JAMES: And so I have. To choose but one, my fondness for the dear Jonathan Sturges, that crippled little demon, resonates unchecked for me even now. How I embraced the precious months he came to stay at Lamb House, with his mordant tongue and bright eyes, full of unprejudiced talk and intelligence. Body-blighted Brother Jonathan! Yet he made his way in London in wondrous fashion.

INTERVIEWER: I'm afraid we're not entirely on the same page.

JAMES: The same page? Would that be an Americanism? With all your foreign influx, we shall not know our English tongue for the sacred purity it once resplendently gave out. A young American cousin, on a visit here, persisted in pronouncing *jewel* as *jool, vowel* as *vowl*, and was driven at last to deem my corrections cruel. "*Cruel*, Rosina, not *crool*," I necessarily admonished. The young ladies of Bryn Mawr College, in the vicinity of Philadelphia, when I lectured there in 1905, had similar American afflictions. They would articulate the reticent *r* in words such as *motherrrr, fatherrrr, millerrrr—*

INTERVIEWER: I admit to that *r* myself. But to come back to your, um, fondness for men. One of your more reckless biographers believes that in the spring of 1865, in your own shuttered bedroom in Cambridge—that's Cambridge, Massachusetts—you had your earliest experience, your *initiation première*, as you yourself called it in your journal.

JAMES: Ah, the epoch-making weeks of that memorable spring! The bliss of *l'initiation première*, the divine, the unique! It was in that very March that my first published story appeared in the *Atlantic Monthly*.

INTERVIEWER: We're definitely not on the same page. He claims that this initiation première of yours was in the arms of the young Oliver Wendell Holmes, Junior, the future chief justice of the United States Supreme Court. He says that you slept with Holmes. Carnally.

JAMES (*recoiling, and pressing his fingers to his temples, as if a familiar migraine is coming on*): My dear lady—

INTERVIEWER (*digging into her tote bag and pulling out a thick biographical volume*): And what about Hugh Walpole? No one burned your letters, after all. Here's what you wrote to your "dear, dear Hugh": "See therefore, how we're at one, and believe in the comfort I take in you. It goes very deep—deep, deep, deep: so infinitely do you touch and move me, dear Hugh." Such obvious ardor! What do you say to it?

JAMES: I say I deeply, deeply, infinitely favor the universalization of epistolary arson. The twaddle of mere graciousness has perhaps too often Niagara'd from the extravagances of my inkpot.

INTERVIEWER: And how about your "exquisite relation" with Jocelyn Persse? A good-looking Anglo-Irishman, the nephew of Lady

Gregory, thirty when you met him, you were sixty. Now it was "my dear, dear Jocelyn." You went so far as to ask for his photo to moon over. And then there was Hendrik Andersen, that big handsome blond Norwegian sculptor—"I have missed you," you confided, "you out of all proportion to the three meagre little days that we had together. I hold you close, I feel, my dear boy, my arms around you, I draw you close, I hold you long." So why shouldn't the homoerotic question come up?

JAMES (*reddening*): Andersen's sculptures, those monstrously huge swollen ugly things. Let us pass over this unseemly subject.

INTERVIEWER: Here in the twenty-first century we pass over nothing, we let it all hang out. You mentioned earlier your despondency over your theatrical failure.

JAMES: Madam, you hurl me from unseemliness to unseemliness! The *sacro terrore* of it all! My charmingly contemplated eloquences were vigorously upon the boards when out of nervousness I slipped out to sample a neighboring drama—*An Ideal Husband*, Oscar Wilde's juvenile folly, flailing its silly jocularity. When I returned to the St. James, the last act was just finishing—there were cries of "Author, author"—and then the hoots and jeers and catcalls of the roughs began—roars—a cage of beasts at some infernal zoo—

INTERVIEWER: You fell into a long depression after that. One of the many in your life, despite brilliant friendships, fame, the richness of travel, Paris, Rome, Florence, Venice, family visits to America—

JAMES: Never say you know the last word about any human heart.

INTERVIEWER: But George Bernard Shaw was in the audience as a reviewer that night, and he praised and championed you. You've had scores of champions and admirers—Edith Wharton, for one.

JAMES: The Firebird! Her motoring habits and intentions, so potent and explicit, bent on catching me up in her irresistible talons, the whir and wind of those great pinions cold on my foredoomed brow! Oh, one's opulent friends—they cost the eyes out of one's head. Edith, always able and interesting, yet insistent and unpredictable. Her powers of devastation were ineffable.

INTERVIEWER: She came with her car and her chauffeur and took you away from your work. But she also facilitated it. There was that scheme she cooked up, getting your mutual publisher to give you a portion of her bestseller royalties—eight thousand dollars—while pretending they were your earnings. It was arranged so shrewdly that you swallowed it whole. And then she took up a collection for your seventieth birthday—

JAMES: A more reckless and indiscreet undertaking, with no ghost of a preliminary leave asked, no hint of a sounding taken—I am still rubbing my eyes for incredulity. I undertook instant prohibitive action. It was shame heaped on shame, following as it did on the failure of my jubilant yet woebegone New York Edition, for which I had had such vain hopes, the hopes, alas, of my vanity—my labors uniformly collected, judiciously introduced by the author, and improved upon according to the author's maturer lights. I have been remarkably unwanted and unread.

INTERVIEWER: Not lately. They make films of your stories and novels. They make novels of your life. You're an industry in the graduate schools. But isn't there something of this frustration in "The Next Time," your tragicomical short story about a literary genius who hopes to turn himself into a popular hack so as to sell, to be read?

JAMES (*gloomily*): With each new striving he can draw out only what lies in him to do—another masterwork doomed to obscurity. Poor fellow, he falls short of falling short!

INTERVIEWER: Which is more or less what happened to you when you were writing Paris letters for the *New York Tribune* at twenty dollars apiece. It ended with your getting sacked for being too good. Your brother saw it coming—he'd warned you not to lose hold of the pulse of the American public. You were over their heads.

JAMES (*with some bitterness*): William instructed me, in point of fact, and not for the first time, to pander. I gave it my best, which is to say my worst. It was the poorest I could do, especially for the money!—Madam, is there to be more of this extraordinary discourse?

INTERVIEWER: Well, I did want to ask about the women in your life. Your tubercular young cousin, Minny Temple, for instance, who inspired your heroines Daisy Miller and Isabel Archer and Milly

Theale . . . she pleaded with you to let her join you in Rome, a city she longed to see, hoping the warmer climate would cure her—

JAMES: The sublime, the generous, the always vivid Minny! Yet in the pursuit of my then burgeoning art, I could not possibly have taken on the care of a dying young woman.

INTERVIEWER: And what of your friendship with Constance Fenimore Woolson? A novelist of sensibility herself, who hung on your every word . . . you stashed her away, you kept your frequent visits to her a great secret from your London circle—

JAMES: I had a dread of being, shall we say, "linked" with Miss Woolson. I feared the public charge of an "attachment." But she was deranged, poor lady. She was not, she was never, wholly sane.

INTERVIEWER: You decided this only after she jumped out of a window in Venice and killed herself. Until then you regarded her, in your own words, as "a deep resource." She put aside her own work for the sake of yours. You exploited her.

James is silent. The fire's flicker darts across the vast bald dome of his Roman head. Then, with a faint groan—he is notably corpulent—he rises from his armchair.

JAMES (*calling out*): Noakes, will you be good enough to escort our visitor to the door?—Ah, my dear lady, let us bring this fruitless exchange to the termination it has long merited. I observe with regret that you possess the modern manner—you proceed rather in the spirit of an assize, you place me in the dock! You scrutinize without scruples. You pry into the dignified celibacy of a contented bachelorhood. Heartlessly you charge on, seizing upon one's humiliations, one's defeats—Mount Ossa on Mount Pelion! You come, in fine, not to praise Caesar, but to bury him. Put it then, madam, that you and I are not, cannot, shall never be, on the same page!

NOAKES (*considerately*): Mind the Master's bicycle don't strike you in the shins, ma'am. Miss Bosanquet, hers was black-and-blue, but she's got used to it, and goes round.

The interviewer picks up her tote bag (unbeknownst to James, a tape recorder is hidden in it), and also one of the jellied pastries, and wordlessly departs.

A Traveling
Coincidence

ANN THWAITE

It is the summer of 1895, and four people are sharing a railway carriage, as I have often imagined them. The carriage, however, is not the type of carriage that would actually have been traveling toward London, into Liverpool Street Station, more than a hundred years ago, but is remarkably like the ones I travel in regularly myself.

The four people are seated round a table, and I am sitting on the other side of the aisle from where I can observe them closely and can even hear what they are saying. The most talkative in the group is a tall, lively, middle-aged man with a fair moustache and neatly cut fair hair. He is sitting comfortably next to a rather plump but equally animated woman of the same age, though she would not like to be reminded of the fact that she is already forty-five. They know each other quite well, Edmund Gosse and Frances Hodgson Burnett, and have been seeing each other a good deal during this year, 1895. They are delighted to have the chance to gossip.

On the other side of the table there is a less likely pair: an elderly widow and a clever young Queen's Scholar at Westminster School. They are not talking to each other. The widow is Emily Tennyson, whose husband, the great poet, died just three years earlier; the boy is Alan Alexander Milne, who is already, at the age of thirteen, beginning to think of himself as a writer rather than a schoolboy mathematician. Lady Tennyson has always had a soft spot for schoolboys. Alan is just a little younger than her own two older grandsons, Lionel's boys, Ally and Charles, both now at Eton. When Alan looks up from the copy of *Punch* he is reading, Lady Tennyson favors him with a bright smile.

Alan Milne has no idea who she is but would be interested if he did. He has been listening to Tennyson's verse and learning it by heart all his short life. One of his first memories is of the visit to his father's school of an actress called Mrs. Robinson (better known later as Dickens's lover, Ellen Ternan) reciting the "Charge of the Heavy Brigade," so much less bellicose than its better known predecessor.

And who loves War for War's own sake
Is fool, or crazed, or worse.

This epilogue had become part of the ethos of the school, an unusual school where one of the masters, H. G. Wells, recalled that corporal punishment was never used. One day A. A. Milne will go on from Westminster to Tennyson's own college, Trinity, at Cambridge. Much later his children's poems in *When We Were Very Young* will sell in their tens of thousands. Geoffrey Grigson (no admirer of Milne) will point out that no poems since Tennyson's have sold so well—and compare Christopher Robin with Mrs. Burnett's little Lord Fauntleroy, "stripped of frills and velvet." Looking at the boy across the aisle, I have in my mind the 1886 photograph that survives of him in his Fauntleroy suit, smiling smugly above his wide lace collar. How much he has changed, inevitably, in the nine years that have passed.

Edmund Gosse, pausing for a moment in his gossip with Mrs. Burnett, now recognizes Emily Tennyson. He had seen that bright smile the one time they had met briefly seven years earlier. This was on the famous occasion when Gosse had called at Aldworth, the Tennysons' house near Haslemere. It was the first time Tennyson had seen Gosse since Churton Collins's vicious attack on one of Gosse's books in the *Quarterly Review* for October 1886—a book that had started as lectures at Trinity College, Cambridge. Henry James had called it a "beastly business," this attack that came near to ruining Gosse's career.

Tennyson's verdict on Collins will be given wide currency years later by Osbert Sitwell when he describes Gosse hearing "the great man roll at him the following alliterative and assuaging sentence:

'He is a Louse upon the Locks of Literature.'" This story was undoubtedly Gosse's own; he was given to making a good story better. In fact (as I know from Gosse's letter to his wife at the time), Tennyson had said nothing of the sort—the phrase came from Smollett's *Humphry Clinker*. All the same, to hear Collins described as a "jackass" by the Poet Laureate had been assuaging, indeed. Now, in the railway carriage, Gosse smiles happily at the poet's widow.

He is remembering how on her honeymoon in 1850 she had visited the Valley of the Rocks in Devon riding on a donkey, just as his own mother, another Emily, did two years later. This had become a family story. Emily Gosse had written about that 1852 holiday in *Seaside Pleasures*, and Edmund's father, Philip Henry, had often spoken of that happy time. Now, in 1895, P. H. Gosse has been dead for seven years. (That is why there are four people in the group in the railway carriage, not five.) It will be another twelve years before Edmund will publish his one major book, *Father and Son*, a "document" that will turn out to be unreliable. But now Edmund Gosse looks across the table at Emily Tennyson, thinking of Emily Gosse.

Lady Tennyson does not notice. She has returned to her book. She is reading a book by a Canadian called Parkin on Imperial Federation, and she is quite "riveted" by it. She always has some serious reading at hand and these days has plenty of time to read, having just finished her acute, meticulous reading of the proofs of the materials that will eventually make the two-volume memoir of her poet husband, published as if by their son, Hallam, but, in fact, a great deal of it written by Emily herself.

"I am afraid, dear child," Emily had recently said to her niece, Agnes Weld, "that my life is not very useful now." She is feeling that her life's work is done. She is nearly ready to die—and will the following year—though visitors still remark on her youthful appearance, her unlined face, and unfaded hair. The boy reading *Punch* on the seat next to her would not have guessed that she turned eighty-two that summer.

Edmund Gosse is unaware of the great work she has been doing since Tennyson's death, though he will, in the new century, have a great deal to say about the image of Tennyson that his friends—invited by his son—will want "to foist on the public," hiding from view the reality ("a gaunt, black, tousled man, rough in speech, brooding like an old gypsy over his inch of clay pipe stuffed with shag, and sucking in port wine with gusto") "in the interests of what was Nice and Proper—gods of the Victorian Age." Edmund knew and admired Tennyson as he was. In 1888, taken in to meet Emily, the poet's wife as part of a tour round Aldworth, Gosse had dismissed her (in spite of her bright smile) as an "old martyr sort of lady." I know he does not know how ludicrous that description is. He has never known her and does not speak to her now. There is nothing martyred about Emily Tennyson, self-deprecating as she can be.

Both the widow and the boy seem able to ignore the gossip that is going on on the other side of the table, but I am myself straining to hear what Gosse and Mrs. Burnett are talking about. I remember how often Gosse's talk was described as brilliant. Robert Louis Stevenson had loved his "graceful gossip," his "singing like the fireside kettle," and Somerset Maugham long afterwards will describe Edmund Gosse as "the most interesting and consistently amusing talker I ever knew."

I realize that on this railway journey there will be no chance, with Lady Tennyson on the other side of the table, of Gosse treating Mrs. Burnett to one of his party pieces. He is an excellent mimic and can "grumble with the growl of Tennyson, giving to the voice the exact burr and mumble of the Lincolnshire Wold." I know this from Arthur Benson's diary. So much of all Gosse's talk turns upon gesture, intonation, look, that it is impossible to reproduce, but I am happy, of course, to have the chance to hear it.

A refreshment trolley rumbles down the aisle between us, and I miss something that is being said. Perhaps Mrs. Burnett is asking for news of Rider Haggard or the Alma-Tademas. They had all dined together at the Gosses' table in Delamere Terrace only a short time before. But when I can hear again, I find their subject, as I might have guessed, is Henry James, their closest mutual friend. A dozen years earlier, the American magazine *Century* (whose London agent was Edmund Gosse) had listed Frances Hodgson Burnett and Henry James together as among those "who hold the front rank today in general estimation." Constance Fenimore Woolson was on that short list, too.

Mrs. Burnett had visited Miss Woolson in Florence at Bellosguardo, not long after Henry James had been there. And now Miss Woolson is dead, a suicide in Venice the year before, and poor Henry James had taken on himself the task of trying to drown her dresses in the lagoon. Though eighteen months have passed since her death, she is still much in all their minds. Claire Benedict, her sister, is in England this summer. There is also another recent death that is too painful to be mentioned—that of Robert Louis Stevenson on the other side of the world.

It is a bad time for Henry James. Both Mrs. Burnett and Edmund Gosse have seen the play, *Guy Domville*, that finally determined James to give up the theater and dreams of popular success. Frances herself has had, from time to time, a good deal of the very success James both craves and despises. Just at this time the play *Fauntleroy* is attracting large audiences in Paris. But it had been rather different with *The Showman's Daughter*, which James himself had reviewed anonymously in the *Pall Mall Gazette* three years before. She has no idea that he found it "pathetic and virtuous" or that, when she took her curtain call in front of a friendly audience, he described her in a letter to a friend as "rotund" and "fatally deluded." What she is remembering is how tenderly he had spoken to her afterwards and the sympathy she received when her play closed prematurely with the country plunged into mourning at the death of Queen Victoria's grandson, the "darling" Duke of Clarence.

"A play is an anxious thing," Frances Hodgson Burnett says to Edmund Gosse. "It always is." She understands exactly how Henry James is feeling. Earlier in this year, 1895, the first night of *Guy Domville* had given James "the most horrible experience of his life." Edmund Gosse had been there. "He told me the whole business sickened him to death," Gosse says. "He had had a hopeless struggle over the years, wrote six plays altogether. Managers would give him their customary loitering and fluctuating attention, and then nothing would come of it. Play after play was turned down. But then we failed to get to *The American* at Southport."

"And I failed to go when it was on in Manchester," Mrs. Burnett admits. "He said he 'rather quaked at the responsibility of encouraging my friendly presence.' Those were his very words—'the whole being, as yet, on so provincial a basis.'"

"And of course *Guy Domville* was *not* provincial," Gosse says. "Everything had been trimmed and adorned for a *London* success. It was at the St. James. Everyone was there."

"I was not," says Mrs. Burnett. "I could not get tickets for the first night, such was the demand. We had to go a day or two later."

Gosse is remembering: "Practically everyone was there. It was crammed with our friends. Close to us were the Burne-Joneses, the Humphry Wards, Norris, Sir Frederic Leighton, Sargent, Du Maurier—all sorts of people." I know, as Gosse does not, that the rising young men were also there, all of whom he would come to know later: Arnold Bennett, H. G. Wells, Bernard Shaw. They were all in the stalls. It was the gallery that did not like the play.

Gosse says: "It was very painful and exciting. When James arrived to take a curtain call—someone had shouted 'Author, Author!'—he was hooted at by a brutal mob. I had lunch with him the next day and he swore never again to get involved with 'a business which lets one into such traps, abysses, and heartbreaks.' Poor fellow!"

"I cannot understand why the audience should have behaved so badly at that first night"; Mrs. Burnett is puzzled. She has never experienced anything like that, I know. She goes on: "The play certainly ends most unconvincingly and feebly—but it was charming in the first act, and I never saw anything on the stage so pretty and so real as that apple tree against the window. It breaks my heart to think of Henry James as the victim of what happened at that first night. It is too tragic to contemplate. And he cares so much about the drama . . . I cannot see why—having such good in it—this play was not better. I've always thought what a *neat* imagination he has. How clever he is." I know that she had been reading him since *The Europeans* seventeen years before.

They would have gone on talking about Henry James for hours and I would have happily listened to them. But it is nearly over, this "frail travelling coincidence"; we are coming into Liverpool Street Station. Alan Milne is already on his feet. Emily Tennyson has closed her book and is putting it into her bag.

"I knew your father," I start to say to Edmund Gosse as he and Mrs. Burnett get up to go. But he doesn't hear me, which is not surprising, as the words in fact stay in my head. The train comes to a stop. I might just as easily say, "I know you all." But looking out of the window at the mass of passengers released from the carriages, hurrying along the platform, I realize that it is no longer 1895. The time for talking has passed. I take my backpack down from the luggage rack and join the hurrying crowd.

Ezra Pound

Rapallo, 1927

WILLIAM M. CHACE

Until the extraordinary technological breakthrough of the early twenty-first century, no one had believed travel backward through time was possible. Of course, that was before one of the last frontiers of superstition—the fixity of chronological linearity—had been exposed for the frail thing it is. Given, however, the severe limitations imposed by the Department of Homeland Security on the number of citizens licensed to override the "past, present, and future" paradigm, I was forced to wait six months before being ticketed to visit Ezra Pound in Rapallo, Italy, in 1927.

It was a trip I had long wanted to make. Until now, my understanding of the poet had to be satisfied with retrospective scholarship, memoirs, and speculations about Pound's life immediately after his departure from Paris and before he was engulfed by political obsessions in the 1930s and 1940s. When, decades ago, I wrote a book about him and T. S. Eliot, all my information was second-hand. But now I would be able to know directly and immediately what he was like when his early work on *The Cantos* was in full swing, when he could look back upon the mark he had left indelibly on the history of literary modernism, and when he was reading—all at once—Dante, Leo Frobenius, Thomas Jefferson, translations of Chinese, Anglo-Saxon, and Provençal poetry, Lenin and Mussolini—while writing an opera, and thinking how history in its most important phases could become embedded in poetry.

Suddenly, there I was in 1927, gazing out from the terrace of a restaurant to the Gulf of Tigullio and the deep blue of the Tyrrhenian Sea. John Keats saw the same vista when composing "Ode on a Grecian Urn," and the town had preserved over the centuries its power to attract tourists as well as distinguished year-round residents —Max Beerbohm, Gerhart Hauptmann, and, on occasion, both Peggy Guggenheim and W. B. Yeats. Pound had come with his wife Dorothy in February of that year; I arrived in the summer. He had immediately made himself known to the fifteen thousand or so residents. Elizabeth Delehanty, a reporter from *The New Yorker*, arrived the same day I did, and she described the appearance of *il poetá*:

> He was tall and broad, with a pointed beard. He had on a white suit that, large though he was, literally flowed from him. The spotless trousers wrapped around his legs as he walked, the shining coat billowed in the breeze. There was a towel tied about his waist and the fringe from it bobbed rhythmically. His hat, which was white too, had been slapped on at a dashing angle. He marched by me, swinging a cane, ignoring the awed Italians, his eyes on an interesting point in space.

He and Dorothy had rented an apartment on the top floor of a six-story building close to the sea. From it he could scan, as Odysseus had once scanned, the glorious panorama of his surroundings. And to gain an even broader perspective on his new habitation, he could ascend for some forty-five minutes a long and graceful *salita* that would bring him to the hills overlooking the Mediterranean. In a few years, he would rent an apartment there for the other woman of his life, his mistress Olga Rudge, the accomplished American violinist.

Pound had left his Paris apartment at 70, *bis*, rue Notre Dame des Champs in Montparnasse, to go to Rapallo, announcing with characteristic executive decisiveness that Paris "has gone to hell." He had brought with him his homemade furniture, his peculiar clothing, and his books, tennis racquet, bassoon, and two typewriters (he pounded them so violently that one always needed repair). Also in the inventory of precious belongings was the "Hieratic Head" sculpture that Henri Gaudier-Brzeska had made of him. Here, at what he called "the navel of the world," he could play tennis in the sun, swim, dine out with friends (Dorothy had long ago declared that she would not cook), and write. From Rapallo, he would edit (as well as publish and fund) the four issues of his new magazine *The Exile*, the distinction of which is marked by its publication of both Yeats's "Sailing to Byzantium" and his own testy comments about politics. And, from Rapallo, he could look back on the extraordinary years, almost two decades, during which he had, with singular power and audacity, transformed poetry in English.

I knew about his achievements; they had become part of the remarkable history of literary modernism: in 1913, Pound had brought the young Robert Frost to the attention of Harriet Monroe's *Poetry*; he had communed with Yeats, seventeen years his senior, for parts of three winters in Stone Cottage in Sussex from 1913 on, and had taught him the discipline of verbal economy and directness; he had gotten James Joyce into print, first his poetry and then *A Portrait of the Artist as a Young Man*; he had received in Paris in November of 1921 the text of a long poem originally called "He Do the Police in Different Voices" and then had directed its author, T. S. Eliot, how to make the many cuts and revisions allowing it to emerge as *The Waste Land*. He had slashed out against all that was old and moribund in poetry; he had jostled here and insulted there; he had gotten money from those who had it to give and forwarded it to the editors who could use it; he was at the center of everything literary and artistic; Ernest Hemingway, William Carlos Williams, Wyndham Lewis, Ford Madox Ford, and the musician George Antheil were among his friends; Iseult Gonne and Nancy Cunard were among his lovers; he wrote letters to everyone.

And then Paris was over, *fini et terminé*, that city suddenly the domain of circles to which Pound did not belong. Although Joyce was there, as was Gertrude Stein, and although Pound knew Jean Cocteau, Constantin Brancusi, André Breton, and others, he no longer dominated artistic life in London and Paris as he had before. Sylvia Beach looked not to him but to Joyce for literary leadership, as did Adrienne Monnier. The Surrealists had nothing to do with him. The avant-garde, perpetually restless, had moved on.

It was not easy for me that day in 1927 to gather up the courage to ask Pound why he had moved to Rapallo, even though I had reason to think that the pride of a man who wished never to be neglected had played its part. Looking at me while at the same time ignoring me, he gave a stentorian response wholly devoid of defensiveness: "It is all in *The Exile*! Quite simply: I want a new civilization. English stupidity and French imbecility drove me here. Italy is now strong, energetic. This is the Third Year of the leadership of the only individual comparable to Thomas Jefferson! It is time to change the calendars! Having marched on Rome in 1922, Mussolini made that year Year One!" And then he strode away, cane in hand, toward the *salita* leading up to Sant'Ambrogio.

But I knew what Pound's fellow writers had been saying about him for some time. Yeats saw him often in Rapallo; together they had coffee in the late morning, talking in a convivial way at cross-purposes, the Irish poet pursuing the occult studies that resulted in *A Vision* in 1925 and the American poet describing the vicious conspiracies that, he contended, had corrupted Europe and the United States. Yeats concluded that Pound was on his way to becoming self-destructive, a man "who produces the most distinguished work and yet in his behavior is the least distinguished of men." In Paris, Joyce, seeing a similar contradiction, had said that Pound could produce both "brilliant discoveries and howling blunders." Wyndham Lewis gave the verdict in summary form: Pound was "a revolutionary simpleton."

Hemingway believed that Pound was suffering the fate of not being read ("like all men who become famous very young") and had become an "ass" who "makes a bloody fool of himself 99 times out of 100 when he writes anything but poetry." In fact, Pound in Rapallo was writing much that was not poetry at all. He had, he told me, escaped the confinements of the purely aesthetic and was alone confronting the political, the economic, and the historical. "The life of the mind doesn't stay in one department fixedly," he said; "after 1924 it wasn't in literature. It was in thinking about civic order, and nobody was doing any of that."

By 1927, Pound had seen a way to order his epic poem, *The Cantos*, by making it a "poem including history." He took what he had thus far written of the poem—a project that was to take him the rest of his life and, even then, would be unfinished—reordered its various parts, and published the results in Paris in that year: *A Draft of*

XVI Cantos of Ezra Pound ("for the Beginning of a Poem of some Length"). The revision placed Odysseus's descent into the underworld as the first canto and thus an essential theme for the entire poem—the struggle to recover the life of the past. The next three cantos would explore the vitality of recurrent myths, with the next two evoking the beauty of Provençal poetry. Cantos VIII through XI would present the virtues of Sigismundo Malatesta, the fifteenth-century ruler of Rimini, as exemplary of the cultural sophistication and political cruelty required to make any society change direction. Cantos XII and XIII, taking the New World and China, respectively, as instances of how societies could be justly governed, would be matched with the next two cantos, the so-called Hell Cantos, as illustrative of the damage that corrupt politicians and usurious bankers could wreak upon the civil world. And the volume would conclude with Canto XVI, an evocation of the bloody purgatory of World War I. Gaudier-Brzeska and the poet/philosopher T. E. Hulme, comrades of Pound, had died in the trenches there; Pound would blame the armament manufacturers for their loss.

Such a structure, he felt, could be employed again and again as the poem moved forward, from its beginning in heroic discovery to its end in contemporary history. The past would always need recovery; societies were always in peril; leaders both good and bad would forever be in power. The poem would embrace everything and become a compendium of all crucial events, an unraveling of the forces making some cultures strong and others weak. It would be diagnosis and cure, the poet as clinician. The project, manifested in no fewer than nine volumes, would engage him for the next forty-four years.

Thus the plan in 1927. But beneath his vigorous declarations of confidence during that year lay haunting doubts. These he freely expressed in a letter to his father, who would join his son in Rapallo in just two years; Pound showed me a copy:

> Dear Dad:-/-/Afraid the whole damn poem is rather obscure, especially in fragments. Have I ever given you the outline of main scheme ::: or whatever it is?
>
> 1. Rather like, or unlike subject and response and counter subject in fugue.

A. A. Live man goes down into world of Dead
C. B. The "repeat in history"
B. C. The "magic moment" or moment of metamorphosis, bust thru
from quotidian into "divine or permanent world." Gods, etc.

I could see that Pound, his doubts notwithstanding, was plunging
on with the poem while simultaneously distributing letters, pam-
phlets, essays, and small books all devoted to politics, money theory,
praise of Mussolini (with an occasional tribute to Adolf Hitler), and
conversational pronouncements. The Rapallo post office officials
saw him every day, with envelopes and parcels in hand addressed to
destinations such as Potsdam, Chicago, Paris, New York, and even
Hailey, Idaho, his birthplace. No domestic realities got in the way of
his industry. Olga Rudge gave birth that year to Pound's daughter,
Mary; the following year, Dorothy had a son, Omar, by another
man. Both children were immediately put into the hands of those
who could look after them. Ceaseless energy, forward motion, un-
compromising zeal, the "unwobbling pivot" fixed at Rapallo, the
fulcrum of the world—this was Pound in that seaside town, in the
years between the wars, making his life, as he had made poetry,
"new."

Speaking to him, I chose not to disclose that I had come from the
academic world. He had little use for professors. Colleges, he said,
were "perverteries and aids to betrayal of the nation." Their adminis-
trators were worse: "American College Presidents ought to be boiled
in oil." His animosity had deep roots: a refractory graduate student
at the University of Pennsylvania who never completed his doctoral
degree and was soon fired from his first and only teaching job at Wa-
bash College in Indiana. Pound told me that "real education must
ultimately be limited to men who insist on knowing, the rest is mere
sheep-herding." As far as he was concerned, universities were where
the sheep and the shepherds gathered. I saw little point in telling
him that by the time of his death in 1972, his only substantial readership resided on campuses and that his legacy had fallen entirely into
the hands of professors and university librarians.

But 1972, and everything that was to happen to Pound, was decades away. I had come in 1927 to see a poet in whose genius, I believed, rested the future of poetry in English. As he had "repaired" it while in England and Paris, he now, I thought, was in an ideal position to make it work again. By reinventing the epic tradition, by taking Homer and Dante and Whitman as his models, he was on his way to building a structure large enough to contain everything that was at stake, or so he insisted, in the culture of the world, past and present. Extraordinary ambition, yes, but nothing out of reach for the poet about whom his colleague T. S. Eliot could say, "Mr. Pound is more responsible for the XXth Century revolution in poetry than is any other individual." It was this Pound, now free to dedicate himself to the great task for which all his training and experience had prepared him, that I had come to witness.

But as I studied him more and more intently in 1927 (I decided that Rapallo would be my home for some time), I began to see, embedded deep within that ambition, an impulse, at first a tic and later an obsession, that was to make his epic poem unlike anything within the ancient tradition from which it had come. One clue to its unusual presence can be detected in Pound's declaration about his poetic method:

> For forty years I have schooled myself not to write the Economic History of the U.S. or any other country, but to write an epic poem which begins "In the Dark Forest," crosses the Purgatory of human error, and ends in the light, "fra i maestri di color che sanno" ["among the masters of those who know"; Dante's praise of Aristotle, *Inferno*, Canto IV]. For this reason I have had to understand the NATURE of error.

For him, "error" would be everything, but I understood that Pound's understanding of it was limited, even reductive. "Error" became all too easy for him to locate—it was certain evil people. First munitions makers, then bankers, then those who did not understand the nature of money. At last, in the years to come, it was to be "the Jews." For Pound, the chain of events driving historical and political reality could be winnowed down to just a few causative agents. If things turned out badly, someone in particular was to blame. Wielding Occam's razor, he did away with everything but what he absolutely needed. For him, a belief in a Jewish conspiracy to control the world through its banks and money supply was ultimately sufficient.

Joined to his notion that cultural decay has but one cause was his belief that supremely bold leadership could arise and right the world. And thus the entry of Benito Mussolini into his life. Olga Rudge was invited to play for *Il Duce* in February 1927, the fifth year of Italian fascism; six years later, in January 1933, Pound himself was invited to meet him at Rome's Palazzo Venezia. A copy of *A Draft of XXX Cantos*, published three years before, had been sent ahead and was lying on Mussolini's desk when the poet got there. *Canto XLI* (published in November 1934) looks back on the encounter:

MA QVESTO,
  said the Boss, "è divertente."
catching the point before the aesthetes had got
    there;
Having drained off the muck by Vada
From the marshes, by Circeo, where no one else wd. have
    drained it.
Waited 2000 years, ate grain from the marshes;
Water supply for ten million, another one million "*vani*"
That is rooms for people to live in.
    XI of our era.

Had I been there at the time (of course Pound didn't invite me), perhaps I could have mentioned to the poet that Mussolini, choosing *divertente* to describe *The Cantos*, was employing the same adjective ("amusing, entertaining, enjoyable") he might have chosen to praise a juggler, a child violinist, or a magician. The situation was sadly poignant: Pound the proud guest had written a profoundly serious indictment of corrupt men and a celebration of strong leaders; Mussolini the condescending host failed to see the point or recognize the praise. Pound's misreading of Mussolini's greeting reveals how confused the poet had become. But his confusion did not end there.

Fascinated by Jefferson and Mussolini because they appeared to him as men who could create societies anew, Pound saw them not primarily concerned with power, but as artists. In *Jefferson and/or*

Mussolini (1934), he wrote that "the great man is filled with a very different passion, the will toward *order*." So Mussolini cleans the swamps, fights a decadent Italian aristocracy, and gives poor Italians new rooms in which to live. Jefferson wills the birth of a nation and, imagining democracy, works the way a sculptor works, to reveal the form that lives within the stone. And Pound, for his part, reinvents poetry in his time. So why not think his work was equivalent to theirs—all three of them creators? Like artist, like politician. In imagining such a fraternity, Pound tried to unite two of his central concerns: poetic order and political order. But the supposed combination proved, like oil and water, unworkable. Jefferson was not a poet but a president. Mussolini proved not to be an aesthete of power, but a brutal and inept tyrant. And Pound was not a politician, but a poet of extraordinary ambition and exceptionally bad judgment. It would take years for Mussolini to meet his wholly undignified end and for his "order" to collapse; and Pound's imprisonment first by the U.S. Army and then by the U.S. government, and all the indignity this incarceration entailed, was still decades away. He was still in Rapallo, as was I, and the war was yet to come.

His energy during these years was astonishing. Every day saw him writing, reading, turning over materials in American history, Confucianism, money theory, Vivaldi musical scores, and Italian fascism. More *Cantos*, more essays in *The Dial*, *The Little Review*, and elsewhere, more letters to hundreds of correspondents, reviews in *The New Masses*, *The Nation*, and *The New Republic*, the ceaseless editorial work for his journal *The Exile*, and then, in 1931, *How to Read*; in 1933 and 1934, respectively, *ABC of Economics* and *ABC of Reading*; in 1934, *Eleven New Cantos* and *Homage to Sextus Propertius*; in 1937, both *Polite Essays* and *The Fifth Decad of Cantos*; 1938 saw the publication of *Guide to Kulchur*, and *Cantos LII–LXXI* appeared in 1940.

Then the war did come. Germany invaded Poland in September 1939, and I left Europe, as did most all other Americans. Choosing to stay behind, Pound found himself stranded in a country with which the United States would soon be at war. He was alone with his British-born wife and American mistress, and now his aging parents.

The mail no longer went through; he listened to the radio for news. Emphatically pledging his support for Mussolini, he denounced Roosevelt. And then, for two years, beginning on January 23, 1941, he broadcast on Rome Radio his support for *Il Duce* and, here and there, for Hitler. Every three days his voice went forth—impassioned, harsh, a mixture of invective, recommendation, folksy twang, rage, anti-Semitic insult, praise for *The Protocols of the Elders of Zion*, and the suggestion that Italy's food shortages could be solved if peanuts were planted in the Alps. Today it is unclear who heard him or, if hearing him, could understand his bizarre harangues, but by July 1943, the Department of Justice in Washington, D.C., which had been monitoring the broadcasts, indicted Pound for treason.

I was away from a poet now alone with his obsessions; soon everyone would be away from him and he would be left with himself, with the sound of his own voice. It was only a matter of time before his world would shatter. By the end of the war, Mussolini was dead, fascism dismembered, the Allies victorious. In early May 1945, Pound was delivered into the hands of the invading U.S. Army, then a federal court in Washington, D.C., and thereafter, for twelve years, the psychiatric staff of St. Elizabeth's Hospital, a facility for the criminally insane, in the nation's capital. He was judged incapable of standing trial and became a long-term ward of the government he despised; he lost even the power to sign a check; most of his friends simply pitied him. Yet he continued to write, returning to *The Cantos*, a poem now wholly different in tone. Looking back on his time under military confinement, the poet knew how close he had come to the edge of total despair and madness:

> As a lone ant from a broken ant-hill
> from the wreckage of Europe, ego scriptor
> . . . .
> we who have passed over Lethe
> . . . .
> Nor can who has passed a month in the death cells
>   believe in capital punishment
> No man who has passed a month in the death cells
>   believes in cages for beasts

. . . .
When the mind swings by a grass-blade
   an ant's forefoot shall save you

My visit with Pound had been as helpful and yet as painful as I knew it would be. While the past can be recovered, it can't be altered. I had wanted to freeze the year 1927 forever, letting Pound's promise at that time define his legacy. But given what happened to him after 1945—his sanity hearing, his twelve years in St. Elizabeth's, his return to Italy, the years of silence then descending on him (he who had spoken so much), and his final expressions of regret ("That I lost my center / fighting the world. / The dreams clash / and are shattered— / and that I tried to make a paradiso / terrestre") and then his pleas for understanding ("Let the Gods forgive what I / have made / Let those I love try to forgive / what I have made")—that legacy will forever be darkened by his errors, rancor, and willfulness. But also by a contrition on his part that, for a writer of such strength and independence, must have been painfully wrenched from him. A poet of remarkable genius, Ezra Pound suffered remarkably as a man.

Orwell's Ghosts

A Play in One Act

PETER FIRCHOW

Cast (in order of appearance):
George Orwell
Dr. Andrew Morland
Alexander Valterovich Litvinenko
First Nurse
Second Nurse
Professor Lionel Trilling
First Student
Second Student
Ex–Prime Minister Tony Blair
Dr. Smythies
Place: A private ward in University College Hospital, London
Date: 20 January 1950
Time: 11 p.m.

The room is furnished as follows, based on Orwell's own description: "washbasin, cupboard, bedside locker, bed table, chest of drawers, wardrobe, 2 mirrors, wireless (knobs beside bed), electric pipe radiator, armchair & 1 other chair, bedside lamp & 2 other lamps, telephone." George Orwell is lying in bed, smoking. He coughs, wipes drops of blood from his mouth with a handkerchief, but continues smoking. He reaches under the bed and pulls out a bottle of rum from which he pours a generous helping into the waiting glass on the bedside table. He then hides the bottle again. From his manner of doing so one can gather that it's something he has done often. He takes a long sip from the glass, replaces it on the bedside table, then returns to the book he has been reading, Dante's *Divine Comedy* in a bilingual edition. From the bed and through the open door Orwell can see in the distance the nurse's station where two nurses chat and pay no attention to what is going on in his room. However, footsteps can be heard approaching the door from a direction not in the line of sight. Orwell puts his book down and looks expectantly at the door. A tall, distinguished-looking, gray-haired man of about sixty, dressed in the white coat of a doctor, with a stethoscope around his neck, enters the room.

ORWELL: Hello, Dr. Morland. Making the rounds?

MORLAND: Yes. Just looking in before I leave for the night; you're my last call. No need to worry, though. If there's a problem, you can always ring for one of the nurses or have my replacement, Dr. Smythies, help you. But I see you're pretty well supplied with cigarettes, drink, and reading material. You shouldn't overindulge, though. You have to rest up and conserve your strength for the trip to Switzerland the day after tomorrow. Besides, cigarettes aren't good for someone with pulmonary problems. And, strictly speaking, alcohol of any sort is off-limits in the hospital. I know you have a bottle hidden away here somewhere, and the only reason I don't have the room searched and the bottle removed is that I don't want you to think of me as another O'Brien bent on torturing his victims. Yes . . . you see I've read your latest book. After all, who hasn't? It's a run-away success. Besides, I like to keep up with what my patients are doing. I don't recall if I've mentioned it to you before, but you're not my first notable literary patient. In 1930, while in the south of France, I was called in to treat D. H. Lawrence for a lung condition similar to yours.

ORWELL: Lawrence died a few days later, didn't he?

MORLAND: Yes, unfortunately, though it was really months rather than days. By the time I got to him, there wasn't much I could do for him. He had neglected his condition shamefully, something you literary folks seem to be in the habit of doing. I did advise him that he needed professional care urgently and told him to go as soon as possible to the sanatorium in Vence where he would get the kind of attention he required. He followed my advice eventually but only after first waiting a couple of months, and then, after he'd finally gone there, he found he didn't like it and left the place after only a few days.

(*Musing.*) He was a difficult patient, though a great writer. I liked him, but I'm not sure he felt the same way about me. He didn't have much use for doctors or even for science in general. You're different in that respect, though mostly in terms of your theory rather than your practice. But perhaps he did the right thing after all, since staying at the sanatorium would at best have given him only a couple of weeks or so more of life—life without much quality, I think it's fair to say. As it was, he died with his wife Frieda and his friends, Aldous and Maria Huxley, close by. Much better to die at home surrounded by people you love and who love you than live on alone in life-sustaining but sterile circumstances.

ORWELL: Well, I hope to have my wife, Sonia, at my bedside when I go. Or, if she can't be there, at least a bottle of rum. I never drank much before, and besides, until recently I couldn't afford to. I remember back in the old days when I was really poor, rigging up, with the help of my sister, a home-made distillery with a glass beaker and rubber hoses to make rum out of molasses. It worked out all right, but the taste of the end-product was awful—undrinkable really. The rubber hoses had contaminated the rum, and I had to throw the whole thing away—another one of my many unsuccessful experiments . . . the poor man's applied science, I suppose.

But now, since you're mentioning odd coincidences, I'd like to say that I've been bothered during the past couple of nights by a strange lot of people coming in and out of my room and looking at me as if I were some sort of exhibit in a zoo. I don't mind a couple of visitors showing up during regular hours—and I certainly don't mind Sonia coming to see me; in fact, she doesn't do it often enough for my taste—but I do mind a collection of strangers disturbing my rest. For example, there's a peculiar person who speaks to himself in a thick Russian accent and is wrapped up in a hospital gown as if he were a patient too. I don't know what to make of him, but I'd be grateful if you'd give orders to have him and his ilk kept out of my room. I'm sick enough without having to be made even more ill by these weird apparitions.

MORLAND: I'm surprised that you're being disturbed. It's the first I've heard of it. I'll tell the nurses to keep an eye out for unannounced visitors or for roaming patients from other wards. Right now, however, if there's nothing else you want me to do, I'll leave for the night. See you tomorrow morning after breakfast.

Morland switches off the light and leaves the room; he can be seen in the distance talking briefly to the two nurses before moving out of sight. A short time passes in darkness during which one can hear Orwell coughing and moving restlessly about in the bed. He swallows repeatedly from a glass—draining the rest of the rum. Slowly a spotlight gathers strength and illuminates the ghostly figure of a man standing by the door. He is dressed in a hospital gown, is in his late thirties, and is so bald that the skull under the skin is almost visible. He moves slowly and with difficulty to the side of Orwell's bed, and a radiant light shines on Orwell as he does so.

ORWELL: Who are you? What do you want? I think I've seen you before. Don't you know that visiting hours were over long ago? Leave me alone or I'll call the nurses.

FIGURE: My name is Alexander Valterovich Litvinenko. I am a patient here in the University College Hospital—or at least I was until a short while ago. I think I am actually dead now, since I was able to walk out of the room unassisted, leaving my body behind in order to come here. Just why I felt compelled to come to see you rather than go somewhere else, I do not know, but I am simply unable to resist the urge. There must be something about you that attracts my spirit and makes me visit you. If I had my own way, I would rather stay peacefully in my bed—and in my own body, for that matter, even if it is dead.

ORWELL: Well, Alexander Valterovich, either you're a ghost or else you're the product of spirits. (*Orwell laughs and then falls into a series of harsh coughs. He again wipes drops of blood from his mouth with the sleeve of his gown.*) That's supposed to be a joke. I know I'm not famous for my sense of humor, and I don't know if ghosts or spirits appreciate jokes. Still, whatever you are, ghost or spirit, you aren't really there, or are there only in some unreal, imaginary, or dreamlike way. To make short shrift of it, I'll classify you simply as a figment of my imagination. No use, then, calling in the nurses or anyone else to get you to leave. I suppose that means I'll just have to humor you (or me, rather) and pretend to talk to you.

I can't really tell you why you're drawn to me here in my hospital bed, but maybe it's because you're Russian. I'm very definitely one of the chief *personae non gratae*—the Latin is because I went to St. Cyprian's and Eton, both places where they force-fed me full of the stuff—I'm very unpopular, let me repeat, in your home country, the Soviet Union (at least with what passes for the government there), more than ever because of my recent writings. But nevertheless it's not a recent phenomenon. I've been denounced there for some years now, ever since I fought in Spain in 1936–37 for the anarchist POUM rather than for the Communist International Brigade. That's also probably where I picked up the tuberculosis that's put me in the hospital for the past several months. All I had to keep me warm in the trenches during the cold Spanish winter were the summer clothes I brought with me from England and a long woolen shawl to keep my neck warm. But the shawl didn't help to keep the fascist bullet out of my neck that nearly killed me. Nor, for that matter, did it—or my miserable clothing—keep the disease out of me that's now killing me. I managed to keep alive then, but it wasn't thanks to the Communist Party, which tried its damnedest to have me and Eileen, my then wife, rot in one of their dank and dirty Catalonian jails.

Despite what I had learned about their less attractive sides in Spain, I was astonished in London to discover to what lengths the Stalinists were prepared to go. Toward the end of the war none other than my ex-publisher, the Party-liner Victor Gollancz, had a contract put out on me to have me bumped off. He just couldn't tolerate what I'd written in *Animal Farm* about his beloved Soviet Union. Later, in spring 1945, when I was in Paris covering the war there and in Germany, I had to borrow a pistol from Hemingway for my own protection. After I got back to London I bought a German Luger automatic pistol and made sure people knew I was carrying it around with me all the time. I still don't quite understand why I did that, since I couldn't get any bullets for the thing—must've been my usual paranoia, I guess.

Actually, if I weren't convinced that you're just an apparition—a ghost or even a dream vision, whatever you prefer—I'd be worried that you too had been sent by Stalin to get rid of me in the way he got rid of Trotsky.

LITVINENKO: This is not possible. Why? Because Stalin died in 1953 and it is now 2011. From what you say, you must be George Orwell, who I know died in this hospital in 1950. You were a notorious enemy of the Soviet Union. While I was still an officer in the KGB, I often had reason to seize copies of your books from dissidents, especially *Animal Farm* and *Nineteen Eighty-Four*. *Animal Farm* even contained a special preface you had written for the Ukrainians and intended to foster rebellion against the Soviet system. I remember you being denounced for being "a former police agent and yellow correspondent" who was successful in Britain because "there is a great demand for garbage there." I believed this Soviet propaganda implicitly then, but now that I have been murdered by Putin, I have my grave doubts—"grave doubts" is good, eh? You see, spirits do have a sense of humor.

By the way, you probably do not know who Putin is. He is the man who was, as it were, "put in" for Stalin, or Big Brother if you prefer, as a dictator a few years after the collapse of the Soviet Union in 1989. Russia is still big and powerful, and Putin still has the ability—and, what is more important, also the will—to get rid of his enemies the same way as Stalin did when he got rid of Trotsky. Nowadays, however, they do not use ice picks, but strange radioactive poisons like Polonium 210. That is why I—or, rather, my spirit—can glow in the dark in the way I am doing now.

It is very strange. I am not entirely sure what to think. If you are really George Orwell, I must have traveled back in time more than fifty years. This is incredible, though I admit it is also incredible that I should be walking about as a ghost. It seems that life—or should I say, death—*is* stranger than fiction, stranger even than your fiction. If I may quote Winston Smith, "We are—or, rather, I am—the dead."

ORWELL: Yes, I agree, though I don't think I'm dead yet. It's very strange. But assuming that it's true that you're really a spirit who has dropped in on me out of the future, you should be able to tell me not only when I die—this very year, I gather from what you've just said, though I don't want to know the precise month or even day—but also whether any of my predictions in *Nineteen Eighty-Four* have turned out to be accurate. Without pretending to clairvoyance, I can say that in my last book I do take a long, hard look into the future, the very future out of which you claim to have come. So far as I can conclude from what you've said, the Soviet Union ceased to exist in 1989, which means that it still existed in 1984. I would say that this fact—if it is one—confirms one of the principal predictions I made in the book, namely, that Big Brother will fail. Not that the reading public or even the critics seem to be aware of it, since the artistic aspect of my novel has gone largely unnoticed. Everyone seems to have forgotten that since 1936 at any rate, I have tried to combine art and politics, especially in my fiction. Although most of the reviews have been laudatory—Bertrand Russell even called the novel a major work of fiction, though I'm a little unclear about just what his qualifications in the area of fiction are—they were all nevertheless so obtuse that they never noticed that *Nineteen Eighty-Four* is a lot subtler than they've given it credit for.

I don't suppose that you as a Russian professional spy (if that's really what you are) have lived long enough in the English-speaking world to know what the literary critics of the future have said about my book, that is, if they are still reading it and writing about it half a century from now. At least I hope that some of them have noticed that the book is ironic about Big Brother's permanent success in putting down any kind of protest. My intention was for readers to notice O'Brien's fanatical pursuit of a rather innocuous Winston Smith, whom he has been manipulating day and night for the previous seven years. A man who goes to such insane lengths to entrap someone who isn't even an enemy, and moreover is utterly powerless, is bound to come to a bad end himself. So much should be clear to just about any reader. After all, no governing class that is at all sensitive and intelligent can be satisfied over the long run with stamping a boot in the face of some hapless fellow creature—forever! That way madness and boredom lie—and boredom's probably more dangerous to any state's long-term stability.

LITVINENKO: I am not a literary critic. But I have read some novels, including your *Nineteen Eighty-Four*, without the help of any literary critics. I do know, however, that both of your anti-Soviet books are required reading in many high schools and colleges in the West and that in the 1950s the CIA even financed an animated film of *Animal Farm* in the hope of discrediting the Soviet Union. But nothing came of it since the satire was too obvious even for the gullible people who usually go to see Hollywood cartoons.

As for my being a professional spy, it is true that I used to be an officer in the KGB and later, after the collapse of the Soviet Union, for a short time in the Russian FSB. But I soon became aware of the filthy game that was being played by the new Russian leaders and asked for, and was granted, political asylum in England. Not long ago I became a British citizen.

ORWELL: Good for you, old chap! A smart move on your part to join our decrepit empire.

LITVINENKO: Yes, I agree. Your empire, decrepit though it may be, is still better than ours, which, by the way, is also decrepit, though in a different way. But we are wasting time. I do not think I was meant to come visit you to chat about literary subjects. I think, as you yourself said, I am here because I am Russian and because I was "liquidated" in a way that only you in the West fully understood was characteristic of the Soviet way of doing things. Perhaps it will clarify the issue if I explain what I have been doing since I arrived in London. I have been working at your old profession, namely journalism, doing much the same sort of thing you became famous for doing, that is, exposing the lies being told, and the crimes committed, by the current Russian leaders. In the old

days of the NKVD and the KGB, it used to be a capital offense to
deny that the Soviet Union was a socialist state; now with the FSB
it is an offense if you question the democratic credentials of Putin
and his cronies. That is why I was killed, and that is also why, I
believe, I have been directed after my death to visit you. As for
who did the directing, I suspect I will find that out pretty soon.
But I am sure at least that it was not Stalin.

ORWELL: So, it looks like you've come to see me because you're really
another version of me. And they've killed you because they aren't
able to kill me anymore, or more likely because they've learned
that it's better to kill someone like me before I—or you—have had
a chance to publish the truth about what continues to be rotten in
the state of Russia.

Suddenly the lights go on. The First Nurse is standing inside the
door with her hand on the light switch. The Second Nurse is standing behind her in the open doorway. The brightly illuminated room
is empty except for the sleeping Orwell.

FIRST NURSE: I could have sworn that I saw a light shining in the
room.

SECOND NURSE: Yes. And I could have sworn that I heard voices
—more than just Mr. Orwell talking in his sleep.

FIRST NURSE: Looks like we're wrong. Look, there's a book lying on
the floor. Mr. Orwell must have dropped it when he fell asleep.
Hmm . . . *The Divine Comedy*. I guess it must be a funny book. I
can't say I blame him for reading something that will cheer him
up. He's not at all well. (*She wipes blood from Orwell's mouth.*)
Hasn't been ever since he came here. It wouldn't surprise me if he
doesn't last the night. I'm sure he has a temperature—look how
much he's perspiring.

SECOND NURSE: Do you think we should notify Dr. Smythies?

FIRST NURSE: No, I don't think that's necessary. Not for the moment
anyway. He's probably just been drinking too much again. I don't
know why he keeps hiding that bottle. Everybody knows he has it.
The smell of rum is overpowering when you come into the room.
Just in case, though, we'd better check on him again soon.

The nurses leave the room, switching off the light as they go. Through the open door one can see them returning to the nurse's station where they resume their chatting. Orwell's room remains dark for several moments. Then an initially faint light grows stronger, and several figures can be seen standing beside Orwell's bed.

MIDDLE-AGED ACADEMIC: Here we are—and there he is, the celebrated George Orwell.

ORWELL: Who are you and what do you want? Do you know what time it is? This is a private room in a hospital, not a railway station. I'd appreciate a little privacy and quiet.

MIDDLE-AGED ACADEMIC: My name is Lionel Trilling. I'm a professor at Columbia University in New York City, and I'm a specialist in modern British literature, including your work. In fact, I'm just in the process of writing an introduction to the American edition of your book about the Spanish Civil War, *Homage to Catalonia*. These other people are some of my graduate students who are very much interested in your books and are even planning to write dissertations on you. They'd be most appreciative if you would answer a few of their questions. We all know, of course, that you are ill, and we'll keep our questions short and will understand if your answers are short too.

ORWELL: Oh, no! A bunch of Americans. I hate Americans almost as much as I hate Russians. And academics to boot! I thought I could avoid them by joining the Imperial Indian Police instead of going to Oxford or Cambridge as most of my friends did. No such luck. They're an obnoxious and persistent lot who even manage to hunt you down in the hospital. You're probably related to Flip and Sambo (otherwise known as Mr. and Mrs. Wilkes), who used to torture me at St. Cyprian's. Now I'd like to know how you got here and who let you in.

TRILLING: Ah . . . that's a good question, one in fact that I'm unable to answer satisfactorily myself. I happened to be talking about you in my seminar on modern British literature, when suddenly we found ourselves in this room. Being familiar with your work and having seen your picture in your obituary a couple of years ago in the *Times*, I knew immediately who you were. Just why and how we've traveled, not only from New York City to London but also into the past, I don't know. There must be some reason for it, though.

ORWELL: I'm sure there is. It's just like in that book I was reading where Dante and Virgil were continually pestering people who were damned to hell and wanted nothing more than to be left alone. I guess you belong to the same category of apparition as that Russian who was here just a little while ago. I finally decided that he came to haunt me because he was really just another version of me. As you probably know, being an expert on my work, all of my novels are really parts of an autobiography—for that matter, so are my documentaries. I suspect you folks are just an extension of that autobiography. No doubt you've also noticed that all of my alternate fictional selves have been victimized, either psychologically or physically, or both. My heroes are all anti-heroes. They're all made to suffer because, like me, they refuse to conform to the prevailing norm. I guess my imagination is unable to make the leap beyond the self—another way of saying, I suppose, that I must be something of an egotist, maybe even a sublime one. If that's the case, then—God forbid!—you too must be a potential me.

TRILLING: It's funny you should say so. Just about all of your critics and biographers are suffering from the delusion that they're Orwell clones. John Rodden has even written a book about the large group of Orwell impersonators, subtitling it *George Orwell's Literary Siblings.* He includes me as one of the most notable Orwell doubles of the latter half of the twentieth century. I suppose I can't help it. Everyone who encounters your work comes to believe that they, too, have been victimized and yet are nevertheless compelled to keep uttering the unpopular truths that will continue to get them victimized. You've set an example for nonconformist conformity.

ORWELL: What's this I hear about biographers? I specifically left instructions in my will that no biography of me should ever be written. Didn't Sonia follow my instructions?

TRILLING: She tried very hard, but biographers will eventually have their way. At last count in 2007, there were at least five biographies, one that even claims to have been authorized. People are naturally curious about your life, wondering how you managed to remain committed to your principles when everyone else seemed to be compromising theirs. After you died, V. S. Pritchett and Noel Annan even went so far as to try to canonize you, calling you a saint. I guess that wouldn't have gone down very well with you if you had been around to hear it, what with your notorious anti-Catholic bias. Of late, however, the references to your alleged sainthood have abated considerably. Now, you're accused of having been antifeminist, antihomosexual, and even anti-Semitic.

FIRST STUDENT: Yes, although Professor Trilling is too modest to say so, he was among the first to criticize you for not being a genius. He maintained that remarkable though you were, your remarkableness didn't quite measure up to the level of genius. What do you think of that, Mr. Orwell?

The students all await Orwell's answer, with their notebooks open and pencils poised.

ORWELL: Well, I don't know quite what to say. I hate to agree with Professor Trilling, but offhand I'd say he's probably right. What's more, he should know, since he's supposed to be a kind of version of myself. If I'm not a genius, then he isn't one either. I'm curious, though, how do you define "genius"?

TRILLING: I don't. That's the beauty of it. I give some examples, though. T. S. Eliot is a genius, or so I claim. I don't give any reasons for his being a genius either, anymore than I do for your status as a nongenius, except to say you're "simple." Clever, eh?

ORWELL: Very. And you claim to be one of my followers?

SECOND STUDENT: What would you tell a budding would-be Orwell? How should I go about being as successful as you've become?

ORWELL: Successful, am I? Well, it looks like the first step you need to take is to get yourself infected with tuberculosis. But perhaps that's something to be avoided, since it's a disease that smacks of literary genius, especially after Keats and D. H. Lawrence died of it. Maybe you should just leave the plush surroundings of Columbia University, which I take to be a kind of Eton College for grown-ups, and plunge yourself into the depths of impoverished Harlem. *Down and Out in New York City* might be a good title for the first book of someone struggling to make a reputation and some money. Then you could write about your experiences as a Texas Ranger watching the occasional lynching after beating up helpless Mexican wetbacks and shooting stray cougars while bragging about your manifold accomplishments in the whites-only bar. Then you could take your .45 and shoot yourself and your dog. That would make a good start, anyway. No chance of your ever making it into the genius category, however. For that you have to be the progeny of a well-to-do family, go to Harvard and Oxford, befriend the rich and especially the famous, write obscure and even incomprehensible poetry, and settle down to a long and comfortable life of spouting *obiter dicta*.

TRILLING: I don't suppose it would make any difference if I apologized for that silly remark I made about your not being a genius? I made it in 1952, at a time when things were difficult for a former fellow traveler like me. I had to tread a fine line between the maniacs in Washington who were holding hearings on supposedly un-American activities and my sometime friends on the left who were keeping close tabs on me to ensure my continued orthodoxy. Not a nice predicament to be in, so I compromised by making you into a kind of ordinary guy who wasn't bright enough to understand the reality of what was going on in Spain and yet at the same time understood perfectly well that, whatever had gone wrong, Stalin was to blame.

ORWELL: Please, please, Professor Trilling, no need to apologize. What difference does it make if I'm a genius or not, as long as my books and essays continue to be read, as I hope they will be?

TRILLING: And as they are. You'll be happy to learn, I hope, that all of your writing is still in print—twenty volumes of fiction, documentaries, letters, essays, and reviews. The University of London has even established a center for the serious study of your work. There are very few, if any, certified geniuses who can boast of the same status among posterity.

Once again the lights suddenly go on, and the two nurses enter the room. As before, there is no one in the room except for the sleeping Orwell.

FIRST NURSE: Not again! Nobody here even though I know I saw a light on and heard several voices.
SECOND NURSE: So did I. I'm beginning to think the place is haunted. Perhaps we should call in an exorcist rather than Dr. Smythies!
FIRST NURSE: Yes, I think it's time to get him to take a look at our patient. (*She touches his forehead.*) He seems to be resting, but he's feverish and there's still blood around his mouth. Let's call Dr. Smythies.

The nurses leave, switching off the light as they go. As before, one can see them returning to their station where one of them picks up a telephone. Orwell's room is left in darkness, but gradually an increasingly loud whirring noise can be heard and an unearthly light begins to illuminate the room. The outlines of an old-fashioned British telephone booth become visible at the side of Orwell's bed. Its door opens and a somewhat harried looking man in his fifties steps out. He is dressed in a suit like a business man, though his loud pink tie suggests a different profession. His permanent smile betrays the politician.

MAN: Hello there! Mr. Orwell, I presume. My name is Tony Blair. I'm the former prime minister of Britain and a member of the Labour Party. I've borrowed this contraption here, which is really a time machine, to visit you. I'm from the future, exactly fifty-seven years in the future. There's a man who calls himself Dr. Who (ha! ha!—that's a joke) who owns the thing. Now that I'm no longer prime minister, I thought I'd take advantage of the opportunity and do a little traveling in time and space. You're one of the first people I'm seeing, mostly because I'm one of your biggest admirers. But we also share a political affiliation—and a last name. Your real name, as I recall, is Eric Blair, though as far as I know we're not related.
ORWELL: Yes, that's true. My real name is Blair, but after publishing

my first book under the pseudonym Orwell, I never went back
to Blair. It's not a name I'm proud of. It sounds too much as if
one were in the habit of blaring away. Is that what you do? Most
politicians, in my experience, no matter what their party, are given
to expending a great deal of hot air. But then perhaps I shouldn't
complain, since journalists like me are guilty of the same sin.

BLAIR: Good old honest Orwell, just as I expected. Never exempting
himself from blame. That's partly why I admire you, along with a
multitude of other folks who do likewise.

ORWELL: Thanks. But I'm not sure what the admiration of politicians, even when they belong to your own party, actually means in
practice. When the Labour Party won in 1945, a number of people
I knew pretty well from working closely with them on the *Tribune*
became important ministers in the new government—Aneurin
Bevan, among others—but did that make a difference to any of
the political changes I was trying to bring about? No, it certainly
didn't. I had hoped that those breeding grounds of privilege, the
private schools—one of which I had attended, as you can probably
hear from my "tony" (excuse the pun) accent—would be abol-
ished. Nothing of the sort; they're flourishing as never before, as
are the so-called ancient universities and even the Royals.

BLAIR: Yes, Labour made a mistake back then, both of going too
easy on some things, like education, as you point out, and too
harshly on others, such as the nationalization of various indus-
tries, like mining and the railways. We also let the unions grow
too powerful, something that hurt us badly with the electorate for
nearly forty years—until I and a few of my friends managed to
radically change the direction of the party.

ORWELL: In what way?

BLAIR: By means of a stroke of genius, I'd say, and one that paid
off with a series of brilliant election successes that have allowed
the Labour Party to stay in power until the present day—sorry,
until the present day in 2011, that is. Our strategy was simple. It
was to transform the Labour Party from a party that had always
supported the interests of the working class into a party that was
in favor of the middle class. In other words, instead of threaten-

ing to turn all the people of Britain into workers, or socialists, we promised to make everyone, including hard-boiled Stalinists, into happy bourgeois quasi-capitalists. The Tories never knew what hit them. No more socialist bogeymen, no more intransigent union bosses, no more fears of increasing nationalization, just smiling, happy faces, with all of us cooperating with our capitalist brothers at home and abroad to make Britain into one of the most successful countries in the world, politically and economically speaking.

ORWELL: So you've sold out the Labour Party to middle-class values? There's no more hope for the proles?

BLAIR: Not at all. There's hope for everybody now—even for our fellow Muslim citizens who don't yet quite grasp where their interests lie. But we'll persuade them. And in the meantime, here in London we've set up the most sophisticated surveillance system in the world. Cameras on every street corner, all being centrally monitored twenty-four hours a day. Your Big Brother hasn't got anything on us, in terms of technology, anyway. Of course, in our case it's meant for the general good, not to maintain a system of tyranny headquartered in the United States. We're still Merrie Old England, not a depressing Air Strip One. We keep tabs only on criminals and terrorists who want to do harm to the rest of the population. It used to be the IRA, but now it's the followers of lunatic Muslim terrorists abroad who are convinced that we want to destroy their religious beliefs. From your own experience as a police officer in Burma, you must remember what it was like dealing with people who have been deluded into thinking that the West means to do them nothing but harm.

ORWELL: Yes, I remember. But I also remember what a racket the British Empire was. One of the few things I still admire about the Labour Party is that it made a start on dismantling that empire, especially the Indian part of it.

BLAIR: Yes, I agree. But what you don't quite appreciate—and really can't, because you died before it happened—is that although our empire abroad has vanished, large numbers of the sometime population of that empire have decided to exercise their right to move to the British Isles and become British citizens. That means that now about 10 to 20 percent of our citizens are either first- or second-generation immigrants, people whose primary national loyalty is often not to our home country but to the country from which they or their parents came. Inevitably, there's conflict.

ORWELL: Well, we may not be blood-related, but even so I suspect you're merely another one of my future selves, a peculiar combination, just as I am, of radical and conservative. That must be why you've come to visit me too. I can sympathize with some of what you're saying, but nevertheless I'm happy I won't live to see the eventual triumph of a Labour Party that's really become a Business Party. I'll happily let another Blair take the blame or credit for that, as well as for transforming London into a city without privacy. I'll let you in on a secret. Though I mostly grew up and lived here or nearby for much of my life (and it now looks like I'll die here), I never did like London. At least my rural utopia on the rainy island of Jura in Scotland will, I hope, be exempt even in the future from all your newfangled surveillance technology.

Good-bye, Tony. This time, for a change, I'll be leaving you behind, along with my various other alternate selves, rather than the other way around. Now, my fellow Orwells, I must bid you all a fond adieu, at least for the time being.

The reclining figure of Orwell convulses, and blood spurts from his mouth. A moment later, the lights go on and Dr. Smythies—a youngish man of about thirty-five—and the two nurses enter the room, which is empty except for the body of Orwell. All three rush to the bed. Smythies puts his stethoscope to Orwell's chest, while one of the nurses checks for a pulse in Orwell's left wrist.

SMYTHIES: He's dead, I'm afraid. Probably a massive pulmonary hemorrhage. It must have suffocated him almost at once, so at least he didn't suffer. No trip for Mr. Orwell to Switzerland, or anywhere else, except perhaps to the next world. The only thing we can do for him now is notify his wife and son.

Smythies covers Orwell's face with the blood-stained sheet. He then leaves, accompanied by the two nurses, one of whom switches off the light as they go out. The room is dark, but gradually in a kind of dim twilight the figures of Litvinenko, Trilling, his students, and Tony Blair can be seen standing at Orwell's bedside, their heads bowed.

END

PART THREE

EVOCATION

Jane Austen's Portrait of the Artist as a Young Woman

EUGENE GOODHEART

The sky was overcast the day Jane Austen and I crossed paths. I am a great admirer of her work, but the weather may have put me in a contentious mood, for the first question I asked was why she chose the disagreeable Emma as the heroine of her novel. She had warned her readers that she was "going to take a heroine whom no one but myself will much like." Novelists these days answer all questions put to them on talk shows. But there used to be a time when they were coy about their intentions, and I expected Miss Austen (she would have bridled at being addressed "Ms.") to resist the directness and aggressiveness of my question. And she replied as expected, "That is for you to discover." Well, I have read *Emma* a number of times, and each time I find it easier to say why the title character is unlikable than why her creator likes her. So I thought I would force the issue by making the case against Emma, hoping that she, Miss Austen, would be provoked to answer.

"In the beginning, Miss Austen, you express admiration for Emma and her situation: 'Emma Woodhouse, handsome, clever and rich, with a comfortable home and happy disposition, seemed to unite some of the best blessings of existence; and had lived twenty-one years in the world with very little to distress or vex her.' There is perhaps a qualification in *seemed*. Three paragraphs down, the qualification is confirmed: 'The real evils indeed of Emma's situation were the power of having rather too much her own way, and a disposition to think a little too well of herself; these were the disadvantages which threatened alloy to her many enjoyments. The danger, however, was at present so unperceived, that they did not by any means rank as misfortunes with her.' An absent mother, who had died

97

when she was very young, a valetudinarian father, and an indulgent governess combine to give her rule of the household. What follows are the promised 'evils,' 'disadvantages,' and 'misfortunes.'

"She begins her 'career' as matchmaker with the successful marriage of her governess, Miss Taylor, to Mr. Weston. What follows is a series of disasters. In trying to arrange a marriage between the vain and pompous Mr. Elton (not her first impression of him) and the young and naive Harriet Smith, Emma simply ignores both the temperamental difference and the social distance between them, and more grievously the desires of Mr. Elton. He is a vicar from a good family with social ambitions, and Harriet, an illegitimate young girl of seventeen, is wholly in thrall to Emma's matchmaking machinations. Emma is callously dismissive of Robert Martin's affections for Harriet. Robert Martin, a yeoman farmer, is a solid and admirable character deserving of the title 'gentleman.' Emma's snobbery prevents her from appreciating his virtues. Only her intervention delays what turns out to be the right outcome, a marriage between him and Harriet. But she seems to have learned nothing from her failure and proceeds to plot a marriage between Harriet and Frank Churchill, again based on a total misunderstanding of their respective natures and desires. Emma takes her cues for her behavior from external circumstances, which she invariably misinterprets. She reads Elton as interested in Harriet when she herself is in fact the object of his interest. She fantasizes a match between Frank Churchill and Harriet on the basis of an event in which Churchill rescues Harriet from an assault by gypsies. If the capacity for accurate interpretation is a sign of intelligence, Emma fails the intelligence test again and again, despite the 'cleverness' that you attribute to her. And then there is a failure of another kind: inconsideration in her behavior toward the kindly but drearily garrulous Miss Bates at the Box Hill outing. Emma cannot resist agreeing with Miss Bates's admission that in the game about to be played, she is 'sure to say . . . dull things.' Tact is a mark of social intelligence, and again Emma fails the test.

"What, then, can possibly redeem her as she goes from misunderstanding to misunderstanding, from misbehavior to misbehavior, from fiasco to fiasco? The extenuations of innocence and youth offered at the beginning are too weak to exculpate her. Years ago Marvin Mudrick made the case that there is nothing to excuse her behavior, except perhaps her honesty, which, he says, 'is a very circumscribed honesty, it operates characteristically in the trough of failure and disaster, before the next rise of confidence and self-delusion.' In other words, she is honest only under duress. Too often she seems not to know her effect or herself, with disastrous results."

As I make the case, I discern a smile on Miss Austen's face, ironic and condescending. "Are you and Mr. Mudrick lawyers, arguing a case in a court of law? You seem to be composing a brief, not reading a novel."

A fair reply, but not fair enough. "After all, Miss Austen, don't you yourself sit in judgment of her both in your own voice and in that of Knightley, her husband-to-be? He takes her to task, for instance, for the 'unfeeling[ness]' and 'insolence' of her response to Miss Bates. His views almost invariably have your imprimatur. So why should we like her? Indeed, why do *you* like her?"

"But you forget," she replies, "that Knightley, always rational and clear-seeing, persists in loving her without being blind to her faults. Why do I like her? She is the favorite of all my characters, and I mean the characters of all my novels. *Emma* is my only novel that is named for the heroine." A pause. "Here's a clue: Stephen Dedalus."

Imagine my amazement! How could she have uttered the name of a character, from James Joyce's *Portrait of the Artist as a Young Man*, that was created more than a century after she died?

"You are bemused. Well ask yourself, how is it possible that I am speaking to you, centuries after my death? As an immortal writer [spoken plainly and without irony], I have met and will continue to meet other immortal writers who were born long after I died."

"So you have met Joyce."

"So to speak," she says slyly. "I found him to be a kindred spirit."

"But you and Joyce are so different in how you write. Your prose has the rational lucidity of the Augustan age. You do know something about stream of consciousness, but you put it in the speech of your most tedious character, Miss Bates, whom Emma can't resist mocking. You make of her an unreadable stream of consciousness, full of repetition, banality, and cloying sentiment, redeemed for the reader only by Emma's perfect-pitch mimicking of her manner to Mrs. Weston when she considers the prospect of a marriage between Miss Bates's niece, Jane Fairfax, and Knightley."

I open my copy of *Emma* and read:

> How could he bear to have Miss Bates belonging to him?—To have him haunting the Abbey, and thanking him all day long for his great kindness in marrying Jane?—"So very kind and obliging—But he always had been such a kind neighbor!" And then fly off, through half a sentence, to her mother's old petticoat—for still it would last a great while—and indeed, she must thankfully say that their petticoats were all very strong. Mrs. Weston mildly reproves Emma: "For shame Emma! Do not mimic her. You divert me against my conscience."

Miss Austen signals to me to stop. "Do you hear yourself? Miss Bates is 'redeemed' by Emma's mimicry of her? Aren't you diverted as well? How does Emma's brilliant performance here fit in to your indictment of her? But you're off in the wrong direction: forget about stream of consciousness. Think about my contemporaries, Wordsworth, Scott, and Byron. I admired what they wrote about love and friendship, and we had something else in common. Can you guess what it is? It's a word that you don't even mention in your indictment—*fancy*. Remember, it is 'the very dear part of her.' My romantic contemporaries exalted imagination. I coined the word *imaginist* to describe Emma."

Strange business. Was Austen allying herself with the Romantic celebration of imagination?

"But," I protest, "Emma's fancy leads to error and folly. The novel seems to warn us about the dangers of fancy. Emma's father speaks of himself 'as very fanciful and troublesome.' And for the moment, at least, he seems to truly know himself. And you tell us that he was 'never able to suppose that other people could think differently from himself.' Of course, the characters of Emma and her father are miles apart? I even wonder how she managed to acquire such a father. And yet something of her father seems present in Emma when after her failure in arranging a marriage between Harriet and Mr. Elton, she realizes that 'she had taken up the idea . . . and made everything bend to it.' You seem, Miss Austen, to be a rationalist making the case against fancy. And what has Stephen Dedalus to do with all this?"

She strikes back, "Use your imagination!"

Stephen, a latter-day Romantic, is Joyce's surrogate in *Portrait of the Artist as a Young Man*. Is Emma Austen's surrogate? What could that mean? Stephen, after all, is an artist or an artist type. Emma has nothing of the artist in her. In fact, as one of Austen's critics, D. A. Miller, notes, "Amid the happy wives and pathetic old maids, there is no successfully unmarried woman; and despite the multitude of girls who seek to acquire 'accomplishments,' not one shows an artistic achievement or even an artistic ambition that surpasses mediocrity." She doesn't even play piano as well as Jane Fairfax, who is no artist.

Austen seems to read my thoughts: "You're looking for Joyce's capitalized Artist and not finding it. Emma doesn't think of herself as 'recreating the conscience of the race.' Neither did I, for that matter. But what Emma and I have in common is . . ."

It suddenly dawned on me: ". . . the social world and matchmaking."

"Yes: Emma may not know it (nobody in the novel knows it), but she is doing my work, trying to re-create her small world by arranging the lives of neighbors in the most fundamental way: that is, by deciding for others whom they should live in intimacy with for the rest of their lives. She is the narrative principle of the novel. I've trusted her to make the plot go."

"But," I object, "she goes off half-cocked and gets everything wrong. Your trust is misplaced."

"Not at all! All her mistakes are part of the design. Do you recall Stephen's remark, 'error is the portal to discovery'? The great Dante 'loses his way in a dark wood.' There would be no story to tell without error. When everything at the end comes together in 'perfect happiness,' the story is over. 'Perfect happiness' is what the storyteller wants to put off as long as possible. Think of Emma's matchmaking efforts not simply as folly, but as experiments in human relationships, which in their failures lead to discoveries about where the truth and happiness of genuine relationship is to be found. She, like Stephen, wants to remake her little world into something more interesting and more vital than the one she has been born into. She doesn't put it to herself that way, and neither do I. Imagine Highbury society without her, defined by the pretensions of the Eltons, the tedious health obsessions of Mr. Woodhouse, the 'tedious prosings' of the Coles, and the mindless talk of Miss Bates. Is it extravagant to see Emma, the imaginist, as an incipient Romantic rebel? Of course, she misfires, as do all artists or artist types who want to rearrange the world to suit their ideal conception of it. Stephen is no different in this respect. But something is gained in the process. Emma would not have learned about the vanity and foolishness of Mr. Elton if he hadn't been exposed in his behavior toward Harriet Smith. The characters of Frank Churchill and Jane Fairfax would have remained a mystery without her creative, though misdirected, efforts. Emma would have never burst the bubble of her conceit if she had not conducted her failed experiments. Storytelling, indeed living, is the making and unmaking of error."

Impressed and surprised, I asked her whether all this was in her mind when she wrote *Emma*.

"Only dimly. You see, that's the advantage of immortality. Having retired from writing, I now have time to read modern writers who are not simply content to tell a story, but also feel compelled to 'theorize' about the stories they tell. Sometimes the theory gets out of hand and the story gets lost in the process, but as a result of reading these writers, I did learn something about what *my* novels were about. But I don't need theory to tell me that your prosecution of Emma leaves out what any responsive reader, not bent on making a case, should find in her—vitality and charm and, yes, a generosity of spirit. Consider the moment when she turns upon herself without tutorial prodding and breaks through, as it were, the brittle manners that govern the social conduct of her little world. Harriet's affection for Emma survives the fiasco with Mr. Elton that Emma had created. Emma is moved by Harriet's unabated love for her despite what she had done." [And then from memory, she produced the passage.]

"There is no charm equal to tenderness of heart," said she afterward to herself. "There is nothing to be compared to it. Warmth and tenderness of heart, with an affectionate open manner, will beat all the clearness of head in the world, for attraction. I am sure it will. It is tenderness of heart which makes my dear father so generally beloved—which gives Isabella all her popularity—I have it not—but I know how to prize and respect it—Harriet is my superior in all the charm and all the felicity it gives. Dear Harriet!—I would not change you for the clearest-headed, longest-sighted, best-judging female breathing. Oh, the coldness of a Jane Fairfax! Harriet is worth a hundred such.—And for a wife—a sensible man's wife—it is invaluable. I mention no names; but happy the man who changes Emma for Harriet!"

"I know," Miss Austen said, "she is too generous in her view of Harriet, too kind in her judgment of her father, ignorant of circumstances in her condemnation of Jane, and perhaps too harsh in her self-judgment. And she is still plotting Harriet's future. But her appreciation of warmth and tenderness of heart, as well as her own deficiency in these qualities, is genuine and moving. And then there are times when she sees things with unimpeachable clarity: 'Emma perceived that her taste was not the only taste on which Mr. Weston depended, and felt, that to be the favorite or intimate of a man who had so many intimates and confidantes, was not the very first distinction in the scale of vanity. She liked his open manners, but a little less of open-heartedness would have made him a higher character.—General benevolence, but not general friendship made a man what he ought to be—She could fancy such a man.' I could not have bettered the perception."

I was about to say something, but she stopped me. "Wait, I am not finished. How can you not respond to a mind that works like Emma's when she discovers that Knightley is in love with her and not Harriet?" [And again from memory, she recited the passage.]

"While he spoke, Emma's mind was most busy, and with all the wonderful velocity of thought, had been able—and yet without losing a word—to catch and comprehend the exact truth of the whole; to see that Harriet's hopes had been entirely groundless, a mistake, a delusion, as complete a delusion as any of her own—that Harriet was nothing; that she was everything herself; that what she had been saying relative to Harriet had been all taken as the language of her own feelings; and that her agitation, her doubts, her reluctance, her discouragement, had been all received as discouragement from herself—And not only was there time for these convictions, with all their glow of attendant happiness; there was time also to rejoice that Harriet's secret had not escaped her, and to resolve that it need not and should not."

"You don't have to tell me," Miss Austen continued, "that Emma's 'velocity of thought' does not always move in the right direction, but when it does it seems to fuse or alternate between fancy and reason in which neither pays a price. And listen to the sound of her joy when she learns that the marriage between Harriet and Robert Martin has been arranged: 'Her mind was in a flutter and wonder, which made it impossible for her to be collected. She was in dancing, singing, exclaiming spirits; and till she moved about, and talked to herself, and laughed and reflected, she could be fit for nothing rational.' You need to see whether you still have a pulse, if you don't find her irresistible at this moment."

What could I possibly say in defense? But I was still not entirely satisfied. Emma may be overjoyed at the *prospect* of marrying Knightley, but what about marriage itself? Are we to believe that she and Knightley, a man almost twice her age, will achieve "the perfect happiness" promised at the end. And what about the dissimilarity of their temperaments, the fanciful Emma and the cool rationality of Knightley?

So I asked Miss Austen, "How could you marry off Knightley and Emma, let alone promise them perfect happiness, when Emma herself says early on, 'I have never been in love; it is not my way, or my nature'?"

"She is young; perhaps she doesn't know herself."

I expected a reply of this sort, but was a little surprised by the "perhaps." Miss Austen seemed unsure, and so I felt emboldened to make the case (there I go again, making a case) that everything about Emma's character suggests not only that the marriage between

Knightley and Emma will not make for perfect happiness, but also that Emma knows herself when she says she is not the marrying kind. If it weren't for the marriage plot, the marriage would never take place.

As I spoke, Miss Austen was uncharacteristically silent. I wasn't finished. "What should we make of the passage in which Knightley congratulates Mrs. Weston on the good marriage she has made? 'You might not give Emma such a complete education as your powers seem to promise; but you are receiving a very good education from *her*, on the very material point of submitting your own will, and doing as you are bid; and if Weston had asked me to recommend him a wife, I should certainly have named Miss Taylor.' You seem more often than not behind the sensible things that Knightley says. But I have to wonder whether his idea of a marriage in which the woman submits to the man is your idea of a good marriage. You don't have to answer me. What is perfectly clear is that it is difficult to imagine Emma or, let me say presumptuously, *you* in the married state under such conditions. Emma is willful, not submissive. What evidence do we have that she will not be up to her old ways after the marriage? Knightley will be there to correct her, but his presence is not an argument for a change in her character. She may learn from experience for the moment, but what she learns will not communicate to her future behavior. I don't have to tell you what your novel tells me, that however much we know our compulsions, we may not be able to overcome them because our wills are stronger than our reason or understanding. Emma acknowledges her mistakes and then proceeds to repeat them. Her fancy and will are irrepressible. She would have to remake herself to become the good, submissive wife the good marriage requires, and there is at least a question whether she is capable of it or even whether it is desirable."

Again Austen was uncharacteristically silent. I believe I struck a nerve, because what I was saying about Emma applied to her as well. I thought I would provoke her by mentioning the feminist critics who have complained about Austen's complicity with patriarchy in upholding the institution of marriage, especially given the submissive role the woman is supposed to play in marriage. She now responded sharply to the question I raised earlier about her view of Knightley's conception of marriage.

"You should know the answer if you read *Pride and Prejudice*. Can you imagine Elizabeth Bennett following in the footsteps of Mrs. Weston—or Emma, for that matter? All marriages are not alike, whatever your radical feminists may think about the matter. Nor do all women have to marry. I didn't marry and never felt diminished by my unmarried state."

I wondered then why Emma had to marry. Unlike Elizabeth and Charlotte Lucas in *Pride and Prejudice*, Emma has financial independence and doesn't have to enter the marriage market.

"Look, I am a novelist, my subjects are courtship and marriage, which, I admit, are endlessly fascinating. The narrative drive of the novel is toward marriage. My readers would have expected nothing less. You may be tone deaf to the irony in 'perfect happiness.' In a neighborhood that contains the Eltons, the Coles, and Miss Bates, do you think that perfect happiness is possible?"

I was prepared to say something, but Miss Austen seemed impatient to leave. She had had enough of me.

So I was left with my copy of *Emma* and my own thoughts on the matter. What became of Emma and Knightley when they settled down to married life? The premature closure in "the perfect happiness of the union" provides no answer to the question, unless, as Miss Austen instructed me, one is naive enough to believe in perfect happiness. Austen-Leigh, the novelist's nephew, said that she had thoughts about subsequent events: his aunt "took a kind of parental interest in the beings she had created, and did not dismiss them from her thoughts when she had finished her last chapter. . . . She would if asked tell us many particulars about the subsequent career of some of her people." Austen-Leigh learned "that Mr. Woodhouse survived the daughter's marriage, and kept her and Mr. Knightley from settling at Donwell about two years; and that the letters placed by Frank Churchill before Jane Fairfax, which she swept away unread, contained the word 'pardon.'" I suddenly remembered having read this somewhere. But it was too late. Miss Austen had made her escape. I would have asked her about what life was like for Knightley and Emma (and, of course, the other member of the ménage à trois, Mr. Woodhouse) at the breakfast or dinner table.

I had recently read a chapter on *Emma* in a book on Jane Austen by Bharat Tandon and came across the following striking remark: "the quotidian talk in which [a married couple] discover and cherish that which they love in their partner may decline, almost imperceptibly into a routine of bickering." And he goes on to say that "only a certain kind of couple could truly be said to thrive in a marriage that was 'a perpetual crisis.' Austen ends *Emma*, a work which unsparingly faces up to solipsism and loss, with a marriage that is a perpetual conversation."

I can't imagine a *perpetual* conversation between spouses or friends that would not at some point become intolerable. I would hope that silences would occasionally interrupt the conversation. But this is carping. What I can imagine are conversations of inequality in which the much older Knightley finds himself mostly in the role of admonisher of Emma's behavior. Does any reader believe that Emma will outgrow that dear, insubordinately fanciful and willful part of her nature? Is that possible, and if possible, desirable? Emma has the wit and style to respond sometimes with defiance and at other times with acknowledgement that Knightley speaks the truth, but it is hard to see how such a relationship can thrive in the long tenure of marriage except perhaps as entertainment in fiction. Emma isn't in the least spinsterish. She, like her creator, is drawn to men, but I'm inclined to see Emma as irredeemable in her autonomy, like her creator obsessed with the idea of marriage, but not made for it. Could it be that there is a connection between celibacy (not chastity, think Maureen Dowd!) and individual autonomy—in Emma's case, the freedom not only to live an independent life, but to shape the lives of others, and in Austen's case, to stand in imagination apart from the world she inhabits so that she can view it with irony, resisting every temptation to submit uncritically to its ways? Ah, but maybe Austen, knowing loneliness as the price of autonomy, wanted to give her favorite character the gift of the only companion worthy of her.

Meeting the Artist

Thomas Hardy

BRIAN ALDISS

One day recently, I was walking along a dusty Wessex lane when I came to a church standing on the edge of a village. A figure was sitting on a folding stool, sketching the church. I stopped and spoke to him.

Although he was an old man with a wrinkled face, his eyes were bright, regarding me. He was evidently summing me up. He showed me his half-finished sketch, asking me what I thought of it. To be honest, I thought it pretty poor, but I strove to be complimentary.

He chuckled. "It's not immensely good. That's one of the reasons I became a writer."

Then I realized I was conversing with Thomas Hardy, certainly one of the most famed English novelists of his time, certainly my favorite writer, certainly he from whom I had learnt many of the essentials of both prose and poetry.

Of course I was paralyzed. But he was wrapped up in his own concerns, frowning at his half-finished sketch. Then he said, without looking up, "I am often reviled because I am an atheist. I do not believe in God, or in this nonsense about his son dying to redeem our sins, two thousand–odd years after his death. Charles Darwin has done away with all that hocus-pocus. So you might wonder why I sit here, sketching a village church."

I agreed it did seem odd.

"It's not odd at all," he said. "This church, and thousands of churches like it, represents not only religion but continuity, the continuity of English life and English tradition. That continuity which neither the upheavals of present-day thought, nor the building of the Great Western Railway, should destroy."

"This shall go forward, though dynasties pass," I said, recalling a line from one of his poems.

"I could not have put it better myself," said Hardy, with a gleam of humor. As if glad to change the subject, he admitted that he preferred the writing of poems to the writing of novels. But it was a rule of life that one had to earn one's living. "Why that should be a rule I am sure I don't know, but there it is. And then of course there's the lure of fame . . ."

"But you speak out for country life and humble folk."

"I dined at the table of the Duke and Duchess of Devonshire only last evening," he said, in a tone that held some reproof.

It was natural to wonder how the conversation might have gone at that distinguished table, and if it had consisted mainly of talk of fox hunting. As though he read my mind, he said, "We stuck to problems of publication and versification. And we talked in general regarding the human pair."

"You must have found that interesting."

"Medium well," he said, with some sharpness. He rose and stretched, closing his portfolio. Our conversation was ended. He nodded to me cordially enough and began to make his way toward the village. Talk of the human pair had upset Hardy, or, at least, it was not a subject on which he was prepared to embark with a stranger.

I went to the village pub and wrote down as much of that conversation with Hardy as I could remember. In our brief exchanges, he had mentioned Charles Darwin. Throughout the most recent biography of Hardy, by Claire Tomalin, Darwin earns scarcely a mention, yet his findings are of major importance in the life of the writer. Darwin spelled out the mysterious labyrinths of terrestrial existence, working meticulously from such small items as the differing shapes of a bird's bill or the activities of earthworms. Such findings had an emotional as well as an intellectual power over Hardy; he felt an affinity with the great scientist, for he too was meticulous, he too was "a man who used to notice such things."

The pairings of humans from the darkness of the past, the human pair of man and woman, had made Hardy uncomfortable.

With some reason. He had been twice married, and by all accounts, neither pairing had been particularly happy. First, he had married Emma Gifford, and then, when Emma died, Florence Dugdale. And he was haunted by a third woman, the ghost of Emma Gifford; he seemed devoured by memories of her and possibly by his neglect of her, his coldness, which had cost them dear. It seems he became emotionally withdrawn from Florence; they hardly spoke—together yet apart in that dreary Max Gate.

Hardy's fame grew. At the beginning of the twentieth century, volumes of his verse began to pour out, from *Wessex Poems* in 1898 to *Winter Words* in 1928. His novel *The Trumpet-Major* apart, it was in these poems that I first met Hardy. I loved him, loved his pessimism, which so accorded with my own, loved his concern with love itself. His isolation was something I could share.

Fame provided some consolation for his disillusion. In "Human Shows," he had written:

> You should have taken warning,
> Love is a terrible thing: sweet for a space
> And then all mourning, mourning . . .

Fortunately, this is not everyone's experience. Although, even as I sat at the table in the village pub, I overheard a trio of drinkers nearby laughing as one of them exclaimed, "Women!—you can't live with 'em, can't live without 'em!" Hardy would have sympathized with the paradox.

Where Hardy would have won more general agreement lies in the difficulties that Charles Darwin's *Origin of Species* (1859) presented to a religious age, with its challenge to the authority of the Bible. In Hardy's grand series of novels, from *Under the Greenwood Tree* in 1872 to *Jude the Obscure* in 1895, we are treated to a tragic vision of a world full of pain—pain easily aggravated by human folly, or the cruel accident of a love letter delivered, but going unnoticed because it was pushed under the door mat.

Upon Hardy's death in 1928, fellow poets in tribute wrote of "the charity of his humour," which was "sweetened" by his "sympathy with human suffering and endurance." These good poets ignore

Hardy's interest in the distant geological past and the vast distances of interstellar space, in both of which he seems to find cause for discomfort—the "monsters of magnitude" being revealed by the rapidly unfolding science in his day. It was the imaginary Wessex that took, and still takes, the reader's fancy: the cottages, the Mellstock choir, the lady farmer, the fermitty seller, the streets of Casterbridge, the milkmaids, the first threshing machine, and, in general, the remembrance of things past, whether factual or otherwise.

The large, the small, did not escape Hardy's shrewd gaze. To take the large, the immense, first, in that brilliant sonnet "At a Lunar Eclipse," the question is asked how the great parades of history, "nation at war with nation," are but shades compared with the immutable functions of the solar system: "Is such the stellar gauge of earthly show?"

That comparatively silly novel *Two on a Tower* treats of astronomy and the size of the galaxy in which we and Lady Constantine live and move and have our being. Up on that eponymous tower, the youthful Swithin endeavors to explain to Lady Constantine the monsters "waiting to be discovered by any moderately penetrating mind." She asks him what monsters he is talking about. "Impersonal monsters, namely, Immensities," he tells her. "Until a person has thought out the stars and their inter-spaces, he has hardly learnt that there are things much more terrible than monsters of shape, namely, monsters of magnitude without known shape. Such monsters are the voids and waste places of the sky. Look, for instance, at those pieces of darkness in the Milky Way. . . . Those are deep wells for the human mind to let itself down into." And, of course, he speaks even of the stars in terms of the transitory: "These everlasting stars . . . they burn out like candles."

As to the small, in "A Pair of Blue Eyes" comes a well-known passage when the lovers, Elfried and Knight, are in trouble. He has slipped over the cliff edge and hangs desperately while Elfried removes her underclothes to knot and make a rope from them with which to rescue him. Some early readers found this positively rude, while more sophisticated readers applauded an aspect of Knight's dilemma as he hung there:

By one of those familiar conjunctions of things wherewith the inanimate world baits the mind of man when he pauses in moments of suspense, opposite Knight's eyes was an imbedded fossil, standing forth in low relief from the rock. It was a creature with eyes. The eyes, dead and turned to stone, were even now regarding him. It was one of the early crustaceans called Trilobites. Separated by millions of years in their lives, Knight and this underling seemed to have met in their death. It was the single instance within reach of his vision of anything that had ever been alive and had had a body to save, as he himself had now.

Hardy goes on to speak of the immense lapses of time before humankind appeared on the scene. "They were grand times, but they were mean times too, and mean were their relics. He was to be with the small in his death." Then comes the following sentence: "Time closed like a fan before him." It is brilliant, Hardyesque, and, consequently, startling.

Marcel Proust, across the Channel from those white cliffs built by extinct life forms, declared this rather trivial love story his favorite among Hardy's writings. I have often wondered if it was not this one sentence that started Proust on the road that led him to the work we English speakers used to call *Remembrance of Things Past*—where time opens like a fan.

. . . .

Looking through my set of Thomas Hardy's *Works*, bound in the somber green of Osgood, McIlvane & Co., 45 Albemarle Street, I decide that *The Return of the Native* is my favorite, even set against such competition as *Tess* and *Jude*, *The Woodlanders*, *The Mayor of Casterbridge*, with its overpowering first chapter, and *Far from the Madding Crowd* (the latter made into an excellent movie, filmed by Nicholas Roeg and directed by John Schlesinger).

In *The Return*, Clim Yeobright, Eustacia Vye, Damon Wildeve, not forgetting Granfer Cantle, play out their drama on Egdon Heath. The novel opens with a description of the heath toward twilight: "The heaven being spread with this pallid screen and the earth with the darkest vegetation, their meeting line at the horizon was clearly marked. In such contrast, the heath wore the appearance of

an installment of night which had taken up its place before its astronomical hour was come: darkness had to a great extent arrived
hereon, while day stood distinct in the sky." Anyone who cannot
respond to such perceptions is to be pitied. Nor is it merely description for description's sake. The coming of darkness, the onslaughts
of time—such are constants in the encompassing heath of Thomas
Hardy's cogitations. We catch a glimpse of the conscious being oppressed by the unconscious, later to be named the Immanent Will.
He was always in conflict with himself; as he says in his "Life,"
"half the time I believe . . . in spectres, mysterious voices, intuitions,
omens, dreams, haunted places, etc., etc. But then, I do not believe
in these in the old sense of belief any more for that."

The old sense of belief? Could that have died with the voyage of
the *Beagle*?

Toward the end of the novel, Granfer Cantle—the novel's main
well of humor—declares: "In common conscience every man ought
either to marry or to go for a soldier. 'Tis a scandal to the nation to
do neither one nor t'other."

But Hardy goes deeper than either of these two alternatives,
though both in fact are staples of his tragic theater. They reappear
in the historical work in which Earth is tortured by an overwhelm-
ing pattern of entropy, later to be called, as we have mentioned, the
Immanent Will—this in the work that appeared toward the end of
his life. This all-encompassing verse and prose drama, *The Dynasts*,
is almost impossibly ambitious. It centers on one of Hardy's lifelong
interests, the Napoleonic Wars. Even those who have not ventured
into this vast and complex panorama, an English version of Tolstoy's
War and Peace, may be familiar with the author's masterly piece of
scene-setting. It must have influenced many a movie director:

> The nether sky opens, and Europe is disclosed as a prone and emaciated
> figure, the Alps shaping like a backbone, and the branching mountain
> chains like ribs, the peninsular plateau of Spain forming a head. Broad
> and lengthy lowlands stretch from the north of France across Russia like
> a grey-green garment hemmed by the Ural mountains and the glisten-
> ing Arctic Ocean.

For all his justified pride in the scope and variety of his poems, Hardy—as we see here—was a master of prose at a period when he strove, following the findings of Darwin and others, to express a new awareness of humanity's predicament.

The formidable *Dynasts* embraces an immense cast list, from Pitt and Fox, Nelson, the Empress Josephine, and Napoleon himself to heralds and soldiers. Even the worms cowering beneath the battle-fields of Waterloo have their say. Above this great concourse fly phantom Intelligences, embodiments of the immensities spoken of previously by Swithin in his tower, Intelligences that comment on the war-torn scene of the planet below: the Spirit of the Years, the Spirit of the Pities, the Shade of the Earth. These are the invisible characters who open the drama, and who, in speech and verse, convey much of Hardy's thought and pain:

SHADE OF THE EARTH
What of the Immanent Will and Its designs?

SPIRIT OF THE YEARS
It works unconsciously as heretofore
Eternal artistries in Circumstance,
Whose patterns, wrought by wrapt aesthetic rote,
Seem in themselves its single listless aim,
And not their consequence.

Not to God, this great hymn, but the first to evolution.

Oscar Wilde

May I Say Nothing?

FRANCIS KING

If Lewis Carroll's Alice were on hand to comment on my life of now eighty-seven years, she might well summarize it: "Curiouser and curiouser!" By that she would not mean that it had become odder and odder—though certainly there has been much oddness in it—but rather that my curiosity, instead of decreasing decade by decade as one might expect, has instead become more and more importunate. I am convinced that it is because of this curiosity that I have been able to survive in turn cancer, heart disease, and a stroke against all the odds. I will not let myself die since I am so determined to know what will happen next.

As a novelist, it is my fate usually to be asked by literary editors to review novels. But if, instead of a novel, I am sent a biography, I seize on it with all the avidity of my cat for a fledgling bird. With luck my curiosity about some eminent figure of the past will, at least in part, be satisfied. There are three writers about whom I am more curious than about any others: Shakespeare (inevitably); the Japanese Lady Murasaki, whom I regard as not merely the first but also one of the greatest of all novelists; and Oscar Wilde. Between the first two of these and the third, there is of course a significant difference. For Shakespeare, few contemporary records exist, for Lady Murasaki, virtually none; but for Wilde, there is a superfluity of documentation—biographies, newspaper cuttings, government reports, memoirs, letters written to him or by him. Yet, oddly, for me at least, Wilde still remains a mystery. He was someone who was always voluble in expressing his opinions and seemingly candid in striking one arresting and even shocking attitude after another. Yet I can never escape the sense that, behind the entire extrovert display, a creature far less confident and more vulnerable is hiding from my gaze. That is why, when I long, in the phrase of the eighteenth-century Scottish poet James Thomson, to "hold high converse with the mighty dead," it is for converse with Wilde that that longing is most insistent.

I should most like to have met Wilde at two periods of his life: its high summer, when he was the swaggering, witty, eloquent, preposterous darling of London society, and the grim winter of it, when, condemned, neglected, and even cut by so many of the people who had once been proud to be his friends and to whom he had given unstinted help and encouragement, he was, as he himself put it with characteristically acute, if now bitter, wit, "dying beyond my means" in a third-rate Paris hotel of which, fortunately, the decent proprietor was lax in demanding settlement for an ever increasing pile of unpaid bills.

During Wilde's high summer, I should like to have called on him at the house, No. 16 Tite Street, in which he was living with his tragically put-upon wife Constance and the two young sons whom, as many eyewitnesses reported, he indulged and adored. I used occasionally to visit this house in the 1960s and 1970s when an impoverished aristocrat, Felix Hope-Nicholson, and his ancient mother inhabited it. Though she never confessed it to me, this mother had every reason to feel sympathy toward Constance Wilde, since she herself had also had a foppish, flamboyant, witty, reckless husband who preferred his own sex to the opposite one. To eke out their finances, mother and son let off rooms to what in those times were genteelly called "paying guests" rather than lodgers.

My chief impression of the house—one of those, on four floors with a basement, that nowadays have all too often been divided into flats because of their unmanageable vastness and the income to be derived from their conversion—was of gloom, both physical and psychological. The old lady often lay out on a day bed, almost invisible in a murky recess at a far end of the room. She would be silent, asleep I assumed, until suddenly some hoarse utterance, preceded by a rattling cough, would interrupt my conversation with her son, making it clear that she had been listening to us and wished to correct or contradict something that one or other of us had been so foolish as to utter.

Were I now to be granted my wish to enter that same house during the period when the Wildes were in occupation, it would look entirely different. My bright, youthful eyes and not my bleary, ancient ones would be darting hither and thither, since it would be as a young man, intelligent, cultivated, and—yes, let me be immodest!—handsome that I'd have chosen to visit the great author, since I knew that in that role I'd be better able to win his confidence and so to extract from him some answers to my prying. Were I to enter as the wrinkled and almost bald man that I am now, I should certainly be far less successful in realizing my aim.

Edwin Godwin, once married to the greatest actress of the time, Ellen Terry, and an architect then in high favor with the artistic avant-garde, spent almost a year creating for Wilde the House Beautiful of which he had always dreamed. The young man (myself) entering this House Beautiful for the first time gazes around him at now some example of the Japanoiserie then so much in vogue, now a pair of Tanagra statuettes, now an array of the blue-and-white china that Wilde began to collect when still an undergraduate at Magdalene College, Oxford, and now a seductive green bronze figure of Narcissus that makes me feel that Shelley's invocation "Spirit of Beauty! Tarry still awhile!," carved on an architrave in the room, has been seductively fulfilled. Then with a mixture of pleasure and envy I watch as Wilde, by now already famous, prosperous, and respectably married, jokes with his two little boys. Behind the trio, the nanny stands motionless and silent, until a wave of the master's podgy, alabaster, heavily beringed hand indicates to her that she can now remove her charges upstairs so that we two can discuss matters inappropriate for their youthful ears. Later, Constance Wilde, handsome but hardly the "grave, slight, violet-eyed little Artemis" once described by Wilde echoing his beloved Shelley, looks in to ask her husband, after he has introduced us to each other, whether she should wear the diamond earrings or the amethyst ones for the dinner party to which they must soon go out. "You'll look divine in either, my goddess," he replies and she then laughs and cries out, "Oh, don't be so silly!"

When she has gone, Wilde shifts in his chair and turns to me. "Now tell me something about yourself, dear boy." But the dear boy wants only to learn more about the large, full-lipped, preening man before him. First of all his questions must be this: To what extent is your wit—destined to be so constantly and so admiringly quoted in the centuries that follow—spontaneous and to what extent contrived? But would I ever dare to put that question? And if I did, would he deign to answer it?

When I was up at Oxford in the immediate aftermath of the last war, Ken Tynan, later to become a formidable and celebrated drama critic, was the most conspicuous undergraduate of our generation, as Wilde had once been of his. Short of spending months with a personal trainer in a gymnasium, Tynan could never have hoped to model his own wispy, epicene physique on Wilde's sturdy one—once described to me by Bernard Berenson as that of an effeminate Irish stevedore. But he produced the same kind of arrogant, outrageous witticisms and referred to his talents with the same towering self-regard that once impelled Wilde to boast "Aeolian harps play in the breeze of my matchless talk." He also copied Wilde's extravagant style of dress. The pea-green trousers, the fuchsia blouses open at the neck, and the gold anklet glittering above a narrow moccasin would nowadays pass with little notice; but at that period they provoked shocked, amused, or admiring stares. It was difficult for any of us to accept the truth: unlike Wilde, this man was not, as we would put it in those days, *queer*.

The leading drama critic of the day, James Agate, notoriously queer, took Tynan under his downy wing. Appropriately, when Tynan visited London, Agate would conduct him to the Café Royal, since that is where Wilde would often entertain either his literary friends or his far-from-literary catamites. Once a crowd had gathered round the table, the two men would engage in a conversation, with Tynan as the wit and Agate as the feed. One would of course have expected it to be the other way about. On the first of the two occasions on which I myself was present, I was dazzled by Tynan's performance and at once thought, as many others had thought before me, that here was another Wilde. But on the second occasion my reaction was different. Tynan repeated two witticisms already familiar to me from the previous occasion and no doubt some others already familiar to some at least of the people in our little gathering. Agate was all too obviously striking the matches to ignite each verbal firework that soared up into the ether. I realized that there had been endless and laborious preparation to achieve so impressive an effect.

During Wilde's lifetime, many people, most famously Whistler, would suspect that, as with Tynan, the brilliant witticisms had been carefully sharpened and polished before they were uttered with theatrical effrontery and nonchalance. There was also, as many of these people noted, constant repetition of this or that particularly successful epigram. I myself share the continuing admiration for a wit so audacious and brilliant. But like those people in the past, I am also suspicious of it. In the course of my dream visit to Wilde I now try to provoke some sally from him. Then, when I have succeeded, I consider: Was that epigram new minted especially for me? Or have Robbie Ross, Alfred Douglas, Reggie Turner, and the rest of that gang of homosexual aesthetes already heard it and laughed at it?

The effect of a paradox depends on the surprise and even shock that it provokes. Each time that one hears or reads it yet again, inevitably its force diminishes. I wish now that I could once again hear *for the first time* the two greatest actors of my youth, Edith Evans and John Gielgud, in a production of *The Importance of Being Earnest* so perfect that in my later years as a drama critic it became the yardstick by which to judge all later ones. None of those later ones—not even ones in which Judi Dench and Maggie Smith essayed Evans's role of Lady Bracknell—ever gave me the same ecstatic pleasure as that first. During those later performances I waited for each epigram instead of being startled by its sudden and glorious explosion. Eventually I could even deliver most of the epigrams myself. How wonderful it would be if those epigrams spoken so long ago by Wilde over the dinner tables of the cultural elite and later recorded in innumerable biographies and dictionaries of quotations could now be uttered for the first time to me during my dream encounter with the most celebrated conversationalist of his times!

It is familiarity not merely with the words of those epigrams, but also with the manner of their manufacture that today sometimes makes me sigh, rather than smile. All too often they are based on some generalization that turns conventional opinion upside down and so makes the auditors first gasp and then guffaw at its daring. "The proper basis for marriage is a mutual misunderstanding" is a typical example. We all know that this is not a revelation of a truth, such as we find in the epigrams of Montesquieu or Emerson. Another typical epigram is "All women become like their mothers. That is their tragedy. No man does. That's his." The statement would be equally true—and equally false—if one were to invert it, substituting *fathers* for *mothers*. As though in self-defense against such accusations, Wilde once declared, "A truth in art is that whose contradiction is also true."

Having listened, rapt, to Wilde's coruscating wit for the first glorious time and so without any sense of tedious familiarity, I at last venture to probe into the murky clouds of gossip and scandal now gathering around him, seemingly without his awareness and so without his making any attempt to exercise more prudence and self-restraint. *The Picture of Dorian Gray* has just enjoyed a *succès de scandale*, but if one is so vulnerable, is it wise to create a scandal as the price of success? This is a society the tolerance of which may extend contemptuously and reluctantly to Wilde's sort of love, but which is nonetheless rigid in its insistence that such love should never dare to speak its name. At the time of our Tite Street meeting *The Picture of Dorian Gray* has received a number of hostile reviews, some of which have contained, in a code all too easy to decipher, innuendoes about a private life that is far too public for the discretion demanded by the society of the time.

I ask him about a report that he went in person to complain to the editor of the *St. James's Gazette* about a hostile review, written by a critic called Samuel Henry Jeyes, titled "A Study in Puppydom." Jeyes defended himself: "What is the use of writing of, and hinting at, things you do not mean?," to receive the reply, "I mean every word I have said and everything which I hinted in *Dorian Gray*." Jeyes abruptly concluded the argument with the prophetic words, "Then all I can say is that if you do mean them you are very likely to find yourself in a police court one of these days."

Wilde now brushes Jeyes aside. "My book is a moral one. In his attempt to kill conscience Dorian Gray kills himself. What could be more moral than that? There is an ethical beauty in the action. As for Mr. Jeyes, have you heard of Jeyes Fluid? It is a foul-smelling disinfectant used to clean the bowls of privies. Mr. Jeyes is aptly named."

Later, I put it to him that he should surely show more discretion when in the company of his—I try to think of a suitable way of referring to them and, having rejected "rent boys" as too harsh, eventually come out with "youthful friends." Is it wise, I ask, to take them to the Café Royal to booze absinthe or to Kettner's to guzzle grouse?

"Oh, dear boy, how conventional you are for someone of your age! Discretion is the virtue of those who lack the courage to be themselves. One day my name will be written in hot water—but who cares about that, if it is still there to be read? I feel sorry for those poor wretches, spawn of the slums. Like all of us, they want to better themselves—and by that they mean, as we all often mean, by making money. What can they barter to achieve that aim other than their beautiful bodies? Their lives are lives of slavery. We try to solve that problem by amusing the slaves."

"And amusing yourself?"

He stares. "Oh, you are sharp, dear boy!" He closes his eyes, then nods. "Yes, and amusing myself. Youth is even more irresistible than beauty. Youth is the sacred fount. The other day I met a lad called Stevenson who is famed all over Wapping as a runner." He sighed and raised both hands. "His left leg is a Greek poem. And all in all—well, I can only describe him as a lily of lilies."

Is he being facetious? I realize that he isn't. "You have your two sons," I remind him. "Those beautiful sons in whose company you were obviously taking so much pleasure just now."

"Yes, I have those two dear boys. And I also have their dear mother. The proper basis for marriage is a mutual misunderstanding. She and I have that. Our marriage is blessed."

Constance has entered. "Oh, Oscar, you must get dressed. It's gone seven. We mustn't be late again for dear Ada and Earnest."

"To be late is a discourtesy only when it is shown by the dead to the living. Otherwise it merely sharpens the pleasure of one's eventual arrival."

She turns to me with a shrug and a raising of the eyebrows. "Oh, he says such foolish things."

A giantess of a maid suddenly appears. In a doom-laden voice she announces, "There's a young gentleman to see you, sir."

Wilde flaps his hand in the air. It is the hand that Max Beerbohm once likened to a dead fish. "Oh, send him away! Send him away! Say I'm too busy tonight."

"He says it's urgent, sir. He says you were to meet him at the Café Royal."

"No, no! He's wrong about that." Again he flaps his hand in the air. "Send him away."

As I quit his presence, he says, "I hope that we shall meet again, dear boy." By then both Constance and the maid have vanished. "You are a delicate flower—yes, you too are a lily of lilies. Please, let us meet again under, er, more auspicious circumstances. No doubt you are familiar with Brighton. I often go there to get the fog of London out of my lungs. We might make a little excursion there together."

But, despite that invitation, we do not meet again until, having run into Robbie Ross in the Louvre, I accompany him, at his insistence, to the Hôtel d'Alsace, where Wilde is said to be dying. There are ten grades of Paris hotels, and the Alsace is in the fifth. Robbie Ross knocks on the door of Wilde's room with the gold knob of his cane and, without waiting for an answer, pushes it open. The room is small and everything in it seems as disheveled as the figure sprawled on the high iron bedstead, his head propped on three pillows, the top one of which is blotched with suppurations, red streaked with yellow, from the infected ear of which Ross warned me on our walk over. Wilde is fully dressed, but for his boots, heels downtrodden and their leather dull, that lie askew beside the bed, and the frayed cravat that dangles from the bedpost. His face is pink and puffed, and his hands, swollen, red, and shiny, rest on the vast tumulus of the belly on which they are clasped. Now he half sits up, supporting himself on an elbow, and shakes himself like a dog that has just emerged from a swim. He blinks rapidly. Then suddenly and miraculously a transformation has happened. From being a figure that I should probably not have recognized if I had not known whom to expect, he has miraculously once again become the smiling, welcoming man that I met in the Tite Street house now denuded of his beloved possessions, all of which were auctioned off for ridiculously low prices after his precipitous fall.

Nauseatingly I am aware of a peculiarly unpleasant odor inadequately masked by what, yes, can only be a liberal use of Jeyes Fluid.

"Do you remember me?" I ask.

"Of course I do! How I could forget a flower so fragrant and gracile."

I am pleased. But I do not believe for one moment that he is telling the truth.

I wanted to bring him a present, and Ross suggested a bottle of champagne. I hold it out and, having taken it from me, he peers at the label. "Ah, a bottle of the Widow! How clever of you to know that that is the champagne I prefer above all others."

"Mr. Ross told me that it was."

At this point Ross excuses himself by saying that he has to see his bank about another remittance before it closes. He has already told me that he is sure that I'd prefer a tête-à-tête conversation with "our dear Oscar."

Wilde now throws first one skeletal leg and then the other off the bed and, groping as though into darkness, staggers toward an armchair. I hurry forward to help him. I notice that there is a hole in one of his socks and that a big toe, grime black under its curved, uncut nail, is peeping through it. He pats the huge bandage over his infected ear, as though to assure himself that it has not become detached.

"So what brings you to Paris, dear boy?"

"I have an uncle who is head of chancery at the Embassy."

"That's not a good reason for coming here—but it's a better one than coming here to die." He looks around him. "What do you think of my wallpaper?" As I hesitate how to reply, he continues: "Terrible. That wallpaper and I are fighting a duel to the death. One or the other of us has to go." He waits for my laughter and is clearly pleased when it comes, since for him it brings the reassurance that the old sorcerer can still work his magic. He points to a chair facing his own. "Sit, *sit*, dear boy! Make yourself comfortable—if it is possible to do so in that horrid little chair in this horrid little room. Look at that object over there." He points to a chipped enamel bidet with an equally chipped enamel jug resting askew inside it. "That might have been bought second-hand from a bankrupt brothel."

I sit. Then I lean forward. "Mr. Wilde, I am a great admirer of yours. I have been haunted by your trial—and your terrible ordeal in prison—and now, now, I am haunted by all this." I make a gesture to take in the whole squalid room. "Yes, all these things have haunted me in their different ways. And yet I have also been puzzled."

"*Puzzled*? Now *I* am puzzled. What do you mean, dear boy?"

"I cannot understand why it all happened as it did. It did not have to happen. Did it?"

"Oh, yes. Yes, it did. I had to fulfill my destiny."

"But why did you choose a destiny of that kind to fulfill?" Suddenly I surprise myself by becoming impassioned. I lean forward: "Why, for example, did you not follow your wife's and Frank Harris's insistent urgings to flee to France as soon as you had lost the libel action against Lord Queensberry? So much that was not merely discreditable but even illegal had been revealed in the course of the trial that surely you must have known that a criminal charge would follow?"

He considers for a while. "To have jumped the Channel to escape my fate would have been so embarrassing. Suffering is more becoming than embarrassment."

It is an answer typical of him. But it is not, I am sure, the true one. I have long been convinced that he suffered from an *amor fati* so powerful that it became for him a kind of insanity.

He looks over to me: "So? Continue! What else? Yesterday a surgeon came to probe my ear. That was far more painful than any probing that you can inflict on me."

I speak of *De Profundis*, which Robbie Ross only recently let me read in the uncut version that will not be available to the public for many years to come. In it Wilde writes of "the terrible strain of Douglas's companionship," his rapaciousness and his shallowness. The whole prolonged letter is suffused with regret for the "sins" of his past life and his determination to make a new one. Yet instead of enduring the probation period imposed on him by Constance before he could rejoin her and his two sons, he once again met up with the man who had precipitated the disaster that had engulfed the family as much as it had Wilde himself. To this man who had ruined his life, he even wrote, "Do remake my ruined life for me."

He sighs and mutters *"C'est Vénus toute entière à sa proie attachée"* in a near-perfect French accent. Then he continues in a voice now plangent with melancholy: "We are by nature our own worst enemies. Each man kills the thing he loves, and the thing that he loves the most is the thing that he is most determined to kill—himself."

I brace myself for the question that I most of all want to put. "Mr. Wilde—how shall I put this? Does this illness of yours derive from some—some indiscretion in your distant past?"

His body stiffens in the chair. "I am not sure that I understand. What precipitated my present unfortunate malady was the enjoyment of some mussels—let me spell that out, m-u-s-s-e-l-s, not m-u-s-c-l-e-s—that were not, er, quite as wholesome as they might have been."

His body slumps back in the chair. He turns his head aside. He closes his eyes.

Although these might well be signs that he has wearied of me or at least of my probing, I amaze myself by persisting with my interrogation.

"I heard a rumor the other day that in your early twenties, when still an undergraduate, you contracted a—a certain disease. Might that explain why, after your marriage and the birth of your two boys, all—all sexual congress ceased between you and your wife and you therefore turned—elsewhere."

He makes no response.

I press on. "In its later stages that, er, malady can cause a certain imbalance in sufferers from it. They become morbidly excitable, imprudent, self-confident, even reckless. Self-destructive. Given to passionate whims and overgenerous gestures . . ."

I break off. I wait. Still there is a silence. Then, suddenly, I hear a stentorian snore. He is asleep.

I decide to leave. From the *vestiaire* at the far end of the narrow entrance hall, I claim my overcoat, hat, and umbrella. Then I hear Robbie Ross talking in French to someone at the other end. I slip away to one side, in the hope that he will not notice me. For some reason obscure to me, I have now had enough.

I hear from Wilde's room, its door left ajar: "Monsieur Gide has come to see you, Oscar. I met him out in the street."

"André, dear fellow! What a joy to welcome you! Alas, you find me in a parlous state. I am, I am afraid, dying beyond my means. Frankly, I'm ashamed to receive you in this wretched little room—with a bidet that would disgrace the cheapest of Montmartre brothels. Sit, sit, dear fellow! But sit where you face the window and do not have to look at this horrible wallpaper. That wallpaper and I are fighting a duel to the death; one or the other of us has to go. I fear that it will be I."

I tiptoe to the front door and whisk through it.

At the close of his trial the presiding judge asked Wilde whether he had anything to say. Wilde replied, "May I say nothing, My Lord?"

After all my vain attempts to establish the truth about Wilde's arrogantly suicidal defiance of the conventions of the day and his essential nature, I can only similarly plead, "May I say nothing, dear reader?"

George Gissing

Why Should I Die, If I Can Help It?

PAUL DELANY

On the night of June 20, 2009, I was drifting into sleep in my Vancouver apartment when something startled me awake. A low, eerie sound was coming from my phone. I picked up the receiver and heard, "Is this Professor Delany?"

I was about to hang up when I sensed something businesslike in the clipped English accent of my caller.

"I have a proposal to make to you," he said.

"Any proposal is worth listening to," I replied, "but who are you?"

"My name is H. G. Wells; I'm calling from Spade House, Sandgate."

"Then you are an impostor, because Wells is dead; though you have taken the trouble to find out the name of the house where he lived in 1901."

"I could tell you much more, enough to convince you. But please don't tell me when I died. No one wants to know that."

"Well, I'm awake now, so tell me your business."

"You are a professor of English, so of course you know of my first great success—*The Time Machine*—which I published five years ago, in 1896. Money poured in as I wrote one best-seller after another, and I built this house to my own design, complete with that wonderful invention the telephone. Before I was a writer I was a practical man, working in the laboratories of the University of London, so I built a workshop in the cellar to carry on my scientific experiments. I had already given a precise description of the time machine, and it was no great task for a man of my talents to go ahead and build one. I recognized the dangers, of course, so my first trial was to connect the machine to my telephone. Since the telephone had conquered space, why should it not conquer time as well?"

127

"You have a vivid imagination," I said, "but why choose me to hear your fantasies?"

"I telephoned into the future, to Hatcherds bookshop in Piccadilly, and learned that you had just published a biography of my friend George Gissing."

I decided to humor him for a while. "Yes, so I know that in June 1901 Gissing is your house guest. You want to save him from his dreadful French mistress, Gabrielle, and her even more dreadful mother. You believe that they've been starving him to death, and you're stuffing him with fried bread, beef dripping, black pudding, and every other lethal English recipe you can think of. This reminds him of his happiest days, when he was a little Yorkshire lad going in search of rare plants with his father, before their Sunday dinner. He's gaining a pound a day, and soon will look like the fat boy in *The Pickwick Papers*."

"You seem to have some odd ideas in the twenty-first century about good food," said the supposed Mr. Wells. "But I'm sure you will agree that Gissing needs to be fed and looked after. Two years in France have made him a shadow of his former self. We would keep him here, but my wife, Amy Catherine, is eight months pregnant and cannot nurse an invalid. If Gissing goes back to France, he'll be dead in two or three years. The safest place for him at present is the future. You have a secure position and can give him understanding and sympathy. Will you shelter him as your guest until he has recovered his strength?"

"I could hardly refuse, though I still think you must be a clever practical joker."

"Mr. Gissing will be with you at tea time tomorrow. My only condition is that you tell no one about the nature of your guest, so that he can pass as a middle-aged gentleman of the early twenty-first century. Can you give him the clothes he will need to do that?"

"Yes, I'm exactly the same height as Gissing. I'll lay in supplies and see what further tricks you may try to play on me."

The next morning I took down my copy of *Mrs. Beeton's Book of Household Management* and went off to the supermarket. It would do no harm to have on hand ingredients for Gissing's favorite dish, roast beef with Yorkshire pudding and plenty of gravy—though I drew the line at tripe and onions and other horrors I remembered from my grandmother's kitchen in Brixton. At four o'clock I put out a tablecloth with my best china and silver. I knew that Gissing had hated the French custom of serving breakfast on a plastic cloth, with the bread just sitting on the table. As I was filling the kettle, I felt a sudden change in the atmosphere; I turned and saw, sitting on my couch, the very man who had been my constant preoccupation for some years past. You could see that he had once been handsome, but now he had the haunted stare of someone at the end of his tether. I was shocked by how careworn and haggard he looked—more like a man of sixty than the forty-three-year-old I knew him to be. He had an old pipe stuffed with shag tobacco, but I did not have the heart to tell him that no one outside my apartment would allow him to smoke it.

"Welcome to the twenty-first century, Mr. Gissing," I said. "Some people find it frightening to be up here on the twenty-seventh floor, with these huge plate-glass windows. It must be a new experience for you. Just sit quietly with your back to the view until you feel settled."

"I'm not frightened, but why should anyone want to be so far above the street? In my novel *In the Year of Jubilee*, Nancy Lord feels an unseemly excitement when Luckworth Crewe takes her to the top of the Monument in London. She isn't sure whether it gives her an erotic thrill or an impulse to commit suicide, or both."

"Neither has happened to me," I said, "but once we have dined we can certainly take a turn in the streets, since that was always your inspiration as a novelist."

"I'm happy to dine, though unfortunately I wasn't able to bring my dress suit. Perhaps we could go quickly and buy one off the peg? Bertie Wells gave me a hundred pounds in gold sovereigns; will they accept them here?"

"We'll have to exchange them, and you'll get about three hundred of our dollars for each one. But no one dresses for dinner at home any more. Instead, I'll give you some informal clothes so that you aren't stared at on the street."

"Thank you. I'll have a rest and change while your housekeeper prepares dinner."

"No one has a housekeeper any more, either. I'm going to cook the dinner myself."

"My goodness. Can you really be a professor? Who washes your clothes and cleans your bath and brings up the coal to keep you warm?"

"In the cupboard there's a machine that washes and dries my clothes. I cook and keep warm with electricity, so there's no coal here, or the dirt that goes with it. Instead of a bath, you merely stand in a little compartment and hot water sprays on you from above."

"Half of the vexation in my life came from dealing with landlords and servants, or trying to make peace between them and my wives."

"No one lives with a landlord now, either. We've stripped down our lives. In a big city like this, nearly half of all adults now live alone—as do I."

"I tried to live alone for years, and it nearly killed me. Even the worst of wives or companions is preferable to that."

"You raise an awkward subject," I said. "Some of the reviewers of my biography complained that I treated you too harshly. I suggested that you could have lived contentedly if only you had settled down with an affectionate and sensible woman of your own class. Instead, you ricocheted between 'work-girls' (as you called them) and fine ladies, each of them making you miserable in different ways. Perhaps—dare I say it?—misery was what you wanted, or at least needed. The best of our recent poets, Philip Larkin, said that deprivation was as necessary to him as daffodils to Wordsworth."

"You don't recognize the power of fate," Gissing replied. "Once I had been in prison, and had gone to America, only to discover how hateful life was in the so-called land of the free, I could not possibly have lived a respectable life in Wakefield, or any other small town where people would pry into my origins. I had to live in London and choose a profession where no questions would be asked, and there was no price of admission. That meant becoming a writer. I was still only nineteen when I arrived in the city. I was not gifted with great imagination, like my hero Dickens, and my experience was limited.

All I could do was walk the streets, sometimes fifty miles a day, and keep my eyes open. What I saw broke my heart and my spirit. London seemed to me the greatest penitentiary ever built, where everyone was sentenced to hard labor and solitary confinement. No guards were needed, because selfishness and indifference did their work for them. No one was publicly executed, as in the old days, but many people in my situation executed themselves. Their hangmen were poverty and despair."

"Why not say that London was equally a great palace of pleasure," I said, "from the luxuries of the rich to the pubs and holiday outings of the poor?"

"There was no comfortable bourgeois home where I would be welcome, and even the poorest people on the street turned away from me. They knew I could never be one of them; perhaps, I have to admit, they knew how much I despised their way of life. Yes, I despised them, pitied them, and envied them, all at once. I hated the person that fate had made me into."

"Yet in your garret you read Stendhal and Balzac," I replied, "and saw how a young man of talent could come to the capital and subdue fate to his will."

"Those young men were able to sleep their way to the top. I could only sleep my way to the bottom."

"Nobody in London forced you to send for Nell Harrison and make her your wife. Your idea of getting her to give up prostitution was naive, and she had already destroyed your future as a scholar."

"The choice was not between living with Nell and accepting a fellowship at Cambridge. It was between starving alone and having someone to share my scanty meals and narrow bed."

"So you had the same reason for taking up with Edith Underwood?"

"Yes. Even when she refused to sleep with me before we were married, I was willing to settle for knowing that she would come to visit me twice a week. Just having her company to rely on helped me, at first, to do some of my best writing."

"Forgive me for asking this," I said, "but your biographers have different ideas, and I was unable to make up my own mind about it. Your friend Morley Roberts said that, when it came to women, you didn't know what love was. Was it just sex that caused your fatal attraction to unsuitable women?"

"Sex is well enough, but when you are in bed with someone, you know one thing: you at least are not alone, even in a city where loneliness kills. Yet I have to admit that part of me also stood outside the bed, in shame and disgust."

"A little after your time," I said, "we had a set of intellectuals called the Bloomsbury Group. One day they were discussing what was the greatest discovery of the twentieth century—the aeroplane, radio, etc. Clive Bell said that 'the greatest discovery was that women like it too.'"

"Like what? . . . Ah, I see, an indecent joke. Well, I know that they like it—some of the time, anyway—but I don't think they should like it too much. The most attractive woman in my novels is Nancy Lord, but her husband wants to visit her, not live with her. Critics have found this priggish and peculiar. For how many men, though, is this their secret desire: to gain a woman's love and then have her only at times of his own choosing, with nothing more expected of him? You spoke of French novels: yes, they order these things better in France. A French mistress would have made me happy; what a pity I could not afford one. I have just visited Mr. James, in his charming house at Rye. He described to me just the woman who would have made me a contented man—Madame de Vionnet in his new novel *The Ambassadors*."

"He also wrote of an English lord with a French mistress in *The Princess Casamassima*," I replied. "She stabbed him to death. In real life, your Nancy Lord would have felt bitter loathing for her selfish husband. Anyway, you have a French mistress now, Gabrielle, and things are not going swimmingly with her."

"She is not my mistress; she is my spiritual bride, and my darling mousie girl. Mr. James also said that a biographer was a publishing scoundrel. If you will show me to my bedroom, I will wish you goodnight."

In the morning Gissing wouldn't say a word until I gave him a second slice of fried bread and a second cup of thick orange tea.

"I'm sorry to have been abrupt with you," he said finally, once he had lit his pipe. "You had a book to write, and I know what a desperate business that is. You could not know that I would come here and take you to task for writing about me. I will answer your questions, but first let us go for a walk to see what this century has brought."

I knew that Gissing would not be impressed by Vancouver's tall buildings and floods of horseless carriages. "This is all well enough," he remarked after a while. "I see a prosperous city, but one with no signs of greatness. I told Wells that I would rather go back in time, to the streets of Rome or Athens. He argued that it would be too dirty and dangerous for a man of my temperament. It's true that when I went to the south of Italy, I realized that the people of antiquity lived with a perpetual stink of excrement in their nostrils. You have made progress in sanitation, at least."

"Our women have made progress, too, you may have noticed."

"They seem to walk everywhere unaccompanied, in trousers made from cloth such as a French peasant might wear. Are these your work-girls? Those mats that many of them carry—do they kneel on them in a local factory?"

"There are no factories around here," I replied, "and the mats are for their yoga exercises, an ancient Indian discipline now very popular with young people. But as your friend Wells would admit, it's impossible to predict all these little details of everyday life."

"If those girls are not poor," Gissing asked, "is there any part of the city where poverty can still be seen?"

"Yes, we've arrived at the Downtown East Side, the poorest place in all of Canada. These alleys are like the dreadful inner courts you described in *The Unclassed*."

"I see people who look as awful as Slimy in that novel. But he had his attic room; where do these people live? Do they sleep on the pavement, in those heaps of rags?"

"Yes, they live on the street and, as you can see, inject a kind of laudanum into their veins."

"I understand," said Gissing. "Laudanum is even cheaper than gin, after all."

"No; it's forbidden by law here, and very expensive. These wretches have to steal and rob in order to get it."

"You have one evil, and then add another one to it. But some of these lost souls simply look demented to me; have you no asylums or workhouses for them? I feared the workhouse, but at least its inmates had clean clothes and enough to eat—as long as they obeyed the rules, which I admit were quite strict."

"We no longer believe in rules of that kind," I said. "Some thirty years ago, we decided that asylums were sinister relics of Victorian times; we closed them down and gave the inmates their freedom. Workhouses were closed long before that."

"I wrote that capitalism kicked people into the gutter and told them to enjoy themselves there. But I never imagined that there would be no refuge at all for those unable to survive in our merciless cities. Are there no social reformers to care for the victims I see here?"

"We speak today of Victorian hypocrisy, but we have our own too. We say that we care for the freedom of our unfortunates, but that often means leaving them to their own devices, which is cheaper than housing or feeding them. In your time reformers hoped to bring salvation to the poor; today we offer them 'harm reduction,' and try to keep them out of sight in this one part of the city."

"What is 'harm reduction'?" Gissing asked.

"It is the philosophy that there will always be people who can't cope with life and who use drugs or alcohol to soften the pain of failure. The state shouldn't judge them, just do whatever it can to reduce the damage they cause to themselves or others."

"Nell was a drinker," Gissing replied. "I suppose I reduced the harm of it by giving her food, lodging, and gin. But when I could bear it no longer, I just gave her money, on condition that she never come near me. When you cannot solve a problem, it may be best to put it out of sight, which helps to put it out of mind. In my time, though, the government put unfortunates out of sight in workhouses, where decent folk didn't have to see them. Whichever way is best, my visit to your century has confirmed what my novels said over and over. The miseries of life in great cities are incurable."

"Perhaps we haven't achieved much when it comes to poverty or mental anguish," I replied, "but for physical pain we have done better. Forgive me for raising a personal question, but I know that your health causes you great grief and anxiety. And you recently wrote to your wife, 'Why should I die, if I can help it?' I have a friend who is a consultant at the University Hospital here, Dr. Mobe Haderas. He has agreed to see you in strict privacy, and you could pay him with a few of your sovereigns."

"Doctors and novelists have similar trades, I often think, and two of our greatest novelists, Flaubert and Dostoevsky, were sons of doctors. I will submit to examination by your friend, and will examine him too, in my own way."

I warned Haderas that my friend had a curious but harmless delusion—that he belonged to the nineteenth century rather than the twenty-first. We drove to the doctor's house, and Gissing came out half an hour later.

"Your friend is polite enough, but not much of a doctor," he reported. "After a few simple questions, and after shining a light into my eyes, he asked for some of my urine and spittle in bottles, as quacks used to do in the Middle Ages. He then drew blood from my arm, though a few leeches would have done a better job. Finally, he asked me to blow into a little machine with numbers that lit up. He gave me no medicine and said he would talk to me again in a couple of days. And does he not own a collar and tie? I would get much more for my guinea back in 1901."

"Early in the twentieth century a revolution took place in medicine, with the discovery of diagnostic tests for syphilis, tuberculosis, and other diseases. Your samples will go to a laboratory, and you'll learn more about your illnesses than the greatest physician on Harley Street could ever know in your time."

"I'm not sure I want to know. Novelists can know everything about their characters, but in real life we are often better off being ignorant of what the fates have in store for us. Doctors should tell us only what will give us hope, once they have done their best to cure us."

"Would you rather I spoke to Haderas about the results of your tests?" I replied. "I could certainly do that. But remember, what might have been a death sentence in the early nineteenth century could be easily curable by the twenty-first."

"Very well; I will go back, and learn the best and the worst of what your modern medicine can do."

For the next two days, Gissing stayed quietly in my apartment; he wanted to read some of the important novels published since 1901. I told him that his greatest admirer was a novelist who wrote under the name of George Orwell. In 1948 he wrote a novel about London in the future, which he called, by reversing two numbers, *Nineteen Eighty-Four*. Gissing looked deeply shocked when he had finished it.

"I predicted terrible dictatorships and wars in the twentieth century, but nothing so terrible as Mr. Orwell's vision of future London. Yet your city here seems peaceful and prosperous enough, and I see no scars of past wars. Was Orwell infected with pessimism by reading my novels, and did the actual history of his time show that he was just a gloomy crank? Did my private miseries give me a distorted idea of Europe's future?"

"I'm sorry to say that you were a true prophet, and you had good cause to fear for your children and your children's children. But the time machine was a way of saving you from the miseries of 1901, and I think you should spare yourself knowledge of all the miseries to come."

At that awkward point the phone rang, and soon we were on our way back to Dr. Haderas's house. He asked Gissing to wait in the car and took me aside.

"I don't know what planet your friend has been living on, but I saw at a glance that he had the bluish complexion and codfish breathing of advanced emphysema and, what I could hardly believe, a giant syphilitic lesion on his forehead. The tests confirmed this, and showed active TB in both lungs also."

"Exactly what I had feared; but what can you do for him?"

"Three shots of Penicillin G in his buttock, a week apart, will knock out the syphilis. Then he has a trillion or so TB bacteria inside him, all busy mutating. To kill them all requires a package of four different antibiotics, taken daily for six months. For the emphysema we can do very little. I would give him five years if he stops smoking that cheap tobacco, two or three if he can't quit."

"Without the syphilis and TB, at least his remaining years will be more comfortable."

"Indeed they would," Haderas said. "I'm not sure they would be happier, though. Mr. Gissing also has clinical depression written all over him. We could give him a stiff right and left: Zoloft and cognitive therapy. But I have to admit that the suicide rate never seems to go down, except when there's a major war on."

"I promised him that you would fix him up, but I suppose some people can't be fixed."

"We could hardly put that on our hospital gowns. There's more, too. Syphilis is a reportable disease in British Columbia. I'll need a list of your friend's sexual partners, so that the STD clinic can contact them and arrange for them to be treated."

"I think I need to break all this to him gently," I said. "We'll just go home now, and I'll be in touch in a couple of days."

"When I wrote your biography," I told Gissing the next day, "I tried to understand your motives for living as you did. That's what modern biographers do. But perhaps another of our novelists, Fay Weldon, had a better idea. She said: 'It's what people do that counts, not why.' So what do you want to do? If you stay here with me, you'll be in the hands of doctors and what we call social workers for the next six months. You'll feel better physically, and you'll be given counseling, which means examining everything in your past life and taking advice on how to live in future. I can't guarantee that it will be a happier life, on balance, and you won't live many years anyway."

"What is the alternative?"

"Without giving you too many painful details, I can tell you that if you return to Gabrielle and her mother, you'll fail completely to get them to respect your idea of a happy home life. You'll write two more novels, and your most successful book, about the joys of being a prosperous retired bachelor in a Devon cottage. But like *Born in Exile*, the novel you based on your own struggles, you'll die in exile too."

"Give me a day to think about it," Gissing replied.

When he first came to my apartment, Gissing had been delighted to see my collection of early editions of his books. Now I noticed that an 1892 printing of *Thyrza*, a novel about a south London work-girl and an idealistic young man who falls in love with her, was missing from my shelf. When I asked Gissing if he wanted to read it again, he blushed.

"There is a young lady I have been chatting to in the grocery shop across the street. She says she likes to read, and I feel she is cut out for higher things. Tiffany is her name. She's a singer, too, like my heroine. I hope you don't mind, but I presented her with that copy of *Thyrza*. She has agreed to meet me for a cup of tea and a bun when she finishes her work tomorrow. She's going to explain to me why the words 'Angry Samoans' are written across her bosom."

That night I waited until Gissing was asleep and dialed the number H. G. Wells had given me. In the morning, Gissing's bed was empty. No biographer can or should change his subject's fate. That was the lesson I took from the time machine.

Talking with Joseph Conrad

ALAN SILLITOE

In his last years Joseph Conrad luxuriously fitted out a redundant coal barge as his residence. Nearby was a main road, and he likened the noise of continuous traffic to that of a never-ending sea wave. That, and pollution, seemed not to bother him.

His wife Jessie had died. Though she too had been given immortality, she was no longer able to put up with the tyrannical exactitude of her husband's habits in their daily life. Not caring to stay in an empty house with so many memories, Conrad decided to establish himself again by the water, even if only on the bank of a river.

I had received permission to interview him, and though not exactly looking forward to the experience, wanted to put certain questions that had been in my mind for years.

He was expecting me, of course, at a precise time. As I walked toward the barge from my car, he was standing at his end of the gangplank, a smart figure in a buttoned jacket and naval-style neatly angled cap. As I approached he looked at his waistcoat watch, paced the length of the deck, did a sharp about turn, and stood by the gangplank again just in time to greet me.

After the handshake he led me down a few steps into what he called his stateroom, and every question I had thought to ask vanished into the mist of my brain.

The large low-ceilinged room ran from one side of the boat to the other and was furnished with a sofa, two armchairs, a plan chest for charts, I supposed, and a desk and swivel chair for his writing—all carefully chosen antiques. The royal blue–and–red porthole curtains were made out of a Polish flag, and a Union Jack fluttered on the mast outside.

I had difficulty taking in his words at first because of his accent, but I said yes to what I assumed to be a question; he lit a cigarette, and with rigid precision, poured a large glass of whisky each.

"Sit down, my dear fellow." We faced one another from our armchairs. He was much wrinkled about the eyes, but not unrecognizably so. They held me and were, on the one hand, those of a cynical old salt, but on the other, suggestive of spaces he had spent a lifetime trying to fill with sense. "You'd better fire away with your questions."

Now that he had me at ease I felt he would give no quarter, but, using honesty as the best protection, I told him, "As soon as I came up the gangplank they fled from me, so I hardly know where to start."

He laughed. "And so they do with me. They flee like quicksilver no sooner do I pick up the devilish pen, and then there's the bother, not always successful, in trying to get them back. So we'll enjoy a bit of jaw-jaw instead. I give few interviews nowadays, but when I do I'm invariably asked what work employs me at the moment. So to forestall you asking I can tell you that I'm still fighting through the jungle of Jim's mind, writing a novel called *The Son of Lord Jim*. I won't tell you what it's about—simply can't. What a novel is about is of little importance, something I hardly dare ask myself till every jot and tittle is done. In between it gives such torment, and goes so slowly most of the time that I'm occasionally tempted to do what I foolishly tried at the age of twenty in Marseilles. But no, my dear chap, ultimate despair is no longer the sort of self-indulgence I can aspire to. I can only tell you the title, therefore, and if you have anymore enquiries, they'll have to be close to those I'm likely to ask myself."

That, I knew, would be an impossible task. The atmosphere, stuffy with cigarette smoke and the fumes of whisky, encouraged me to be flippant. "Why was there—or is there—never any humor in your novels and stories? I've wondered all my life, though before you throw me out at the impertinence, let me say that I have enjoyed and profited by everything you've written."

His eyes became gimlets of pride and satisfaction. "Were there any you liked more than others?"

I rattled off a few titles—thank God they came to me—but said I preferred *Nostromo* above all, which I'd read more than once. "It's a masterpiece. I always delight at dinner parties in telling friends that Joseph Conrad, though born in the Ukraine, is one of the greatest English novelists."

He hadn't listened, I thought, though he had. "What about the other books?" he asked sharply.

"Those as well, all of them, but *Nostromo* is supreme."

"You asked about humor," he snapped. "Let me say that humor has no place in literature."

I blanched at such egotism. "What about Shakespeare? And Dickens?"

"They were English, don't you see?"

"So are you," I reminded him, "as a novelist."

"But with a Polish soul. Quite unavoidable, but you must see what I'm getting at. England was never split three ways by tyrannies. Humor couldn't tell me anything, possibly because it was never in me to use it. Only tragedy enables you to reach more truthfully what you are aiming for, or hoping to get at for the embellishment of the universal human spirit."

I had to be satisfied with that, and went on: "Why do you think Henry James was, as you often said, your *master*? I admire him, of course, and have read most of his novels with pleasure, but in some instances I've absolutely lost patience with him, as being unnecessarily woolly."

He lifted his head higher, his trim beard jutting back and forth. "Well, you know, dear fellow, art can't do without a certain woolliness, as you call it, when you're trying to get at the essence of things."

"But none of your work was ever that. You strove to make it clear and simple."

The powder keg went up and I, bloody fool, had not seen the burning fuse snaking toward it. "Simple!" he shouted. "My dear sir, you have my fullest admiration for having the courage to take such a liberty with my tolerance, in uttering so appalling a word as *simple* with regard to my work."

He was the sort of man who could easily upset someone, but he immediately tried to make amends: "I fully realize that your comment could only have come out of misplaced understanding. Still, as you say, the master did occasionally stray a little into the realms of woolliness." The subtle smile indicated he had sometimes thought so himself. "But you would never have dared to hint at it, no sir, not in the slightest. The level of his sensibility would be upset for weeks, perhaps months, but damn it, he was a master, you know. I have to insist on it."

"While we're on the topic of Henry James," I said, "why was he so reluctant to have you to dinner with his friends?"

He laughed, but dryly. "That never worried me, but since you ask, might I be permitted to suppose that it was because he hadn't been to sea and worked in that way for a living? Just imagine if he had!" He laughed openly—almost heartily—for a full minute at the picture. "But if he had, don't you see, he might have been cured of such uneasiness, not to say prejudices." His desire to change the subject was plain: "I see you're carrying a gold watch in your waistcoat?"

I told him I'd bought it from a Polish watchmaker in Nottingham many years ago, a man who had been with the Polish Army in Italy during the Second World War. "Let me see it," he said.

Detaching it from the chain, I passed it across, and he handled it as gently as if he too had been a watchmaker. When he gave it back I told him I'd recently read a book about the Polish Air Force, which had also fought so bravely in the war.

He pointed to the curtains made out of the Polish flag. "Yes, they did fight like lions, didn't they?" Was that a tear in the corner of his left eye? "Poland is free again, no more Germans or Russians or Austrians strutting about. I never thought I'd live to see it."

"The Jews also fought like lions," I reminded him, "in Warsaw and other places. And you were rather scornful when you saw them muttering about money and percentages in the markets of Berdichev. I wondered whether you weren't anti-Semitic, though when people say to me that all Poles are I do try not to believe it."

He frowned and cracked his empty glass down on the walnut wood table between us. "Every man's soul is sacred to me, whoever he is, and if you don't believe that, we can't go on talking."

"Of course I believe you, though I recall that Balzac, in his letters, also made invidious remarks about the Jews in that area."

"Alas, so did many others, old chap. Life is full of regrets, and all we can do is use them in our work to enlighten us as we go into the unknown." He was a man who could laugh more readily than smile. "Nevertheless," he went on, "I have to say that I admire all of Balzac's yarns."

"And so do I, but did you also ever look on *your* work as a kind of human comedy, of sailors on land and sea?" Such a foolish question might well have received a dusty answer, but the whisky was having an effect on me, and I believe on him.

He thought about it, however, glancing to make sure our glasses were well topped up. They weren't, so with a shaking hand he stood to pour refills. "Anyone who writes a dozen novels and a score of stories, against a single backcloth of common experiences, might well have such an idea in mind, but he who imagines shaping what you call a human comedy, and hopes to use it as such, can only be the biggest comedian of all."

I had been let off lightly so tried to pull back some of the questions that had deserted me. It was good that none came, because however skillfully I used them, it was unlikely that I would have received straight answers. He was, though, so punctilious and kindly as a host that a further large ration of whisky kept him talking for more than an hour, spellbinding me with his reflections on art and authorship. Had I been in any condition to take notes I could have written an interesting critical essay.

He expatiated in detail on those periods of his life that biographers know little or nothing about. I never realized he could be so loquacious and even, at times, humorous. If only I could have recorded all that the wise old man said!

It pleased him when, on my unsteady departure, I admired the beautiful sextant in its mahogany box. A faraway look came into his eyes: "My dear fellow, the older you get, the more you dwell with poignant longing on the times of your youth."

A Tardy Talk with
Edith Wharton

JOHN HALPERIN

We meet by appointment in the former dining room of The Mount, the sumptuous home Edith Wharton owned from 1902 to 1912 in Lenox, Massachusetts, in the heart of the Berkshires. For some years it had been a boarding school for girls. Nowadays, it's a putative Wharton museum. The room has been painted sky blue and cream, the better to reflect light. Outside, remains of the spectacular gardens that Mrs. Wharton designed are visible from the spacious windows.

INTERVIEWER: Thank you so much for seeing me.

WHARTON: It's the least I could do for someone who is so interested in poor, dear Henry.

INTERVIEWER: Why "poor" Henry?

WHARTON: Well, you know, he was very unlucky. He lived at a time when the love that dare not speak its name really did not dare. He was terribly repressed. Did you know that all of his life he suffered from constipation? And then, of course, those wonderful novels of his never sold very much. People thought of him as rich, but he wasn't. After he gave up part of his income to support his sister Alice, he depended entirely on his literary earnings, which were never enough. How pleased and proud he would have been to know that he has become such a giant of literary history.

INTERVIEWER: Did he have no idea of what his posthumous reputation would be?

WHARTON: None at all. You know I tried to raise some money for him, but he wouldn't take it. It embarrassed him. I don't think he ever forgave me.

INTERVIEWER: Turning to your own work and life: why did you put a thirty-year embargo on the papers you left to Yale University?

WHARTON: Oh my dear sir, it would have been impossible otherwise. Everyone I grew up with had to be dead, you see, as well as those who grew old with me.

INTERVIEWER: Because of the revelation of your relationship with Morton Fullerton, or of the erotic dreams you had of your father—

WHARTON: Please. I have always believed in being honest, telling the truth. But not everyone can face having the truth given to him. I did not want to be around when things like that came out.

INTERVIEWER: What were your feelings about Fullerton?

WHARTON: I loved him. I did not love all of those clandestine meetings at the Charing Cross Hotel—a very uncomfortable place, by the way—but there wasn't much else we could do.

INTERVIEWER: Do you mind my asking if this was your first sexual relationship?

WHARTON: I mind, but I'll answer. Yes, it was the first. Whatever people thought, I never slept with Walter Berry. And Teddy—impossible.

INTERVIEWER: Do you remember a Canadian graduate student named Leon Edel who visited you in Paris in the 1920s?

WHARTON: I'm afraid not.

INTERVIEWER: He told me an interesting story. He was searching at the time for every scrap of paper Henry James had written on, and he visited you to ask whether you had any presentation copies from James whose inscriptions he could read.

WHARTON: I'm getting a glimmer.

INTERVIEWER: You said that of course he could read them, and you handed him a book. He opened it to find that it was a presentation copy from James to a man he'd never heard of—Morton Fullerton.

WHARTON: Oh yes.

INTERVIEWER: He said you took it back and gave him something else, and he was puzzled by the incident until your papers were opened forty years later. Then at last he realized why you would have a presentation copy from Henry James to Morton Fullerton.

WHARTON: A forty-year mystery solved at last. Yes, Morton left me his library. He had a wonderful collection.

INTERVIEWER: Including some Edith Wharton presentation copies?

WHARTON: Inevitably.

INTERVIEWER: We come now to some questions I'd like to ask you about your own work, if you don't mind.

WHARTON: By all means.

INTERVIEWER: Did you ever regret the very broad satire in *The Custom of the Country*? It is of course a wonderful novel, but no one would describe it as subtle.

WHARTON: You're quite right; it's not at all subtle. Those were bad years for me, just before the war. I had left my husband, sold The Mount, migrated to France, and was awaiting my divorce decree—in Palermo, of all places—and all the horrible publicity that would entail. As a matter of fact, my divorce was granted in 1913, the year in which *The Custom of the Country* was published. I was very *distrait*. I had divorce on my mind. I was angry. And I'm afraid it got through into the novel.

INTERVIEWER: There are two or three divorces in the novel, highly publicized.

WHARTON: Yes. It was on my mind, as I say.

INTERVIEWER: One of them required bribing the pope.

WHARTON: Yes. Such things have always been possible, going back to the Middle Ages.

INTERVIEWER: Mind you, it's a wonderful book—

WHARTON: I should have given Undine a few sympathetic traits so that everyone wouldn't hope she'd fall off a building or get run over by a train. I think I managed that with most of my other heroines.

INTERVIEWER: Did Lily Bart in *The House of Mirth* commit suicide or did she die by accident?

WHARTON: Ah, now that's a good question. Ultimately readers have to decide these things for themselves—I'm not in the business of answering all questions. I present a situation and let readers interpret it as they will.

INTERVIEWER: Do you have an opinion?

WHARTON: My opinion is that she killed herself. She was at the end of her rope and there was no way out. She had reached rock bottom. She couldn't know that Selden had decided to marry her. But of course, as always, he was too late.

INTERVIEWER: Could one see it as an accidental overdose?

WHARTON: Of course one could. Sometimes that is what I think—though I do remember trying at the time to find out how an overdose of chloral would affect someone. But you know, as Henry says somewhere, the whole of anything is never told—you can only take what groups together. The critics often accused him of not finishing his novels, but after all, a novel is a finite form and has to end somewhere. Readers can imagine the story going on, if they like, but the poor novelist has to write *Finis* somewhere.

INTERVIEWER: Some critics say your male characters—Selden being one example—are weak.

WHARTON: They're not weak, they're just men. Men are far more cowardly than women. They have all the social and financial advantages. Women have to be strong, to fight for every scrap. George Eliot understood this, and so did Miss Austen.

INTERVIEWER: Does Lily give up?

WHARTON: Given all of her bad luck and the divisions within her, she has little choice. Had she lived one more day, everything might have been different. But she didn't live one more day. She is always unlucky—unlucky to have scruples in an unscrupulous world. When that happens, you are bound to be defeated.

INTERVIEWER: You were never defeated.

WHARTON: I had resources. For a woman without them, that world was a very difficult place.

INTERVIEWER: I'd like to ask you some questions now about *The Age of Innocence.*

WHARTON: Please do.

INTERVIEWER: Do you think the upper-crust New Yorkers of the 1870s were more innocent than their descendants—or is the title, as many have suspected, ironic?

WHARTON: Well, in some ways the society of the 1870s was more innocent—or perhaps I should say less knowledgeable about certain things, like how to make money and how to manipulate your social status upwards, and how to have a satisfactory emotional life. But in some ways—perhaps in a more personal way—they were not innocent at all. They understood the society of which they were a part very well indeed.

INTERVIEWER: The apparent apotheosis of innocence in the novel, May Welland, is the most manipulative and perhaps the most cynical character of all. She's a very tough cookie.

WHARTON: As you say, a "very tough cookie" indeed.

INTERVIEWER: Why else would she tell Ellen she was pregnant before she tells Newland?

WHARTON: Quite right. I meant her to fight for what was hers. Is that lack of innocence? I don't know.

INTERVIEWER: There is certainly nothing innocent about that famous farewell dinner she gives for Ellen.

WHARTON: As you say, there is nothing innocent about that. She employs, perhaps, some measure of Realpolitik, a word that was in the air in those days.

INTERVIEWER: The "innocent" in the novel seem to have an iron will. All the would-be rebels are defeated by them.

WHARTON: Yes, innocence can be very destructive, can't it? A novelist of my later days understood this very well: Elizabeth Bowen.

INTERVIEWER: Why doesn't Newland go up to see Ellen in the novel's final scene?

WHARTON: Ah, my dear fellow, that's not for me to say. As we know, the whole of anything is never told.

INTERVIEWER: Could the "innocence" in the novel be retrospective— that is, the way you saw the 1870s from the perspective of 1920?

WHARTON: That's a shrewd question, and the answer is possibly yes. As things got more and more brutal and unsubtle, those days seemed more desirable to me. Perhaps the innocence was only in my own mind.

INTERVIEWER: I'd like to move on to some of your other books, which, in my opinion, have been inexplicably neglected by readers and critics.

WHARTON: Which of those far too many volumes are your favorites?

INTERVIEWER: I would have to say *A Son at the Front, The Fruit of the Tree, Old New York,* and *Glimpses of the Moon.* And how I wish you'd been able to finish *The Buccaneers.* Finally, you are a largely unacknowledged master—or mistress—of that anomalous and difficult form, the novella. I'm thinking of *Ethan Frome, Summer*—

WHARTON: Yes, Henry and I used to speak of the novella a good deal. A perfect length, about a hundred pages. Long enough to develop some interesting characters without having to get involved in numerous subplots. But in the group of your favorite lesser-known novels of mine, you don't include one of my favorites, *Hudson River Bracketed.*

INTERVIEWER: What did you most value in that one?

WHARTON: The sort of *Age of Innocence* ambiance—the idea of wanting to go back and live in old New York as if the Great War had never happened. I found the whole idea very moving.

INTERVIEWER: To return to the novella—

WHARTON: And of course *Old New York* is one of my best books, and that is four novellas.

INTERVIEWER: You, James, and Conrad seemed to master the form simultaneously.

WHARTON: Well, they came along a bit before I did. But I agree with you—we all interested ourselves in the form.

INTERVIEWER: *Old New York, The Buccaneers,* and *Glimpses of the Moon* seem to touch on what were familiar subjects for you, but *The Fruit of the Tree* and *A Son at the Front* were quite unusual—an industrial novel about factory owners, with some euthanasia thrown in, and an antiwar novel. How did those come about? What did you know about factories in America in the first decade of the twentieth century?

WHARTON: Very little at first, but I worked it up. I didn't see why women should know nothing about labor relations. The book was too long—I should have shortened it. But I don't regret the theme of mercy killing, which turned out to be the most controversial part of it.

INTERVIEWER: And *A Son at the Front?*

WHARTON: Well, that came more naturally. After all, I was living in France during the Great War, so I didn't have to work it up. I found the relations between parents and their children at this time tragically complicated. Every family wanted to feel that the son of the house was doing his bit. On the other hand, it was excruciating to see him go. I agree with you that this novel has been underappreciated.

INTERVIEWER: Your near neighbor Monsieur Proust deeply regretted the disappearance from Paris of all the good-looking men.

WHARTON: I know he lived a few doors away, but I don't think I ever met him. There were tales of his locking himself up to write. Apparently they were true.

INTERVIEWER: Do you have any comment on the explosion of criticism of your work in recent years?

WHARTON: I suppose people can always say what they like. It's a relief to be taken seriously as a writer—you know, not just as a New York gossip columnist but as an artist. I felt that was the case, especially after *The Age of Innocence* won the Pulitzer Prize. That was the first time for a woman, you know. But I think *The House of Mirth* is a better novel.

INTERVIEWER: Why?

WHARTON: Lily doesn't have the rather more sumptuous choices that the characters in *The Age of Innocence* have. Lack of money makes all the difference. How is a young lady to get along in life if she has nothing of her own but won't marry a dull millionaire? She is too ethical, too fastidious, for her world. It traps her. For the characters in *The Age of Innocence* these are not matters of life and death—only questions of being "in" or "out." In Lily, I think I must have been imagining myself without any money. What would I have done?

INTERVIEWER: One of our most prominent writers, John Updike, classifies you as a literary naturalist, very much in the school of Dreiser. What's your response to that?

WHARTON: Well, in the sense that our environments, where and how we grow up and live, are seen as controlling influences in our lives, I would probably concur. Lily Bart, for example, is almost entirely a product of her environment and her family and its values and seems to have little free will. But if Mr. Updike means it in the sense of a novelist being like a scientist in a laboratory, objectively examining slides, a pathologist who presents evidence but takes no side, then that's obviously wrong. Can a satirist and a naturalist be the same person? Satirists—and of course I'm one—take sides.

INTERVIEWER: As you grew older, you also grew more tolerant of the old ways of doing things?

WHARTON: That's quite true. I was more of a rebel when I was younger. But aren't we all? If you run into Pearl Buck, please let her know that that Nobel Prize should have gone to me.

INTERVIEWER: Do you accept the view of Sinclair Lewis, Scott Fitzgerald, and others that you were the first indigenous American novelist to write about American manners rather than European ones?

WHARTON: That's probably quite true. Cooper, Henry James, and others wrote about Americans in Europe, not in America. Hawthorne's novels seem more historical than contemporary, and Melville's go on interminably about whale blubber. I did try to give a close reading of contemporary American manners, at least in New York, and I suppose I was the first to do that, along with Mr. Howells. It's good to be the first at something, especially if you're a woman.

INTERVIEWER: How disadvantageous was it being a woman?

WHARTON: Was Miss Austen given an education? A few weeks at a boarding school. Like her, I educated myself in my father's library. George Eliot? Self-taught, entirely. Even Mrs. Woolf received no formal education, or so I'm told. How disadvantageous was it? My dear sir, it meant you had to do everything for yourself. One's stupider brothers received a very expensive education, but it doesn't seem to have done them much good. Being from a rich family did me no good at all when it came to education. I had to learn everything on my own. Now may I ask you something?

INTERVIEWER: Of course.

WHARTON: Which of my books is your favorite?

INTERVIEWER: That's easy. *The House of Mirth.*

WHARTON: Why?

INTERVIEWER: I'm not sure. It's one of the few novels you wrote that's set contemporaneously. The scene is meant to be the turn of the century, and the novel was published shortly after. There's no uncertainty in that novel about how you feel toward New York. It's brutal and unforgiving in its upper echelons. I like the lack of ambivalence.

WHARTON: Well, I have your answer. Thank you.

INTERVIEWER: No, thank *you*, Mrs. Wharton.

WHARTON: You're quite welcome.

A Visit with
Mr. Frost

JAY PARINI

This happened some years ago, perhaps a decade. I forget exactly. It was past midnight at the Homer Noble Farm in Ripton, Vermont—the house that once belonged to Robert Frost. He acquired the farm in 1939, soon after his wife's death, and kept the place until he died in 1963. He called it his summer place, but he often arrived in early spring and stayed on late into the fall. He frequently visited the farm in winter, too. There was hardly a season when he stayed away for long.

Because I was writing a biography of Frost, I was allowed to occupy the house for discrete periods, a week or two at a stretch. One can learn a lot about people by staying in their homes, sleeping in their beds, lying in the tubs in their bathrooms, or sitting at their breakfast tables. You get to see the morning light as they saw it, with its idiosyncratic glow as it comes through certain windows, at particular angles. It's not surprising that Sigmund Freud once suggested that any dream about a house is a dream about one's own soul or self.

On the night in question here, I found myself unable to sleep, terrified by the wind. I'm always scared by wind, and Frost's is an especially windy house, built in the mid-nineteenth century—a typical farmhouse of the era, with drafts that curl up from the basement, circulate with impunity, and make their way into the musty attic. The chimneys in these houses always seem to wheeze. Somehow, there always seems to be more inhalation than exhalation in these old places.

It was late summer, with a touch of fall in the air, and this high thin wire of wind rushed through the tall trees that circled the house. Hearing the sound, I suddenly understood in a gut way that early poem by Frost, "The Sound of the Trees." There is, indeed, something about the trees one cannot quite fathom. The huge hemlocks immediately beyond the bedroom wall tossed and turned their limbs anxiously; they brushed aggressively against the house and frightened me with their unearthly sound.

I was working on my book, wondering what to make of Frost's long depressions. For weeks at a time, at various points in his life, he would stay in bed, hardly capable of rising by noon. He kept the shades of his windows drawn. His wife, Elinor, found him irascible or unresponsive. His children learned to avoid him. This was, indeed, a lonely and difficult man. On the other side of this syndrome, he was hyperactive, walking in the woods till midnight, talking excitedly to anyone who cared to listen. During these phases, his wife and children also tried to keep him at bay.

But how could I explain these swinging moods in the mind of a great poet? I hesitated to use the term *manic-depressive*. It seemed way too modern, technical, and inexact. Isn't everyone something of a manic-depressive? Is it really a question of the height of the peaks, the depth of the valleys?

Sleep eluded me. Finally—it was near four in the morning by now—I made my way down the narrow and crooked stairwell to the kitchen, where a black potbellied stove stood cold in one corner. I liked to imagine Frost at night, unable to sleep, sitting by the stove on a winter's night in a cane chair. I could see him as an old man here, not unlike the lonely figure in "An Old Man's Winter Night," that incomparable poem about the isolation of a human being at the end of life, a man who can no longer "keep a house," a farm, a countryside.

That was a favorite word of this poet: *keep*. It comes from an Anglo-Saxon root-word: *cepen*. It means to seize or hold, to possess. The mind keeps a house, a farm, a countryside. It holds the landscape in place, it occupies the land with dignity, its surveys the house of the spirit: a particular ecosphere. But an old man has a hard time with this work of keeping. Dignity itself is often difficult to obtain in this late phase of any life. Loneliness becomes fierce, almost debilitating.

As in "The Most of It," the old person calls out upon the universe in vain, hoping for more than mere echo; he or she wants "counter-love" or "original response." Frost knew this deeply. I cannot doubt that he, too, wanted love.

I sat by the stove now, drinking a cup of mint tea. I had my notes before me and was trying to write something, to add a few sentences to the biography. It had been stalled for a long time, as I wondered about what Frost was really like. A man has a "personality," that hideous word. It helps to think of that term, *persona*, with its roots in Latin. The word means mask. One puts on masks, and speaks through these masks to the world. The eyeholes may reveal the reality behind the mask. But it's the voice one hears, the voice sounding through the mask: *per-sona*. In the best of circumstances, the mask becomes the face, as reality inheres in the performance of self.

As I was thinking about these things, the phone rang, startling me. It's not an ordinary phone in Frost's kitchen but an old-fashioned black ring-down device. One cranks the crank, and it rings—but only in the cabin on the hill behind Frost's farmhouse. This cabin, built in 1928 for hunters, had become Frost's favorite hangout in his last decades. He would sleep there in a pine-walled room, eat there at a three-legged table, write there in his favorite Morris chair, with a lapboard across his knees. It was only a brief walk down a woodsy path through maple and poplar to the main farmhouse, and he could easily call or "ring down" from the cabin to the house on this phone.

His dear friend and secretary, Kay Morrison, would answer. He would ask whether the mail had come, or whether she could bring him a pot of coffee. He would check in: "I'm alive," he often muttered, as if to reassure her. By then, he was in his eighties and had acquired a Mount Rushmore face. It was a face that Americans knew well.

But was this phone ringing now? It was impossible. I knew that the cabin was locked, and—unless invaders had broken the lock—nobody could crank the cabin's phone. I had locked the door myself the previous afternoon. Perhaps I had imagined the ring?

I put the ringing down to an overactive imagination. But then it rang again. I knew, by now, that I must be hallucinating. Yet in this waking dream I walked to the phone and lifted it, and wondered aloud, "Mr. Frost?"

"I'm here, yes." The voice was unmistakable, and his.

"In the cabin?"

"Yes, I'm here."

"Is there anything I can do for you?"

"I'm out of sorts," he said. After a pause: "Come up."

Anybody who has been dead for many decades has good reason to feel out of sorts, but I decided to go. I got a big flashlight from the drawer and headed up through the woods under a hunter's moon. The wind rustled the ferns, which seemed unworldly, the feathery tongues in apparent conversation. I smelled a dead animal in the ditch nearby, and hurried past it. Here and there I stumbled. Was I going mad?

The cabin glowed in its hilltop clearing: a skull of sorts, the logs silvery in the strange light. There was a small blaze in the sitting room, by the stone fireplace. I could see the white helmet of Frost's hair through the windowpane. It was definitely him, that much I could swear.

I had the key with me and opened the door gingerly, my hands shaking. That Mr. Frost had not needed a key to get in did not escape my attention.

"Hello, Mr. Parini," he said.

"Please, call me Jay."

"You can call me Mr. Frost," he said.

"Of course."

"Sit down, boy."

I was a boy again, although over fifty. It felt odd to think of myself as a boy; in fact, I disliked the arrogance of this old poet. He radiated arrogance, sitting in his wooden rocker, in stiff canvas trousers, an open-collared shirt, a rustic jacket. He looked like a dead man, the skin barely real; one could almost see through the papery cracks in his cheeks. But I liked the stubby hands: like claws. He had worked with these hands, and even death had done nothing to diminish their potential to grip something, anything.

"I'm pleased to meet you, Mr. Frost," I said.

"Everyone is."

"What brings you . . . back?" I wondered.

"You," he said. "This book you're doing, the biography of this man called Robert Frost."

"You've heard about it?"

"It's one of the advantages of heaven: you can look down. You see what they're up to."

"Have you by any chance read what I've written?"

"Skimmed it." He rocked in silence for a few moments, gathering his thoughts. "Not bad," he said. "But you fail to connect the dots."

"How's that?"

"You split me in two. Sometimes I seem like, well, somebody's benevolent uncle, a generous fellow, full of grace notes. Other times I growl and grouse. I do nasty things, say them, too."

"So which is the real you?"

"Robert Frost is a fiction," he said firmly. "Remember that."

"Meaning?"

"Meaning what I said. It's a shaped thing. *Fictio.* That's Latin. It means shaping. I put a man on stage whenever I go to read. I speak these poems by Frost. They often seem to me like the words of another man. They feel alien to me, too often. But when I recite them, when I inhabit them, they become me. Or I become them."

"You become Robert Frost."

"Good boy," he said, smiling now. "You're a quick learner."

"But what happens when you step off the stage? What about now?"

"I'm just like you when I'm not reading those poems. I'm nobody. Or everybody. It's the human spirit we're talking about here. The wind in the trees. Wind, you know, is *spiritus* in Latin. This spirit blows through the trees, rips off the leaves, does a lot of damage."

"And maybe some good as well?" I wondered.

He just glowered. "Sometimes it lifts the hem of the garment, perhaps so."

"The garment of the world: I like that."

"I'm too old for compliments," he said. "I'm beyond old."

"You're dead," I said.

He laughed at my frankness. "I believe you don't have a very clear understanding of life and death. These are fictions, too. Have you never read my poems? If you have, you know Robert Frost, and you know he is not dead, and can not die. I'm not really gone, you see. I'm here. I'm always here, in this cabin, in this house."

"What about the Old Man in that poem of yours?"

"He's here, too. In this cabin. But he can keep it, and keep the farm, and keep the countryside. I occupy this place."

"Genius loci," I said.

"Don't be too clever," he warned. "It's never good to be too clever. You miss out on life, always trying to make a joke. Life is no joke."

I felt chastened. I also felt anxious to push forward with the interview. Here was a unique opportunity to talk to Frost personally, to ask the questions that had been pounding in my brain for years now. I'd been trying to write this biography since I first stepped onto the campus at Dartmouth, Frost's old college, back in 1975. I remember walking into the Rare Books and Manuscripts Library, wondering what it had that might interest me. I said to the small gray man at the desk, "So what have you got?" "Frost," he answered, and fetched from the dark bowels of that building a boxful of moldy letters, manuscripts, notebooks. I began to read, and kept reading, and the questions arose: thousands of questions. I wanted answers.

"I need to ask you a few things, Mr. Frost," I said, with some urgency.

But the light of dawn had begun to creep through the adjoining forest. The Norway pines bristled. The wind, which had been so loud and insistent throughout the long night, almost horrifying, died. And the rocking chair was empty.

I rose in panic and looked in the bedroom, in the bathroom, in the kitchen. No Robert Frost, none. The figure a poet makes had departed as mysteriously as he came.

Disappointed, I stepped outside, stood on the stone steps of the cabin, and saw the mountains, range after range, under the sunrise, far into Vermont. The meadow below the cabin glistened, covered with a fine lace of dew. The air stung with freshness.

I walked slowly back to the main house, thinking over what had transpired. I was, of course, pleased that I had caught a glimpse of the man himself, but as certain as ever that it would be difficult, perhaps impossible, to catch him. One can never hold the wind in one's own hands, and that's the truth. One simply can't.

William Faulkner

As I Lay Dreaming

CARL ROLLYSON

I've been having strange dreams lately. I woke up this morning after a vivid half-waking reverie about attending a theater performance. It starred Susan Sontag, who seemed thrilled about her role and responded to questions after the performance with an appetite that astounded me. She was so well known for her surly, even contemptuous treatment of interlocutors, especially during the last phase of her career—and yet her mood was not entirely surprising. As a student she had acted in plays at the University of Chicago, befriending Mike Nichols, then a fellow student who became a lifelong friend. My wife and I had tried to interview Nichols for our biography of Sontag, but he was always "too busy," too involved in a project to see us—or so one of his assistants would say.

This sort of friendly brush-off often frustrates biographers. Most of the time, though, biographers are like brokers cold calling. How to get the attention of people who don't know you? Biographers don't even have a hot stock tip to entice their marks.

This sort of brooding entered my reverie about the Sontag dream as I began to wake up and remember she was dead—dead since 2004. I've had many dreams about my biographical subjects. Sometimes the subjects are friendly, but I wake realizing I've learned nothing. The dreams seem to be about the irreparable gap between biographer and subject, the same one Henry James dramatizes in "The Real Right Thing" when he has a biographer (sanctioned by the subject's widow) confront the ghost of his subject—a forbidding apparition that does not speak but seems a projection of the biographer's own dread that he has been deprecating his subject's life by invading his space. And yet, here I am dreaming of these charming encoun-

160

ters with my subjects! There is obviously a yearning for contact with them that my conscious and calloused view of my work scoffs at.

The Sontag dream was provoked, I see now, by my reading of Philip Baruth's *The X President*, set in 2055. In this science fiction scenario, a new technology allows the insertion of key players into past scenes, thus altering the course of history. The technology has never been used, but now the U.S. government is desperate because it is losing a war against the Eastern Alliance (Russia and China have teamed up).

Forget whether you like this sort of hypothetical narrative and concentrate on what it speaks to: our desire to be at another place in another time in order to witness, if not to change, an important moment in history. I don't believe in the possibility of time travel. I understand that a group of scientists recently declared they could now say definitively it is not possible. Yet what is biography if it is not time travel?

. . . .

As William Faulkner writes in *Requiem for a Nun*, "The past is never past." We don't really go forward or backward. One can turn a corner, as I understand biographer Jeffrey Meyers did, and find oneself in the eighteenth century talking with Dr. Johnson. This sounds absurd, I know, but biographers are a bunch of Billy Pilgrims. Kurt Vonnegut describes the phenomenon: "Billy Pilgrim has come unstuck in time. . . . Billy is spastic in time, has no control over where he is going next, and the trips aren't necessarily fun. He is in a constant state of stage fright, he says, because he never knows what part of his life he is going to have to act in next."

Biographers believe they have control over their narratives, but their dreams suggest another dimension to their work, one in which the subject remains in charge.

. . . .

July 15, 2007

Reading *The X President* has induced early morning reveries that are becoming longer and longer. I feel I'm in some sort of middle state between sleeping and waking, a Kubla Khan realm, that has been building and building toward. . . . Well, here is what happened.

Faulkner has always struck me as the most unapproachable of figures. He never seemed to want to talk about his work. I know—he did interviews and patiently answered student questions at the University of Virginia. But early on he formulated a sort of generic defense, a patter that varied little, which makes reading his interviews an exercise in repetition. And then he published those essays about how privacy was no longer respected. He even claimed if he had to do it all over again, he would have published his work anonymously. I wrote my first book on Faulkner, a study of his uses of the past, and knew that while he is famous for his statement "the past is never past," his novels are all about how hard it is to know the past, to get inside it, as Quentin and Shreve attempt to do in *Absalom, Absalom!* Faulkner, it seems to me, represents a rebuff to the biographer.

"Subjects have the whip hand. Subjects have the whip hand," I chanted as a sort of mantra this morning as I was trying to wake up. Lately I've been having trouble rousing myself. Most unusual for me. The only time I ever had this trouble before was when I was trying to write my dissertation on Faulkner, and the words wouldn't come. I kept getting up later each day.

My doze was suddenly disrupted: "I've never understood why it is supposed that characters in novels speak for their authors." That soft southern drawl I used to listen to intently on a Caedmon record album was unmistakable. It was WF, for sure. He seemed to be musing on what I was thinking. Although subjects had spoken to me in dreams before, I woke up never remembering what they said. But now I swear I wasn't dreaming. For one thing, I had this voice to go on. I lay still, sensing my only hope of hearing more from WF was to remain *silent*.

Pillow talk with WF? I know it sounds absurd, but in any other setting, in any other kind of meeting, how could I ever get him to talk to me? Now he had come calling, so to speak, as if he were riding one of my brain waves. If I didn't press him, if I proceeded by indirection, if I remained in bed—a biographer at rest—perhaps this line to WF (however it had been established) would not be cut off.

Of course, I had all sorts of questions I wanted to ask. How do you think your drinking affected your writing? Regarding *To Have and Have Not* and *The Big Sleep*, how did you feel about having to adapt other novelists' works? Do you think your experience with Hollywood ended up detracting from your fiction writing? Do you think Estelle really meant to commit suicide when she walked into the sea shortly after you married her? Why did you have Ben Wasson arrange that meeting between your mistress, Meta, and Estelle? I had written an article about that incident, speculating on Faulkner's motivations. But if I blurted out any of this, the voice would surely go away.

"I'm almost gone as it is," the voice replied, because of course Faulkner was reading my thoughts. Frantically, I tried to suppress my questions and jam the frequency we shared with Faulknerisms: "Between grief and nothing I will take grief." "I feel like a wet seed in the hot blind earth." "Delicate equilibrium of periodical filth." And my favorite, "Women!"

I had met Meta Wilde while doing a biography of Lillian Hellman, and she had told me a little anecdote about meeting Hellman that I did not use. It just went nowhere—one of those cul-de-sacs biographers frequently end up in. All it amounted to was greeting Hellman, who promptly let out a huge fart.

Faulkner laughed. "Serves you right," he said. This seemed to break the ice. What a relief to think like a biographer but not have to explain myself.

"Meta," Faulkner seemed to breathe out her name.

I remembered attending an MLA conference when her tell-all book was published. Faulkner scholars rushed to scorn it.

"Not *all*," said Faulkner raising his voice, adding, "much obliged."

"For what?" I thought, but that was it: he understood that I was not one of the scoffers. I understood that the man who had written the tormented *Wild Palms* had been deeply in love with Meta and yet convinced that their love for each other was doomed. Indeed, I had come to believe that he had engineered—even forced—his fate by contriving that meeting between Estelle and Meta. Otherwise, what he had done was just perverse.

"Hold on, hold on," Faulkner said with considerable desperation in his voice. I could imagine that this was just the kind of speculation that drove biographical subjects mad, the one-upping biographers claiming to know their subjects better than the subjects knew themselves. "Best not get ahead of yourself," he cautioned.

"Between grief and nothing I will *make* grief," I heard myself say *out loud*, throwing out a challenge. I marveled at my effrontery, expecting the worst.

But Faulkner only groaned.

Then it occurred to me that I should tell a story—his story, as I conceived it. I had a better chance of getting on with him that way, rather than trying him with questions.

He sighed. "Go on." He sounded resigned, but just a bit inviting too, as if he welcomed my story—at least it would be a story and not the usual academic rot that clotted around his work and made readers all the more certain that he was "difficult."

I felt now as if I could read his mind, as if a bridge had been established, and so I ventured: "I always liked your response to that student in Virginia who said he didn't understand one of your books. I forget which one."

"And I forget what I told him," Faulkner replied.

"You said, 'Read it again.' And that is what biographers . . .'"

"Hold on, hold on," Faulkner stopped me, commanding: "*THE STORY!*"

"A story that proceeds by indirection," I ventured, "by a series of interviews with and speculations about the female witnesses to your life, so that like Sutpen, you appear as the oblique center of the biographer's own *Absalom, Absalom!*"

"Hah!"

"Estelle knew damn well that she was, in part, your creation. The same was true for Helen Baird, Meta, Joan Williams, and probably all the women in your life. Remember what your character, Jeffrey Almoner, says to Amy Howard (Williams's stand-in) in *The Wintering*, 'I like to think I made you, as you made me over.'"

Not a word from Faulkner.

"Should I go on?" I asked.

"Only if you stop using the second person and refer instead to 'Faulkner.'"

"So you won't have to commit yourself?"

"So I can at least pretend you're telling a goddamn story."

"Faulkner was no womanizer," I continued. "He could not use women without being influenced in return. Estelle wrote, 'Meta was a skilled musician . . .'"

"My mother painted," Faulkner murmured. "Estelle couldn't write."

"She tried. She played piano for you . . ."

"Watch it!" Faulkner nearly shouted.

"Faulkner drew pictures for Estelle, and the young lovers grew up almost as twins of each other until her family put an end to scruffy Billy's courtship because he wasn't good enough for their daughter. It opened up a gap between them. Catching Estelle on the rebound, Faulkner could never recoup their youth and went looking for it in other women, even though she remained the slim, white, youthful figure of his poetry, an androgynous dancing form—both a projection and fulfillment of desire."

"The phantom that I thought was you," Faulkner recited a line from one of his early poems.

"Faulkner returned again and again to this image of the elusive female, no more able to resolve what had happened to him in early manhood than Sutpen could articulate what happened to him when he was turned away from the master's front door."

"The butterfly became a wraith," Faulkner said quite bitterly.

"Estelle looked frail and careworn, skeletal and wasted, even in her thirties," I continued. "She drank and flirted, but she was already so far past her prime that she disgusted Faulkner."

Faulkner grunted.

"Hollywood, for all his complaints about it, gave Faulkner the chance to reinvent himself as the long-suffering, misunderstood but stoical and staunch family man, the rock Meta could count on. She knew her man drank, but perhaps for her own self-protection she couldn't abide the idea that Faulkner might be as culpable as Estelle."

"Ach!" Faulkner sounded disgusted.

"Back home, Faulkner was 'Billy,' and Estelle scoffed at his swelling romances and condescended to his nubile infatuations. 'Certainly, I do not blame Joan,' Estelle wrote to Faulkner's editor, Saxe Commins: 'In all probability, had *I* been an aspiring young writer and an elderly celebrity had fallen in love with me—I would have accepted him as avidly as Joan did Bill.' Faulkner would often say that Estelle never took his writing seriously, and biographers have suggested that he was not fair to her, but her own words to Commins suggest she enjoyed cutting him down to size with formulations such as 'elderly celebrity.' Joan, of course, thought of her man as a world-class writer. But oddly enough, none of these women—perhaps because they were besotted with Faulkner's fame—ever saw their mentor/lover as a man who couldn't reconcile himself to his wife's aging even as he aged himself. Although Faulkner remained married to Estelle, he put her aside nearly as ruthlessly as Sutpen had cut Eulalia Bon from his life, rejecting her, spirit and flesh. Both men, Sutpen and his creator, were design-bound personalities. The trouble was that while Estelle sometimes played according to Faulkner's script, at other times she asserted herself in such a way as to thwart his efforts to make their lives conform to his fictional representations of them to his young lovers."

I heard Faulkner move. He cleared this throat and began, "I . . ."

But I cut him off with, "*THE STORY!*" Biographers often make a big show about empathizing with their subjects and not judging them, as if biographers are channeling the story but not actually making it their own. But in fact, one must be rather ruthless to write biography, developing a narrative that takes on a life of its own. And so I overrode a writer that in my nonbiographer's moments I revered.

"Let me tell it," he insisted, breaking in just like Shreve in *Absalom, Absalom!* And sometimes the biographer does have to go with the flow—in this case relinquishing control to Faulkner describing the character 'Faulkner':

"Meta said Faulkner was her rock of Gibraltar. Loving him was a way of—Joan said I . . ."

"Hah!" I shouted. But he did not respond to my biographer's bait.

"Joan said Faulkner made her a woman. Estelle had nothing to do with it. Might as well say the matrix of his life had expanded in the love of these women as to say he was seeking some kind of pathetic return to youth. What a magnificent effort that old man was making even as he knew such love was doomed. Estelle just tried to make him look silly."

I interrupted, "But it has been said her letters evince a 'tragic wisdom' and that Faulkner and Estelle remained together out of fealty to their youthful love."

Faulkner snorted.

"The past is never past . . ." I began but was overridden.

"Estelle would not *let go*, and Faulkner understood it was too late to begin again with another woman. Did Faulkner *ever* live as though the past *dominated* his actions? A consequence of that proposition is Quentin Compson's suicide. Estelle made too damn much of her 'devotion' when Faulkner asked her for a divorce. He did not want to lose himself to a love like Harry Wilbourne's, or stand convicted of a contempt for women that that old convict expressed even as he was trying to save one. You can't ever save a woman, though that is what some of them wanted from Faulkner."

"How did Faulkner know that?" I asked, deciding to try to steer him toward what I wanted to know.

"Well, he put it all to a test."

"Ah, that meeting between Estelle and Meta."

Faulkner laughed and chewed his bitter thumbs, you might say. "Hollywood had to be good for something," he said. "Estelle had pestered him about a trip West just when he was anticipating a fine time with Meta. Estelle didn't belong in Hollywood. It was pitiful watching her try to compete."

"But what does it say about Faulkner that he wanted to *expose* his wife in that way?"

"Do you mean he was a son of a bitch?"

"Well . . ."

"Listen! Estelle had been at him for *years*!"

"And what about Meta? Was it fair to her?"

"She wanted a good look at Estelle. Faulkner could tell. Was Estelle really that ghost of a woman her lover had pitied and raged against? Meta wanted to see for herself."

"Ben Wasson, who set up the meeting, thought it was Faulkner's first move in a divorce proceeding."

"What did Ben know? He was just doing Faulkner a favor."

"But why upset Estelle and trouble Meta? Surely neither woman really needed this confrontation?"

"But what about Faulkner? What did *he* need? It was hell going back and forth between Hollywood and Oxford. It was all so make-believe."

"But introducing Meta as Ben's girl?"

"Well, Faulkner knew Estelle wouldn't be fooled, but he also knew that she would rather have a charade than an out-and-out conflict."

"She was passive-aggressive."

"Ah, well, if you must use that kind of language. Estelle had dried up. All she cared about was her position as Mrs. Faulkner. She objected when anyone called her Mrs. Estelle Faulkner. She wanted his first name, too."

"Surely there was more to it than that."

"That is the biographer's need, isn't it? To say there was more to it than that."

"Not just the biographer's, surely. What about the novelist's need?"

Faulkner ignored the question. "Faulkner never romanticized Estelle as much as has been supposed. He always had misgivings about her."

"Then why marry her?"

This question was a conversation stopper. My guess is that no one spoke for a full five minutes. Then he said, "A man marries . . . well, it was like that convict caught in a flood. He assumes responsibility for the woman even though . . ."

"But marriage?"

"My God, is it really so mystifying? Faulkner had something to prove after Estelle returned without Cornell."

"Marriage as a kind of vindication of his own worthiness?"

"Nothing so exact . . . more like the marriage was a part of the mode of life he wanted when he wasn't about to go elsewhere for it, and Estelle was already bound up in his imagination of a place he could not disentangle himself from without sacrificing the sense of the kind of man he was in the place he could not, dared not, repudiate."

"I had a design," I began quoting Sutpen.

"An unrooted romance . . ."

"Are you thinking of Meta?" I asked.

"You mean, is Faulkner thinking of Meta?" he corrected. "The encounter between Estelle and Meta was certainly part of a design."

"Showing both women why they couldn't trade places?"

"Showing why for all the conflict there was nothing to resolve, nothing to get out of 'winning.' Faulkner wasn't going to settle for being someone's prize."

"But isn't that what Estelle got anyway? Like Mary Hemingway hanging on to the end?"

"And so she had to pay the price of that. Why blame Bill?"

"And Meta?"

"That girl could always take care of herself."

"Still, what an awkward—some might say perverse—way to handle his two women."

"'His women'? They had their own desires. Faulkner was never the kind of man who thought of himself as the center of the universe—not even when he was in love."

"So did playing out that scene between Estelle and Meta prove anything? Neither woman could have performed at her best, Meta wary of saying much and naturally subdued, Estelle frenetic with an effort to be both ingratiating and in command. Didn't Estelle despise Faulkner for this kind of ruse? Didn't Meta feel as humiliated as Estelle?"

"Didn't Faulkner contrive the encounter as a way to show them all how hopeless it was to think there was some sort of romantic solution to their dilemma? Wasn't he showing them that any decisive move would simply tear him apart?"

"So Meta eventually faded away, took care of her own life. But what of Estelle?"

"I suppose Faulkner would say she had little left to her, not much more than that wraith Henry Sutpen at the end of *Absalom, Absalom!*"

"She is a haunting figure. Faulkner must have given her that."

"I think he did. But you know it is a mistake to think he came to some sort of final acceptance of her—or even effected a truce in their lifelong struggle over him. Novelists' lives are not novels, their characters are never traceable back to their creators."

"Isn't this where you came in? Isn't this where I object . . ."

I didn't complete the sentence. He was gone. How I could tell, I can't say, but the line between us was dead. The rest was silence.

PART FOUR

CONSOLIDATION

Questions for the Master

Alfred Edward Housman

COLIN DEXTER

As a gentle (pretty needless, really) introduction to what I have to say, let me recount how I first met Housman. It was a surname that I would certainly have misspelled when, in summer 1946 I was a sixteen-year-old schoolboy in a Lincolnshire grammar school, studying Latin and Greek, and when the headmaster came into our class one morning and (à propos of nothing, as I recall) read to us *A Shropshire Lad* LXII ("Terence this is stupid stuff . . ."). At the time some of the lines meant precious little to me—and indeed how otherwise with such couplets as

> The cow; the old cow, she is dead;
> It sleeps well the hornèd head.

Yet there were other couplets that struck a happy chord with my classmates and me, since we were already enjoying our regular underage intake of local ale:

> Say, for what think ye were hop-yards meant,
> Or why was Burton built on Trent?

And since we were there also studying the early books of *Paradise Lost*, we were delighted that, at least in Housman's eyes,

> . . . malt does more than Milton can
> To justify God's ways to man.

But it was not until a good many years later that I came to treasure other lines from that same poem. And when the *Sunday Telegraph* asked a group of writers to submit their favorite couplet from the whole of English literature, my choice was

And I will friend you, if I may,
In the dark and cloudy day.

Fourteen words only—all but one of them a monosyllable—yet for me a wonderful promise that Housman has always so faithfully kept.

As a result of that fortuitous introduction in 1946, I was immediately and permanently hooked, very soon realizing that Housman, as a scholar-poet, had few if any equals in the controlled and profound tenor of his poetry and in his unrivaled status as the greatest Latin scholar of his age. And some four or five years later I began to collect—and still now collect—anything and everything connected with his life and works, very early on learning that he had joined that extraordinary group of figures in English literature who had departed from the University of Oxford without obtaining a degree: Johnson, Gibbon, Shelley, Swinburne, Betjeman, et al. In the hierarchy of the heroes established in my youthful years, he had already been promoted to the top four (all H's): Homer, Hardy, Housman, and Len Hutton, the latter an incomparable English opening batsman.

No, dear reader, I have not forgotten my brief of trying to decide upon the question(s) I would wish (and indeed would not wish) to ask AEH, but one point—for me a profoundly important one—requires some elucidation: I have just used the phrase "life and works" as though the two words were a pair of yoked oxen. This, in my view, is a bit (a lot) misleading. Let me explain.

When, after teaching Latin and Greek in English schools for only thirteen years, deafness (which has blighted my life) drove me to quit the classroom, I took up a post with the Oxford University Delegacy of School Examinations, supervising the syllabuses, the administration, and the examination of Latin, Greek, ancient history, and English. In this post I was fairly quickly initiated into a very different mode of pedagogic thinking. From the start my elders and betters sought to impress on me two major principles. First, to go to the books themselves, rather than to the books *about* the books. And I needed such a lesson. In Higher School Certificate in the late 1940s, I took English as a subsidiary subject, but I never read the actual texts prescribed at all. *Far from the Madding Crowd* was one such text, and I read nary a word of it, just a very fine introduction to it, which I duly studied—and with great profit, because I became a successful candidate. The only thing I missed, of course, in this shoddy process, was the huge delight of reading the novel itself and making some personal response to it—which should have been the object of the whole exercise. Instead of which, what I learned was when Hardy was born and when he died and what he did betweenwhiles.

In most realms of literature the role of biography has been steadily increasing, with the unstated implication that the artist's life is intimately and intrinsically connected with his or her work, that the one cannot be fully understood or appreciated without the other. But please let us draw the line somewhere between the two. I well remember a question set in A-level English, "Was Hamlet mad?"— and thereafter reading many worthy and knowledgeable answers beginning in the following sort of way: "Before considering this important question, we must look with some care at the social mores of this period and the personal circumstances under which the play was written. As a famous and perceptive critic has reminded us," and so on, two or three pages of it, all of which can be and should be—and was—ignored by the examiner. And well, too, I remember one candidate, a girl from Portsmouth, who began her essay "Yes! Hamlet was as twisted as a corkscrew. For example, in Act something, Scene something, he says . . ." This opening was greeted with universal joy, rewarded with "Hurrah!" and with three ticks in the margin from the senior Awarder. First then, let it be the text; and then, if it be required, the biographical details second. And it was the text I wrote about when I described the death of a man with whom Inspector Morse shared a hospital ward in Oxford—a character who in fact was based upon my greatest friend in life, and who invariably referred to Housman as "The Master." I quote (if you'll forgive me) from that novel:

> The curtains around the bed of the late Colonel were now standing
> open in the normal way to reveal the newly laundered sheets, with the

changed blankets professionally mitred at the foot of the bed. Had Morse known how the man could never abide a chord of Richard Wagner, he would have felt much aggrieved; yet had he known how the Colonel had committed to memory virtually the whole of Housman's poetic corpus, he would have been profoundly gratified.

In short, let me emphasize once more that a great many poets—and in this case, particularly AEH—were not saying look at *me*; they were saying look at what I *wrote*; look at my works, since that is what is important about my achievements as a poet, or a classical scholar, or whatever.

What did such a fundamental shift of emphasis mean to me in a practical, personal way in my love of AEH?

I was very proud in 2004 to be invited to give the annual Housman lecture on "The Name and Nature of Poetry." In my talk I was particularly critical (I now think rather unfairly) of that fine scholar Carol Efrati, who had just published a book on AEH, *The Road of Danger, Guilt, and Shame*. The title of this work has at least one merit, since it features the splendid Oxford comma after the word *Guilt*. Yet had I taken the trouble to read the first two words of the first sentence of Chapter 1, I would not have bought it. It reads: "Housman's homosexuality may be the true explanation of the dream poem in his manuscript notebook D . . ." etc., etc. The Master's "homosexuality" is a donné—rather like Patricia Cornwell's definitive certainty that Jack the Ripper was Walter Sickert. Did Miss Efrati's AEH opus further my affection for the great man? Not one whit. His sexuality is clearly of considerable interest to some. To me it is of no concern or interest whatsoever.

Quae cum ita sint (as Cicero would say), it will come as no surprise perhaps to readers that there are a good many questions that I shall definitely *not* be putting to our scholar-poet:

(i) What were his sexual proclivities? And how far did thoughts of Moses Jackson torment (monopolize) his melancholy and vulnerable temperament?

(ii) Why, with his supremely gifted mind, did he fail so dismally in the final examinations in Literae Humaniores ("Greats") at Oxford University?

(iii) Why was it that he spent some thirty or so years editing the works of the obscure Latin poet Manilius?

(iv) How is it that a man of such acute observation, with such a treasury of vocabulary, should write (I generalize a little!) such tedious letters?

(v) On a more flippant note, why had he refused (a well-authenticated anecdote) to allow the philosopher Ludwig Wittgenstein to make use of his personal loo in Trinity College, Cambridge?

Why wouldn't I be particularly eager to learn from AEH himself the answers to these questions—pretty fundamental as they are for any potential biographer? Simply because I think I know the answers to them myself. And, more importantly, because for the most part they are concerned with the *life* of AEH, and with the teasingly puzzling personal traits of that great man. Now if someone discovers how many minutes he took to boil an egg, I would probably be interested enough to register the fact—for a while, I suppose. But I must confess to having forgotten far more about such things than I ever knew. Life is short, and AEH is not the greatest figure in English literature. But for most of my adult life he has been the brightest star in the firmament—not in any way because I wish to know ever more about his life and his habits, but because I wish to luxuriate—and increasingly to luxuriate—in his poetic output and in his academic achievements.

What, then, are *my* answers to those nonquestions?

Moses Jackson? Never in the whole of his life would AEH love a fellow human being as he loved his former roommate. He thought of him continually (if not continuously), and all his waking and doubtless sleeping life he heart-achingly regretted Jackson's nonreciprocation.

Failure in "Greats"? AEH's interest in Latin and Greek centered, perhaps almost exclusively, on the *literature* written in each of those languages and its transmission through the ages in the classical manuscripts we have inherited. He had little genuine interest, I believe, in ancient history or in early Greco-Roman philosophy. If this is not wholly true, he probably had sufficient conceit in his already voluminous knowledge to believe that he could answer, with comparative ease, any of the questions likely to be asked of him. As a result he neglected all (if any?) of the necessary revision. If, in turn, this explanation also is not wholly true, let me suggest—I know about these things!—that he entered the wrong index number on his answer sheets.

Manilius? AEH himself has told us the answer. He once described this minor Latin writer as a "facile and frivolous poet, the brightest facet of whose genius was an eminent aptitude for doing sums in verse"; but he insisted, as always, that classical textual scholarship had next to nothing to do with literary criticism and appreciation. And whatever impression AEH sought to present to others, he pretty clearly had a secret desire for posthumous fame and harbored the hope that future generations of scholars would mention him in the same breath as Scaliger and Bentley, both of whom he admired greatly (especially the latter). The dedicated work that these two famous emendators had done on the five books of Manilius's *Astronomica* had left more than sufficient virgin territory for a mind so enormously subtle as his own to explore and to exploit. *And* to improve and to perfect that earlier toil—for I have become increasingly aware that AEH was ever a perfectionist. (Let it not be forgotten, either, that both Manilius and AEH were strangely addicted to matters astrological!)

AEH as correspondent? He was seemingly little interested in letter writing, with no wish to be remembered for any distinction in this particular genre—quite unlike, let us say, Byron, Keats, D. H. Lawrence, etc. This is somewhat surprising since he was no less a master of prose than of poetry, frequently exhibiting the same qualities of incisiveness and clarity—as well as the additional one of scathing and flashing invective. So many of his letters are extant, and a two-volume, monumental, and definitive collection has recently been published by Oxford University Press (edited by Archie Burnett).

But they are, for the most part, of pedestrian appeal and of only minimal interest to lovers of his poems, revealing little of his inner feelings—apart from those heartbreakingly poignant few written to his close friends on the death of Moses Jackson. Pity, really, since he could be wonderfully and wickedly contemptuous about his less skilled fellow practitioners in the field on textual criticism. Consider the following: "I do not know upon what subject [he] will next employ his versatile incapacity. For he is very well—dangerously well." Alas, there are very few passages in his letters where he writes in such memorable—and memorizable—vein! Nothing like the marvelous Keats, who in a letter to a friend—not in a formal ode—describes the tide coming in on the southern coast of England and leaving an "untumultuous fringe of silver foam." Whew! (And what other word in English contains five *u*'s?)

What about Wittgenstein? Let me be flippant about answering this final nonquestion. Quite simply, either AEH disliked the philosopher for some reason; or, perhaps immediately before that request he had made use of his own WC himself and was embarrassingly aware of the malodorous miasma that still lingered around that room.

Reader, your patience is finally to be rewarded.

Dear Mr. Housman,

Why are you so unappreciative—and indeed often dismissive—of a good many other poets—as well as of yourself?

Yours truly,

Colin Dexter

Now, in view of the gravity of my charge, and the unlikelihood of my receiving any definitive reply from AEH, I ought, if I can, to try to substantiate it.

Housman himself suggests that a worthy literary critic appears at the outside once a century or so, as rare as Halley's comet, and that the odds are quite astronomical against such a critic appearing amid the tiny band of classical scholars. Even if he does (says Housman) "all I know is that I am not he." And a good many of us would agree with him. But he does cite, presumably with full admiration, the major influences on his own poetry: the songs of Shakespeare, the border ballads, and Heinrich Heine. (He must surely have just forgotten the huge influence of the King James Bible.) We can all surely approve of his tastes. But other passages from The Master's pen appear to me to be extremely dubious and eminently questionable.

As regards his assessment of a few other people's poetry, we learn that Dryden and Pope were not his cup of tea. Quoting Isaac Watts's lines—

> Soft and easy is thy cradle;
> Coarse and hard thy Saviour lay,
> When his birthplace was a stable
> And his softest bed was hay—

Housman maintains that this "simple verse," bad rhyme and all, is poetry beyond Pope. This is a strange and almost inexplicable thing to say, although he may well have had his tongue in his cheek at the time.

When we come to the nineteenth century, we find, in Housman's personal copy of Palgrave's *Golden Treasury* (1897), thirty-nine of the printed poems completely crossed through with a neatly ruled vertical pencil stroke, including "The Charge of the Light Brigade"— surely a poem of great élan and power that we can still hear in Tennyson's own voice:

> Then they rode back, but not,
> Not the six hundred.

Including, too, Clough's "Say not the struggle nought availeth," a poem that almost every anthologist has recognized as a poem of great power and fortitude.

I have already referred to AEH's distaste for much of the poetry written in the eighteenth century, and it is only fair, and very interesting, to look at the poets writing during those years that he *did* enjoy, and in which he detected the true "poetic" voice. These four: Collins, Smart, Cowper, and Blake. And what did these poets have in common? They were all mad. Now, we remember Plato's view that all poets were mad—had to be, in fact. But this assertion does seem to me to be Housman arguing a very flimsy philosophy. What did Plato mean by madness? What did Housman mean? How would modern psychiatrists categorize the varied degrees of paranoia exhibited by his chosen quartet? I don't know. I have never read a full biography of any of these four—for life, after all, is short, and none of them has played any significant role in my own enjoyment of English poetry. But what of John Clare (I know he is a nineteenth-century man)? After being officially certified as insane in 1837—and thereafter recertified—Clare spent the rest of his life in Northampton General Asylum. So what did Housman think of *him*—a genuine madman? Just three of his poems are printed in the Palgrave anthology (including the moving "I am! Yet what I am who cares, or knows?"), and through each of them Housman has ruled that fatal penciled line!

But let us be fair to Housman, for there are clear instances of an extremely deep sensitivity and appreciation of fellow poets. What am I thinking of? From *The Name and Nature of Poetry*, for example (in Housman's own words):

> Even Shakespeare would sometimes pour out his loveliest poetry in saying nothing.
>
> > Take O take those lips away
> > That so sweetly were forsworn . . . etc.
>
> That is nonsense; but it is ravishing poetry.

Of Milton (in the same lecture): "'Nymphs and shepherds, dance no more'—six simple words that can draw tears, as I know it can, to the eyes of more readers than one." From the Latin poet Horace, Odes IV 7, a translation of *Diffugere Nives* (*The snows are fled away . . .*), a poem by which Housman was deeply moved. One of his former pupils tells us that after he had completed his exposition of the text, he unprecedentedly turned to his audience: "I should like to spend the last few minutes considering this ode simply as poetry." Then he read the poem aloud, with deep emotion, first in Latin, and then in an English translation of his own, ending in quick, choked accents: "That I regard as the most beautiful poem in ancient literature."

This last citation lies at the heart of my question to AEH, viz that he seems to me (to put things rather cruelly) to be more than some-what defective in his literary judgment, especially with regard to his own poetry. The translation just mentioned is to be found in *More Poems*, that posthumously published volume of what I suppose we must think of as Housman "rejects" but which (praise be!) Laurence rescued for us, although not without his brother's blessing. I must add, too, at this point, the fact that my own (perhaps) excessive and exuberant admiration of *More Poems* is not shared by every member of the Housman Society. At the biennial weekend meeting of members in Bromsgrove in 2007, we all took part in a general session at which we read to each other our favorite AEH poem. Not a single choice was taken from the forty-eight entries in *More Poems*. Perhaps I comforted myself with the knowledge that twenty-four of the forty-eight were chosen by F. C. Horwood in his hundred favorite poems in *A. E. Housman: Poetry and Prose* (Hutchinson Educational). But, yes, let us please remember that not one of them was chosen by Housman himself.

Why? Although one may readily advance reasons for Housman's reluctance to see these poems published in his lifetime—they were unfinished, say, or they were unrevised (for Housman *was* a perfectionist), or they were too personally referenced, or simply that some were not really up to his customary high standard—it is very difficult to see why a good many of them were not published in his lifetime, with considerable pride and gratification to the author. Which poems do I have particularly in mind? Well, too many to quote or even to mention here. But it is extraordinarily difficult to explain the omission of such superbly crafted poems as "I lay me down and slumber," "Smooth between sea and land," "I to my perils," "On forelands high in heaven," and "How clear, how lovely bright." But I will (finally) quote the last of these choices in full, and to explain why I find it so splendid.

> How clear, how lovely bright,
> How beautiful to sight
>   Those beams of morning play:
> How heaven laughs out with glee

Where, like a bird set free,
Up from the eastern sea
   Soars the delightful day.

To-day I shall be strong,
No more shall yield to wrong,
   Shall squander life no more;
Days lost, I know not how,
I shall retrieve them now;
Now I shall keep the vow
   I never kept before.

Ensanguining the skies
How heavily it dies
   Into the west away;
Past touch and sight and sound
Not further to be found
How hopeless underground
   Falls the remorseful day.
              (*More Poems XVI*)

This is a poem of dry, wry, gentle humor, and "humorous" is hardly the epithet we can usually apply to AEH—although we have it on Laurence's authority that his brother would laugh considerably more heartily than other members of the family at facetious and jocular verses. Indeed could *write* them, too. But this is also a poem of great charm and honesty, its "remorse" centered upon unrealized resolutions and unfulfilled intentions. The stanzas are beautifully structured and balanced, framed from the opening to the closing of day; from the beams of early morning to the ensanguined skies of eve; from the "Soars" of the seventh line to the "Falls" of the last—and with the powerful central stanza stating the poet's determined, albeit disappointed, resolve. The metrical form is unusual, with its very demanding aa–b–ccc–b pattern, which in AEH's masterful hands (as here) flows so happily, so fluently from his pen. In sum, the poem focuses upon the well-nigh universal regret of humankind over the countless days that have been "lost," days that once they are over can never, never be retrieved.

I have suggested (*vide supra*) three possible reasons for AEH's rejection of such poems. How do they apply to this one?

(i) Unfinished, perhaps? Well, there is some remote possibility that a line of dots found in some early copies of the original (unique) draft, dots between stanzas two and three, mean that AEH would possibly have added another stanza at that point. But this is wholly discounted, I feel, since Laurence later claimed that he had himself put in the dots on the grounds that there seems (is) a big break of time and mood at that point in the poem.

(ii) Repetition of a theme found earlier in his poetic corpus? Not that I can recall—and I have read of no one else who can.

(iii) Too personal, too personalized? Not at all. AEH is commenting upon a weakness of virtually the whole of the human race.

To what else can we put down the omission of this poem? There is only one remaining cause: AEH's inability to recognize that here he had written yet another memorable masterpiece.

The prosecution rests its case, m'lud. But the chief prosecutor wishes to express his gratitude to AEH for providing him with the title of the final Inspector Morse novel, *The Remorseful Day*, and furthermore wishes to submit a strong recommendation for mercy.

Rudyard Kipling

Thinking in Ink

CATHERINE AIRD

I'd like rather more than an AfterWord with Rudyard Kipling. Not that his wife, Carrie, would have ever admitted me to the presence to tell him so and thus distract him from his work—I nearly wrote "his great work," but somehow I don't think he would have liked it called that. Rather the "honoured craft," which is how he put it himself.

The trouble would be in knowing where to start. It would be no use, for instance, telling him how much I have always admired what he has written—thousands upon thousands of readers have done that already. Nor, I am sure, would anything be gained by saying how persistently undervalued I think his work is in these post-Colonial days—in which view I am quite certain I am not alone.

No use touching on the biographies and critiques of him, either. There have been plenty of them, all detailing a long and rather sad life as a man and a full one as a writer, and most of them attempting to clamber inside that very unusual mind. It was a mind that stayed focused on his work through Life's Handicaps, but that's another story: good writers just write. I sense, though, that no biography would ever have cut the mustard with him. No man who summed up his own work thus in the preface to *Life's Handicap* (1891) could have been at all precious:

> I write of all matters that lie within my understanding, and many that do not. But chiefly I write of Life and Death, and men and women, and Love and Fate according to the measure of my ability, telling the tale through the mouths of one, two or more people. Then by the favour of God the tales are told and money accrues to me that I may keep alive.

As credos go, few authors could better that.

But if by some happy chance I had been able to make my way firstly into the Punjab Club in Lahore in northwest India or lastly into that study at Bateman's in Sussex (or into the several places in between where he lived and wrote), there would indeed be some things I would have liked to ask Kipling. For instance, how did he make that unusual transmogrification from working journalist to great writer?—although in his autobiography *Something of Myself* (1937; not "Everything of Myself," mind you), he does set out what he calls "the Higher Editing": it is a counsel of perfection:

> Take of well-ground Indian Ink as much as suffices and a camel-hair brush proportionate to the interspaces of your lines. In an auspicious hour, read your final draft and consider faithfully every paragraph, sentence and word, blacking out where requisite. Let it lie by to drain as long as possible. At the end of that time, re-read and you will find it will bear a second shortening. Finally, read it aloud and at leisure. Maybe a shade more brushwork will then indicate or impose itself. If not, praise Allah and let it go, and "when thou hast done, repent not."

I like that mention of "an auspicious hour," but first of all I would want to tell him how damaging I thought that exceedingly well-known poem of his called "If" must have been to many of its readers—including me, and I'm not even trying to be a Man, my son. It was an impossible standard to set, and impossible not to feel a failure if one didn't attain it.

It was especially those lines about risking all and never breathing a word about your loss that I have always found so upsetting:

> If you can make one heap of all your winnings
> And risk it on one turn of pitch-and-toss,
> And lose, and start again at your beginnings
> And never breath a word about your loss; . . .

They are the exact opposite of Shakespeare's more practical:

> Give sorrow words: the grief that does not speak
> Whispers the o'erfraught heart, and bids it break.
> [*Macbeth* IX:iii:208]

No use speculating though on how a modern-day bereavement counselor would try to help with the loss of two of his "Beloved Kids." The grief at the death of young Josephine found its way into print obliquely in that haunting story about dead children called "They" in *Traffics and Discoveries* (1904), with an insight into Kipling's own stiff upper lip being put into the words of the blind woman, who says, "You've got such good defences in your eyes—looking out—before anyone can really pain you in your soul."

Similarly, the restraint of Kipling's stoical poem "My Boy Jack" (1916) would probably be condemned today, just as his reticent reference to the death of his son John in his two-volume history of *The Irish Guards in the Great War* (1923) has since been deemed to be too detached for some.

Rudyard Kipling died in 1936. In the late 1940s two very elderly lady missionaries, who had retired before the Second World War from India, were neighbors of mine and were kind enough not to mind being questioned by the importunate teenager that I must have seemed. They had not only known Kipling but remembered his parents, J. Lockwood and Alice Kipling.

India had then not long been independent and partitioned (something Kipling was not to know), and these one-time expatriates spoke sadly of having had to leave behind family graves that they would never see again in what had been British India. I thought then and I think now that it was a subject worthy of the pen of him who declared "I write of Life and Death." Kipling could have written of that very particular sorrow better than anyone I know, brought up as I had been on John Buchan's poem "Fratri Dilectissimo—W.H.B." about his dead brother and how grateful he was because that brother had been able to die in his native Scotland:

> One boon the fates relenting gave
> Not where the scented hill-wind blows
> From cedar thickets lies your grave
> Nor 'mid the steep Himalayan snows.

Were I really granted an AfterWord, I would ask that Kipling put this specific deprivation of mourners into his empathetic verse.

And there is something I definitely would want to ask him: where exactly did he have in mind when he wrote the poem "The Way through the Woods," published in *Rewards and Fairies* (1910). Kipling was a frequent visitor to the village where I live—he had great friends at the manor house here—and there is indeed a very ancient way through the woods two miles north of the manor that was not so much shut "seventy years ago" as having gradually fallen into disuse since a new Turnpike Road Plan for a metaled road had been published in 1813. Turnpikes, though, as is their function, exact a toll, and the old road continued to be used by those averse to paying it until the great gate on the Turnpike Road was taken down in 1877. I have walked this road—weather and rain have not quite undone it again—and found vestiges of little brick bridges, although I never heard "the swish of a skirt in the dew."

Greatly daring, I wrote to Kipling's surviving daughter, the redoubtable Mrs. George Bambridge, in my capacity as editor of the parish magazine (a role more exacting than might be supposed, Best Beloved, and one not to be undertaken lightly, since the readership lives on one's doorstep and is apt to be quite combative about muddled initials or missed deadlines). She answered amiably enough, giving me permission to reproduce the poem and state my theory but said that she would neither confirm nor deny that the poem in question had been based on that particular old road. My AfterWord would include asking her father himself.

Rudyard Kipling, the writer, was to touch my life even more closely in the middle of the 1960s when a book of mine was reviewed kindly in one of the literary journals. Well, "kindly" with the caveat that it showed rather too many undertones of one of the great man's short stories. Since I had never read the one cited, I naturally made haste to do so—and found that my tale did indeed have rather more than undertones of the story in question, *pour cause*. We had both taken the names of some of the characters from the same source—the gravestones that lined the path toward the church from the little gate leading to the manor house, all there in his day as well as mine.

But it is quite another short story that I would wish to explore further with him. "The Children of the Zodiac" has always intrigued me. Out of a quite phenomenal output—Kipling must have been "thinking in ink" all his life, and there can be few who have read his entire corpus—this and the poem "A Death-Bed" (and the two are oddly linked) have stayed with me longer than most.

I am not alone in puzzling over "A Death-Bed." That formidable literary critic Marghanita Laski confessed that of all the writings she had chosen for her 1974 BBC radio program *Kipling's English History*, she understood this poem least of all. She found it compelling—it is mainly about the death of the Kaiser's father, Crown Prince Frederick the Noble (and later—for ninety-nine days only, and as a sick man—Frederick III), from cancer of the throat. In 1888 there was a right royal, and very public, row between English and German surgeons during the patient's illness—and after his death—about how to treat the cancer. Interspersed between the narrative of the poem, which comprises the many different ways death can come in wartime, and the different manners in which men—and women—may die ("Some Die Eloquent"), is a description of the operation on the crown prince, the "All-Highest."

Kipling certainly got his medicine right when within the narrative of the poem he has the surgeon speak thus:

> *[This is the gland at the back of the jaw,*
> *And an answering lump by the collar-bone.]*

And

> *[It will follow the regular course of—throats.]*

And again

> *[Since it is rather too late for the knife,*
> *All we can do is mask the pain.]*

Leading to

> *[Don't be afraid of a triple dose;*
> *The pain will neutralise half we give.*

Here are the needles. See that he dies
  While the effects of the drug endure . . .]

But it is much more than a clinical account of dying from a disease (or from the doctors) as opposed to dying on the battlefield. There is the statement in the opening verse—still up for discussion surely:

"This is the State above the Law.
The State exists for the State alone."

If this poem is compelling, Kipling's short story "The Children of the Zodiac" is something between a fable and an allegory—or even a parable—and again shows a preoccupation with death and disease. It is a complicated tale about wanting to die and not wanting to die, and I would like to ask Kipling what made him publish it as early as 1893, including this extract: "He said that he wished to die, and when Death came he tried to run away. He is a coward."

The six Children of the Zodiac—the Ram, the Bull, Leo, the Twins, and the Girl—are afraid of the Houses that belong to the Scorpion, the Balance, the Crab, the Fishes, the Archer, and the Waterman, which they say trouble the Children of Men. Although men treat the Children of the Zodiac as gods, the Children themselves do not understand human happiness until Leo kisses the Girl. ("I write of Life and Death . . . and Love and Fate," remember). The Bull is harnessed but lives in fear of dying by the sting of the Scorpion, while the Ram is afraid of being shot by the Archer, and the Fishes have told the Twins that one day they will come and carry the Twins away.

Running through the rest of the story, though, is a looming awareness of the danger that comes from Cancer, the Crab—a fear that Kipling is said to have had of a genetic inheritance of the disease. Leo dies from cancer of the throat—as Frederick III had. The breast of the Girl is as hard as stone, and the Crab tells her, "You were born into my House, and at the appointed time I shall come for you." Kipling was being very prescient here, since at the time when he penned this story the genetic element of cancer was not really recognized.

Were he here in person to answer my questions (not so much the autocrat at the breakfast table as the literary polymath at the dinner table), I would ask him first what made him write that last about Cancer the Crab and how did he know so much about cancer—both his parents were still alive at the time, and he can't have been more than twenty-seven years old when he wrote about a disease so much on his mind. I'd ask him that—oh, that and so much else besides.

But, then, the man who once wrote, "Seek not to question other than / The books I leave behind," mightn't have liked being asked about his preoccupation with cancer or indeed anything else.

Now, there's a thought . . .

Arnold Bennett

A Great Man

MARGARET DRABBLE

I have many questions for Arnold Bennett. I thought I got to know him well while writing his biography several decades ago, but the more you get to know about a writer, the more questions you have. Some of them he would not be able to answer. To begin at the end, I would like to know more of the particular details of his death. This may seem a morbid curiosity, but it is not wholly trivial. It touches on some of the important issues that plagued his life and divided his friends and family. Was his common-law wife, the actress Dorothy Cheston Bennett, in attendance? Or his formidable sister Sissie? Or both of them? (They did not get on, and disagreed about what happened that night, each claiming superior rights. Dorothy certainly claimed to be there, but we have only her word for it.) And was his legal wife, Marguerite, who had long refused to divorce him, still sitting it out downstairs in the lobby of the large apartment block near Baker Street, hoping to be in at the end? At that point in time, in 1931, Bennett was famed as the most highly paid writer in Britain, perhaps the most famous writer in the English-speaking world, and there were rival claims to his legacy.

He died in Chiltern Court of typhoid fever, which he is said to have contracted from carelessly drinking tap water in Paris. His widow Dorothy, who talked to me a great deal about his last illness, told two stories to account for it, one of them strangely self-incriminating. This version had it that in the hotel where they were staying, in December 1930, she noticed that the water in his Evian bottle was low and meant to replenish it from the bottle in her own bedroom. But she forgot, and he filled his carafe in the middle of the night from the tap. The second version, or incident, which has been more widely disseminated, relates that some days later, in the hotel restaurant, Bennett helped himself to water from the carafe on the table and was reproached for his carelessness by the waiter with the words "Ah, ce n'est pas sage, Monsieur Bennett, ce n'est pas sage."

Either or both of these stories could be true, and it is also possible that he contracted typhoid in some other place or some other manner. We shall never know. One of the gossip mongers of literary London reported to me that Dorothy had poisoned him with a pork chop. I did not put this in my book, as Dorothy was still very much alive at the time of publication in 1974, and she would not have liked it. Bennett died in the small hours, in the early morning of March 27, which accounts for the fact that the date of his death is sometimes given as March 26.

My interest in Bennett originates in his family background in the Five Towns of Staffordshire, which provided him with so much of his material. My mother's family also came from the Five Towns, and my aunt's middle name was Bennett. This was enough for us to believe that there was a connection, but whether there was or not, we certainly had a good many of his books at home. I read them when I was young, before anybody told me what I ought to think about them, and I recognized the world of my grandparents—its perversely proud provincialism, its little snobberies, its heavy polished furniture, its high teas, its cultural interests, its curiously agnostic view of the Methodism that had dominated the region in the nineteenth century. The Five Towns folk were full of stubborn contradictions, and they still are.

The first thing I would like to say to Bennett, when I meet him, is "Well done!" He immortalized a region and its way of life through keen observation and through an insight into human motivation as disenchanted and acute as Freud's. Although almost always good humored, he was never sentimental. This, in a popular writer, is a highly unusual combination. He modeled himself on the great French realists, Balzac, the Goncourts, de Maupassant, and Zola, and brought their sociological objectivity to bear on English morals and manners. It is an unlikely and a brilliant fusion.

I would like to sit him down in a comfortable chair, and flatter him with my admiration, and try to get him to talk about himself and his career, which began so unpromisingly, and which he pursued with such determination and such prolonged success. He liked women, so, despite his stammer and shyness, he might unbend a little for me. He liked forthright, high-spirited, forward women like Sophia Baines of *The Old Wives' Tale* and Hilda Lessways of the Clayhanger series. He liked pretty women. He liked artistic women. He liked outsiders who were never quite at home in society. He liked lame ducks. I could surely fit myself into one or two of these categories, and ask him how he came to have such faith in his own talent. Was he just born that way? Or did he inherit it? Or was it a chance meeting, either of a book or of a person, which set him on his path? And at what age did he know he was going to make it? I would like to know which were the periods of his life that were most strongly marked by self-doubt. Several times, in his fiction, he sketched the path of the man he might have been if he hadn't made it—the lonely and frustrated failure, the perpetual provincial yearning for the big city, the man "born to be a Londoner" who never quite got there. Maybe he had moments, in the small hours, when his worldly success seemed like a mirage, when he saw his reputation slipping away from him as a new generation of writers rose to challenge him. His last coherent words to Dorothy are reported to have been something like, "It's all going wrong, my girl"—words that authors, with their instinct for Schadenfreude, love to repeat. What did he mean by them? Even Dorothy wasn't sure. He may have been referring to an awareness that he was fatally ill, to a sense that their relationship was deteriorating, to the dismal state of the stock market, to dwindling American profits, to his own overstretched and overworked creative powers. His last novel, *Imperial Palace*, seemed to some (including Dorothy) to be a parody of his earlier successes. Maybe he had reached the end of his talent.

If I were bold enough, and if he seemed to be in the mode of stoic and ironic detachment that came naturally to him, I would like to ask him whether he was surprised by the decline of his posthumous reputation, and by the higher status of his one-time rival Virginia Woolf. Bennett is no longer a household name or a best seller, as he once was, and he is not part of the canon. His best books remain in print, and since he came out of copyright, some of the lesser titles have appeared in cheap editions, but he rarely features on a university syllabus. Recently, the small and discriminating Churnet Valley Press has reissued several volumes of his work, with illuminating introductions by John Shapcott, who is chair of the Arnold Bennett Society. Shapcott, in his foreword to *The Price of Love*, a novel that was written during peacetime but published on the first of October 1914, writes brilliantly of Bennett's sense of elegy, of his knowledge that the provincial world he had known was changing and passing forever. Shapcott applies structuralist language and insights to Bennett's realist prose and makes us see it and the Five Town with fresh eyes. He also addresses Bennett's involvement with the new art of the cinema, suggesting that *The Price of Love* is the first work of fiction in the English language to attempt to document its effect on provincial life, on the mentality of the wider (and undereducated) public, and on artistic representation.

Bennett today would certainly not be surprised by the extraordinary success of the new medium of film, for he was one of the first to spot its potential. It is far easier to imagine Bennett sitting in the cinema than Virginia Woolf, and it would be amusing to hear his reactions to the latest excesses of Hollywood. Maybe, like his literary heir J. B. Priestley, he would eventually have recognized the devil's threat to the literary novel and learned to sup with a long spoon. But maybe he would have taken to it with zest. In his lifetime he certainly made efforts to enter the cinematic world, although his success as a screenwriter was limited. He would have enjoyed Shapcott's twenty-first-century appreciation of the "flaunting modernity" of the nightlife of Edwardian Bursley that Bennett evokes: "Innumerable organised activities were going forward at that moment in the serried buildings of the endless confused streets that stretched up hill and down dale from one end of the Five Towns to the other—theatres, Empire music-halls, Hippodrome music-halls, picture-palaces in dozens, concerts, singsongs, spiritualist propaganda, democratic propaganda, skating-rinks, Wild West exhibitions, Dutch auctions." The fictitious Imperial Cinema de Luxe, built next to the new Primitive Methodist Chapel and ablaze with electricity, is a wondrous place to the characters of Bennett's novel, and Shapcott traces its history with loving care: it was based on the Moorlands Picture House, which in turn became the Globe, Kino's, and the Imperial Palace before becoming a fishing tackle shop that now advertises itself as "The Largest Tackle Shop in the Globe." Bennett relished sociological commentary like this and would be pleased that at least some readers were still paying attention to the mutability of modernity.

The passing of time was one of his great themes, and he took pleasure in noting trends and fashions. What would he make of the changing role of women? The rise of feminism has certainly contributed to the displacement of Bennett from the pantheon, along with Galsworthy and, to a lesser extent, H. G. Wells. This is just as Woolf predicted. Yet, ironically, Bennett and Wells were both in their time champions of the New Woman, cared about women's rights, were aware of their subjugation, and created memorable female characters. (Wells was less consistent in this vein than his friend Bennett, but Ann Veronica is an achievement not to be overlooked.) Would Bennett now consider that "things have gone too far" and that women have got too much of the upper hand? I doubt it. He was immensely fair-minded and would have applauded the progress made on this front since the mid-twentieth century.

There is evidence that at times he could be a domestic tyrant, like his father Enoch and his father's fictional counterpart Darius Clayhanger. He was fierce about mealtime punctuality, and the marital rows between Hilda and Edwin Clayhanger are clearly based on quarrels with his French wife Marguerite. In his minor works he could write glibly and patronizingly about female foibles and inconsistencies over matters such as shopping and hats and was not above enlisting a cliché to make a trite gender-based joke. But underlying all of this was a consistent and stalwart appreciation of the overworked and underpaid and underthanked role of the female domestic servant. The sympathetic treatment of servants in the Clayhanger trilogy is unsurpassed in English literature and enters a realm of feminism of which Woolf, for class reasons, knew little. For this alone I would like to bring him back from the dead to thank him. He knew what domestic labor was. Poor young plain bespectacled Minnie, turned out of the house when found to be "in trouble" by the dying and relentlessly religious Auntie Hamps; the loyal maid Elsie, in *Riceyman Steps*; the charwoman Mrs. Tams, in *The Price of Love*: they are part of a long succession of women whom most novelists considered beyond the realms of polite fiction. Bennett learned here from the French models of Zola and the Goncourts, but he took his lessons to his heart. Here is Mrs. Tams:

> a woman of nearly sixty, stout and—in appearance—untidy and dirty. . . . Human eyes so seldom saw her without a coarse brown apron that, apronless, she would have almost seemed (like Eve) to be unattired. It and a pail were the insignia of her vocation. She was accomplished and conscientious; she could be trusted; despite appearances, her habits were cleanly. She was also a woman of immense experience. In addition to being one of the finest exponents of the art of step-stoning and general housework that the Five Towns could show, she had numerous other talents. She was thoroughly accustomed to the supreme spectacles of birth and death, and could assist thereat with dignity and skill. She could turn away the wrath of rent-collectors, rate-collectors, school-inspectors, and magistrates . . . [and] she could coax extra sixpences out of a pawnbroker. She had never had a holiday, and almost never failed in her duty.

The hint of the mock-heroic here, early in the novel, is misleading, for Mrs. Tams does indeed eventually prove to be the moral anchor of the book, superior in honesty, sensitivity, and pragmatism to her morally dubious young employers. Bennett takes her seriously.

Bennett was one of the first to point out that conditions of employment for women like Mrs. Tams were based on injustice and inequality, and one of the first to dramatize their plight. He would have approved of the new and cleaner world of household gadgets we have been lucky enough to inherit, which have assisted feminism in a practical manner by making domestic work and therefore the woman's lot easier. (He liked electricity, central heating, well-plumbed bathrooms, and the vacuum cleaner.) He would have been curious about the new forms of slave labor that have succeeded the old, and might have asked why we do not address them more often in fiction. (It is partly, I would reply, a question of language: the new slaves of the Western world speak foreign tongues.) But on balance, I think he would be pleased with the evolution of the roles of Minnie and Elsie and Mrs. Tams.

Finally, I would like to transport Bennett back to his birthplace and ask him what he makes of it today and whether it has altered in ways that he would have expected. There is much still that he would recognize. Some of the buildings of Burslem are exactly as they were in his youth, a little shabbier, but otherwise unchanged. For good and ill, there has been less redevelopment and regeneration here than in many of Britain's industrial regions. He would see the golden angel on the Old Town Hall, the street frontage of the old coaching inn known as the Leopard, the ornate terra-cotta façade of the Wedgwood Memorial Institute. The Baines's shop from *The Old Wives' Tale* is still there, though it looks neglected. There are a few picturesque bottle kilns dotted about the landscape, and one working Victorian pottery survives. The Trent and Mersey canal, which opened up the region at the beginning of the Industrial Revolution, flows still, though it is far less busy than it was and has not yet caught up with the vogue for tourist waterways. He would be able to locate some of the homes and workplaces of his fictional characters, garnished with historical maroon plaques, though others have been demolished. He would find enough points of reference to help him to find his way from borough to borough through this muddled conglomeration. His keen sociological eye would note that this is a region where a cinema was converted into a theater and a theater into a cinema, and that the best purpose-built theater-in-the-round in Britain is to be found here on Etruria Road, a tribute to the devotion and persistence of one dedicated theater director, Peter Cheeseman, who died in 2010. He was, like Denry, the hero of Bennett's novel *The Card*, a man who made things happen. And Bennett would find a restaurant called Denry's, after this enterprising hero, and rejoice that Denry was not forgotten.

But he would find no statue of himself, and that might disappoint him. J. B. Priestley, in 1933, two years after Bennett's death, noted that there was no memorial to Bennett and that nobody ever mentioned him. He recorded this fact in his chapter on the Potteries in his classic travel book *English Journey*, published in 1935, in which he protested that public life and public monuments celebrated local industrialists and "empty big-wigs" decorated with medals, but not their greatest writer. The Five Towns did not wholly admire their successful son. There is a large statue of Priestley in Bradford, but no statue of Bennett in Burslem.

Bennett was shrewd enough to know why the Potteries did not appreciate him more. He had deserted them for the metropolis, and in his novels he had exposed them to anthropological analysis, as though they were some dark exotic realm inhabited by savages. He felt a little of the guilt of this and knew he would not be wholly forgiven. From his lodgings near Fontainebleau, from his Queen Anne country house in Thorpe-le-Soken, from his comfortable London apartments, from his yacht, from the Savoy and the Riviera, he had looked back at his birthplace with a shudder, and yet he had exploited it and its people for artistic and financial profit. Would he now, in the twenty-first century, survey the continuing blight that hovers over much of the Five Towns and consider it their due?

At his deathbed, the representatives of the stages of his mortal life assembled, amidst the news bulletins charting his imminent departure and the respectful laying of straw upon the noisy cobbled streets of London. It was a very Bennett scene. He had kept in touch with his past, despite his reluctance to revisit the neighborhood of his youth in person. He remained until death a good family man, supporting relatives in need, and was generous to a fault in some of his dealings. He had escaped to Paris when his father died and had married a Frenchwoman whose flamboyant and demonstrative behavior was as surprising and shocking to the Bennett clan as the appearance of Sophia's monstrously Gallic French poodle to the citizens of Bursley at the end of *The Old Wives' Tale*. Then he had escaped from the Frenchwoman to live with an actress, whereupon the Bennett clan decided to side with the Frenchwoman. Bennett knew the perversities and vagaries of human nature and would not have been much surprised by any of this. He could have written some telling dialogue for those assembled in Chiltern Court awaiting his death. He was good on wills and inheritance, on financial hypocrisy and self-serving self-righteousness.

Maybe he would think that the Potteries today represent the dying end of the long life of realism, that literary movement which he embodied with such dignity and high artistic commitment. We have moved on, into the fantasy world of the virtual, into the glittering screen of pornographic Internet merchandise, and left behind the smoky streets, the restraints, the inhibitions, the long silences, the darkened rooms, the battle against dirt and squalor, the slow canal. These made Bennett, and these he abandoned, for a busy life at the center. But these he also preserved, in his slow and patient prose. I think Bennett would be surprised by how little his hometowns have changed since he was born above a pawnbroker's shop on Hope Street in 1867. He might have expected, as did Priestley, that by now they would be glittering with high technology, as indeed parts of them are. But something in them has resisted modernization. Realism may be dead, but the world that produced it lives recognizably on.

In 1976, ATV showed a twenty-six part adaptation of the Clayhanger trilogy, which allowed the story to develop at its own slow, cumulative, meditative pace, recording in careful period detail each epoch in the lives of its closely observed characters. We see Edwin Clayhanger and his sisters when they are young and rebellious; we see them as they grow into conformist middle age; we see youth and hope slip away from the young and hopeful. It is faithful to the spirit of the novels, omitting little. The death scenes are particularly unsparing. Step by step we suffer the mental and physical decline of Edwin's father Darius (magnificently played by Harry Andrews), and step by step, literally, we stagger up the stairs with him to the bedroom he knows he will never leave again. We see the vain, controlling, highly bedizened Mrs. Hamps (memorably embodied by Joyce Redman) as she is slowly stripped of her formidable frontage of curls, her shaking plumes, her black brocades, her bullying power, and her dignity. They die slowly, as did Bennett himself.

You can't make television like that in the twenty-first century. We don't have the concentration span. Something happened between

1976 and the year 2000. It wasn't human nature that changed, it was the means of production. If anything, we die even more slowly than we used to, but we can no longer bear to tell it as it is. Our technology has outstripped our content. Bennett, who always prided himself on being up to the next trick, would have been fascinated by the evolution of storytelling. Some aspects of literary modernism dismayed him, but he was a champion of the artistic avant-garde and would have been annoyed to find himself adopted by John Carey as a spokesman for masses. His mind was more subtle, more open, less partisan than Carey's alignment suggests.

Bennett knew that he was writing at the end of the dominance of realism and its precocious and provocative French offspring, naturalism. His work foreshadows aspects of modernism (Shapcott claims that his novel *Riceyman Steps* is a modernist masterpiece, although Woolf described it as "dishwater"), and he was aware of the shape of things to come. In 1910 he wrote in praise of the notorious postimpressionist exhibition at the Grafton Galleries, which elsewhere aroused much ridicule; he rejoiced in Cezanne and Gauguin, condemned London's scorn of them as humiliating in its insularity, and rightly foresaw that in twenty years London would be "signing an apology for its guffaw" and "writing itself down an ass." In the same article, more interestingly, he revealed that the exhibition had shaken his faith in his own poetic: he reflected, in *The New Age* in December 1910,

> I have permitted myself to suspect that supposing some writer were to come along and do in words what these men have done in paint, I might conceivably be disgusted with nearly the whole of modern fiction, and I might have to begin again. . . . Supposing a young writer turned up and forced me, and some of our contemporaries—us who fancy ourselves a bit—to admit that we had been concerning ourselves unduly with essentials, that we had been worrying ourselves to achieve infantile realisms? Well, that day would be a great and disturbing day—for us. And we should see what we should see.

Bennett's willingness to ask himself these questions and to allow himself to be disturbed is a measure of his stature as a writer and as a critic. He was a great man.

One Word Less

Questioning Samuel Beckett

ALAN W. FRIEDMAN

The notion of an AfterWord would doubtless have struck the famously taciturn Samuel Beckett as excessive. When asked if he were an English playwright, Beckett replied "au contraire." Walking through a London park on a particularly beautiful day with a friend who exclaimed that it was the sort of day that made one glad to be alive, Beckett said, "I wouldn't go that far." Asked to explain *What Where*, one of his late works for the stage, Beckett said: "I don't know what it means. Don't ask me what it means. It's an object." And responding to an inquiry from Alan Schneider, his American director, for insight into *Endgame*, he wrote, "the less I speak about my work the better"; he similarly told Mel Gussow, "I'm tired of talking about my work."

Yet in reply to my request for a new play to be performed at a conference on his work that I was organizing in the mid-1980s, the unfailingly polite and responsive Beckett wrote: "Nothing left. All used up. What's your deadline?" Although the comparative fulsomeness of this reply led us to assume we had a firm commitment, in the end there was only silence. Yet Beckett's silences were never devoid of substance; and rather than disappoint us when he failed to produce a new play, he offered us permission to stage *Human Wishes*, his first, aborted attempt to write drama, and one that he had long suppressed. The experience was exhilarating, even revelatory.

Beckett considered James Joyce, his sometime mentor and friend, a synthesizer (expansive, encyclopedic) and himself an analyzer (a reductive minimalist): "The more Joyce knew the more he could. He's tending toward omniscience and omnipotence as an artist. I'm working with impotence, ignorance." Joyce accreted and encompassed; Beckett diminished and denied: "I realised that Joyce had gone as far as one could in the direction of knowing more, [being] in control of one's material. He was always adding to it; you only have to look at his proofs to see that. I realised that my own way was in impoverishment, in lack of knowledge and in taking away, in subtracting rather than adding." As opposed to Joyce, who dismayed his publishers by writing vast swaths of his texts at the copy proof stage, Beckett produced work that became ever more constrained and constricted as he moved from early draft to published work, and from published work to performance script.

For Beckett, even very little could be excessive, whether it was about his texts, his characters, or himself. Elaborate opening mimes in the texts of *Film* and *Krapp's Last Tape* disappeared from productions on which he worked. He was reticent about the lives of his characters, about whom he said he knew nothing beyond what he had written. In a letter to Kay Boyle, he wrote, "I know creatures are supposed to have no secrets for their authors, but I'm afraid mine for me have little else." When Billie Whitelaw, with whom he worked closely on many productions, asked *"Am I dead?"* about a character she was playing in *Footfalls* under Beckett's direction, he answered as best he could, "Well, let's just say *you're not quite there.*" Whitelaw says that this was the only time she ever asked him about one of his characters, perhaps because she quickly realized not that he was withholding information, but that, as he always said, he knew only what was in the text.

He was most often asked about Godot ("Was he God?" for example, a question that makes no sense since the play was conceived and written in French) and answered that he knew only what was on the page. Even Alan Schneider, at his first meeting with Beckett, asked who Godot was; Beckett said that if he had known, he would have said so in the play. He did not, he insisted, write symbolically or allegorically, nor did his works contain hidden meanings: "no symbols where none intended."

Beckett's writings were, in a sense, a lifelong vanishing act. Godot, his most famous character, never appears onstage; other characters appear in reduced form: as torsos (in *Endgame, Happy Days,* and

Play), as merely a Mouth (in *Not I*), or as disembodied voices (in *Eh Joe, That Time, Ghost Trio, . . . but the clouds . . .* , the offstage Mother in *Footfalls*, V in *Rockaby*). Beckett sought refinement into silence and absence, moving ever closer toward his ideal goal: not a Joycean compendium of human experience, but the blank page or the empty theater that he told Schneider would be achieved if *Godot* were performed "my way." Struggling to translate his late text *Worstward Ho* (1983) into French, "With an urgency," he said, "I've gagged myself," then added in a moment of Beckettian humor, "Life's ambition," acknowledging that his being blocked was utterly appropriate, given his inclination toward silence.

Reclusive and intensely private, Beckett was as reluctant to talk or write about his life, which he considered "devoid of interest," as he was about his work. As various drafts demonstrate, he took pains to reduce or eliminate autobiographical and Irish allusions when he revised *All That Fall*, *Krapp's Last Tape*, and *Not I*, among others, although they would leak through despite his efforts. In response to Mel Gussow's request for a comment on his upcoming eightieth birthday, Beckett wrote: "I have nothing to say about the sad un-event and its sad effects—for publication or otherwise. Forgive." But of course this response was itself quite revealing. When he learned he had been awarded the Nobel Prize for literature, he hid out for as long as he could from what he considered a disaster because it meant the end of his privacy. Yet as several recent biographies and memoirs reveal (see Deidre Bair, Jasmes Knowlson, Lois Gordon, Anne Atik, for example), much is now known of his life that Beckett would have preferred to keep private, and much more will soon be known as his four-volume *Correspondence* has begun to appear.

For me, the greatest gap in our knowledge of Beckett's life, and the period about which I would most like to ask, concerns what were in many ways his most crucial years: 1940 to 1945. Beckett rarely referred explicitly to this time, his correspondence reveals little, and his biographers provide insufficient detail to explain the remarkable transformation that occurred to an obscure author who, before the war, published and sold little, suffered acutely from various ailments, was often at loose ends, drank excessively, was dominated by a manipulative mother, had debilitating bouts of depression and despair for which he underwent intensive Kleinian psychoanalysis, displayed little interest in political matters, and often sank into "apathy and lethargy." How did the war experience enable and inspire this failed author to launch the career that, in 1969, culminated in his being awarded the Nobel Prize?

Here's my summary of what is known about those years. In the late 1930s, Beckett famously said, "I preferred France in war to Ireland in peace," and proved his seriousness of purpose by leaving the safety of Ireland as soon as war broke out in order to embrace, under the most difficult circumstances, the country that had received him in exile and for which he felt a great cultural affinity. His commitment to French freedom and his antipathy toward Hitler were genuine and profound, though based more on friendship than on an abstract cause: "I was fighting against the Germans, who were making life hell for my friends, and not for the French nation." For Beckett, all politics were local and personal.

Beckett joined the French Resistance in Paris, performing "liaison or secretarial work" as translator, transcriber, and courier. After his cell was discovered and broken, he fled to Roussillon in unoccupied southeast France, where he eventually came to support the Maquis by collecting and hiding arms and supplies for them. The war years were an even more difficult time for Beckett than the prewar years, a time of danger, depression, physical exhaustion, and boredom, alleviated only partially by manual labor, heavy drinking, long walks, chess, his writing of the novel *Watt*, and his war work. Beckett subsequently dismissed his wartime service as "Boy Scout stuff," but it was acknowledged, after the war ended, by his being awarded the Croix de Guerre and the Médaille de la Réconnaissance Française for "his effectiveness as an information source in an important intelligence network."

The year the war ended, 1945, was a watershed for Beckett. He returned to Ireland, where he was dismayed by the excess of food and the indifference to wartime suffering that his neutral homeland had escaped. He commented, "My friends eat sawdust and turnips while all Ireland safely gorges." He returned to France by way of the devastated French town of St. Lô, which he worked with the Irish Red Cross to reclaim from its status as what he called "the Capital of the Ruins" and to build a hospital; he experienced what he called his "revelation" that transformed his life and his writing; and he began to write fiction and drama in French. The "revelation" inspired Beckett to break with all that had gone before, with what he called "my own folly. Only then did I begin to write the things I feel." He somehow suddenly recognized that he would never succeed in suppressing or extirpating his debilitating depression and dark pessimism, but that he could transform them from a weakness into a strength, into both inspiration and subject matter. This revelation, which he mockingly dramatizes in *Krapp's Last Tape*, inaugurated the period of extraordinary creativity that he referred to as "one great spurt of enthusiasm" and that, in the half decade immediately following the war, enabled him to write *Eleuthéria*, *Waiting for Godot*, *Mercier and Camier*, *Molloy*, *Malone Dies*, and *The Unnamable*, as well as several pieces of short fiction.

The question for me, then, the one I would most like to ask Beckett, is exactly what happened during the war years that wrought this change? He has said, "I became a writer, because all else failed"; but before the war he had also failed as a writer, as his mother liked to tell him and as he acknowledged himself. Although it is almost never overt in his writing, the Nobel Prize committee understood the significance of Beckett's war experience, viewing it as the "foundation" of his postwar writings: "these works are not about the war itself, about life at the front, or in the French resistance movement . . . , but about what happened afterwards, when peace came and the curtain was rent from the unholiest of unholies to reveal the terrifying spectacle of the lengths to which man can go in inhuman degradation—whether ordered or driven by himself—and how much of such degradation man can survive." Without designating the historical causes, Beckett's postwar writings relentlessly depict a landscape and its inhabitants devastated by world war and the Holocaust: the scrounging for food and growing despair in *Godot*; the crippling, postapocalyptic world of *Endgame*; the rationing and disappearance of basic supplies in both, as well as in *Happy Days*; the burnt-out landscape presided over by an omnipotent offstage force in *Act without Words I* and *Happy Days* (Winnie and Willie were originally depicted as war survivors); sadistic autocrats and their victims in *Godot, How It Is, Catastrophe*, and *What Where*, among other works; and characters reduced to bodily parts and remnants in many of the late plays.

Despite his reputation for being apolitical, such depictions are, among other things, political statements, just as his decision to write in French seems to have been at least partly a political act: a gesture of solidarity with the people with whom he had fought and suffered the privations of war. More directly and overtly political actions followed, including his signing of both the United Nations–sponsored "Manifesto by Nobel Laureates against Hunger and Under-development" (1981), an appeal for relief of those suffering deprivation, and a petition in support of Salmon Rushdie (1989); he also dedicated *Catastrophe* to Václav Havel, jailed at the time as a dissident. As James Knowlson writes, "He was deeply committed to human rights; he firmly and totally opposed apartheid and was hostile from an early age to all forms of racism; he supported human rights movements throughout the world, including Amnesty International and Oxfam; he supported the freedom movement in Eastern Europe."

What exactly did Beckett himself make of the epiphany that transformed him? I would like to ask, though he perhaps provides as full an answer as one could expect in *Krapp's Last Tape* (1958), his most autobiographical work. The play is pivotal for Beckett in many ways: it is his first major postwar work written in English; it inaugurates his increasingly economic theatrical style of writing as well as the kind of technical demands that impelled him to begin directing his own plays; and its protagonist is his first dramatic monologist. But its chief significance for my present purpose is that it offers his fullest self-representation, though less than he did in the early draft of the play. *Krapp* retains allusions to the long widowhood and death of Beckett's mother (1933–1950); an early love (disguised as Theodor Fontane's character, Effi Briest); the humiliation of the French version of *Murphy*, which sold only seventeen copies; walks on the heath with his dog; and, most important, his 1946 epiphanic revelation of his creative path: to accept his bleakness of vision and to write out of personal experience and largely in first-person mono-logist form. Reacting with typical wryness to the revelation, Beckett saw himself as "doomed to spend the rest of my days digging up the detritus of my life and vomiting it out over and over again," and he realized that "optimism is not my way. I shall always be depressed, but what comforts me is the realization that I can now accept this dark side as the commanding side of my personality. In accepting it, I will make it work for me." The revelation induced a new sense of purpose and resolve that, despite writing blocks, depression, and near breakdowns, remained with him the rest of his life. Because its representation is at the heart of the play, the revelation could not be excised without destroying it. So Beckett, who often refused to take himself too seriously, self-mockingly referred to it as "the vi-sion at last" and has Krapp disgustedly fast forward the tape past it three times in order to listen instead to his younger self recalling the last moment of romantic intimacy in a life desiccated by the conse-quences of his epiphany.

The bleak picture of Beckett that emerges initially from the outline of his life seems two-dimensional: withdrawn and reclusive, despair-ing and gloomy, profoundly pessimistic, demanding and inflexible about the production of his work, apolitical. But everything of the sort is immediately qualified and complicated by its opposite. So, for example, this most "apolitical" of writers was deeply if not overtly political. Similarly, his singularity of vision concerning the transi-tion from page to stage made him extremely sensitive to and notori-ously specific about how his texts should be realized in performance. After watching the young Peter Hall's production of *Endgame* in London for several excruciating nights, Beckett would whisper in anguish to Alan Schneider, "They're doing it ahl wrong." When he learned that the American Repertory Theatre in Boston was setting the play in a burned-out subway tunnel and incorporating music by Philip Glass, an agreement was finally reached that the production could proceed but the program would include an insert written by Beckett: "Any production of *Endgame* which ignores my stage di-rections is completely unacceptable to me." Putting actors through their paces, Beckett often seemed to become as one with his own sadistic autocrats: Pozzo in *Godot,* Clov in *Endgame,* the light in *Play* (which under Schneider's direction was nicknamed Sam), offstage, omnipotent deities in *Act without Words I* and *Happy Days,* and D (Director/Dictator) in *Catastrophe.* He once asked Billie Whitelaw to change a three-dot pause to two dots, and the sensory deprivation he caused her when rehearsing *Not I,* which she thought of as "a form of torture," led Beckett to cry out in anguish, "Oh Billie . . . what have I done to you?" But the rehearsal soon resumed. Perhaps fully acknowledging and finally repudiating his own authoritarian instinct, Beckett's last two plays, depicting that tyranny in the guise of D in *Catastrophe* and V/Bam in *What Where,* license revolt in a way that, with a few notable exceptions, he had largely denied actors and refused to sanction in productions by others.

Yet over the years Beckett came to trust certain actors and directors with whom he had worked closely. He despaired of even trying to answer Alan Schneider's questions about the origins and circumstances of Mouth in *Not I*: "I no more know where she is or why than she does," he wrote. There was only the text and stage image, both of which he had provided for us. "The rest is Ibsen." Schneider nonetheless writes of wishing that Beckett had been present when he was directing—to answer questions, to make his intentions clear, to resolve "all those inevitable differences of opinion or interpretation of each word and each moment," and, especially, "to adapt and change something . . . [that] doesn't seem to be working, or might be more interesting with some slight variation." Schneider had to settle for writing to Beckett and explaining the latest crux in a production and then waiting for the inevitable clarification or else acceptance ("Yes, of course") of the decision he had taken. In response to Schneider's questions about staging *Play,* Beckett wrote: "What matters is that you feel the spirit of the thing and the intention as you do. Give them that as best you can, even if it involves certain deviations from what I have written and said," and ultimately he went so far as to say, "Do it anny way you like, Alan; anny way you like."

As his own director, Beckett's relationship with his texts became highly fluid. Walter Asmus, who worked as Beckett's assistant director on several productions in Berlin, writes that Beckett constantly interrogated and critiqued his own scripts: "He is also open to suggestions any time, and he even asks for them. He is not at all interested in carrying out a rigid concept, but aims for the best possible interpretation of his script." Discovering the need for flexibility and compromise, Beckett altered his plays so that his productions often deviated as much as anyone else's from his published stage directions: the tape recorder in *Krapp* could be played offstage; *Not I*'s Auditor could be omitted; and *Play*'s initially prescribed identical repetition became optional: "The repeat may be an exact replica of first statement or it may present an element of variation."

And, yes, Beckett was instinctively withdrawn and reclusive, avoiding strangers and publicity as much as he could. Yet although the innumerable requests for his time that he received mainly caused him grief and anguish, Beckett was almost invariably kind and polite in response to them: the intruders into his life who asked to meet with him, the actors and directors who sought his assistance, the numerous correspondents and interviewers to whom he revealed more about himself and his life than perhaps he intended—a courtesy that only encouraged more such requests. He had even hoped *not* to receive the Nobel Prize, hiding from the resultant fame to which he felt "damned," declining to go to Sweden to accept the award. Yet unlike Jean-Paul Sartre, he did not refuse the prize—because to do so would, he felt, have broken faith with all those who had long praised and supported his work. And it provided him an opportunity to display his generosity by immediately giving away the prize money.

Beckett was also commonly viewed as a despairing and gloomy writer who portrayed the human condition as, in Hobbes's words, "nasty, brutish, and short." Yet he perhaps came closest to labeling himself accurately when he subtitled *Waiting for Godot* "A Tragicomedy," for he saw the two as inseparable: "Nothing is funnier than unhappiness," as Nell says in *Endgame*. He had a great wit and sense of humor, and his favorite target was himself. The narrator of his short prose piece *Enough* seems to be speaking for and of Beckett: "He was not given to talk. An average of a hundred words per day and night. Spaced out. A bare million in all. Numerous repeats. Ejaculations. Too few for even a cursory survey. What do I know of man's destiny? I could tell you more about radishes"—as he does in *Godot*.

And, finally, he was a deeply pessimistic writer whose very depths seemed to produce its opposite. Beckett actor Jack MacGowran consistently maintained that Beckett's writings were not about despair, but that contained within their silences, repetitions, and sometimes hysterical outbursts lies a profound optimism: "He's written about human distress not human despair. Everything in his work ends with hope. Hope, hope, in everything he writes. I've never met a man with so much compassion for the human race." This is the same note struck so eloquently by the Nobel Prize award: out of "the depths of abhorrence, a despair that has to reach the utmost bounds of suffering to discover that compassion has no bound," he produced work that "rises . . . like a *miserere* from all mankind, its muffled minor key sounding liberation to the oppressed, and comfort to those in need."

Such paradox is extremely rare and far beyond mere ordinary complexity—as Beckett himself seemed to know, and at times sought to articulate. Here is, perhaps, his clearest statement concerning what drove him: "The expression that there is nothing to express, nothing with which to express, nothing from which to express, no power to express, no desire to express, together with the obligation to express." Would Beckett now be willing to offer an AfterWord, to explain exactly what he meant by this statement of what drove him? *Could* he?

Acknowledgments

Grateful acknowledgement is made to the following for permission to reprint previously published materials: Margaret Atwood and Cambridge University Press for "Descent: Negotiating with the Dead," excerpted from *Negotiating with the Dead: A Writer on Writing* (2002); and Cynthia Ozick, Houghton Mifflin, and the Melanie Jackson Agency for "An (Unfortunate) Interview with Henry James," excerpted from *The Din in the Head* (2006).

I would like to record my great debt to Jeffrey Meyers, who read and responded to earlier drafts of the introduction and index, generously helped me to acquire eight of the contributions to this book, and, along with Catherine Aird, suggested ideas for the title.

Notes on the Contributors

CATHERINE AIRD is the author of more than twenty detective novels, the latest of which is *Past Tense* (2010), and two collections of stories, *Injury Time* (1994) and *Chapter and Hearse* (2003). She has edited a number of parish histories and has produced a *son et lumière* and a video on local subjects. She is past chair of the Crime Writers' Association.

BRIAN ALDISS's novel *Walcot* (2008) is the history of one family throughout the twentieth century. He has other novels in the pipeline. His selection of poems, *A Prehistory of Mind*, also appeared in 2008. Meanwhile, along with lecturing, he is working on his isoles (similar to collages, but pure color) and hopes to have an exhibition one day soon.

MARGARET ATWOOD was born in 1939 in Ottawa and grew up in northern Québec, Ontario, and Toronto. She received her undergraduate degree from Victoria College at the University of Toronto and her master's degree from Radcliffe College. Throughout her forty years of writing, she has received numerous awards and honorary degrees. She is the author of more than twenty-five volumes of poetry, fiction, and nonfiction and is perhaps best known for her novels, which include *The Edible Woman* (1969), *Surfacing* (1972), *The Handmaid's Tale* (1985), *Cat's Eye* (1988), *The Robber Bride* (1993), and *Alias Grace* (1996). In 2000 her novel *The Blind Assassin* won the Booker Prize for Fiction. Her work has been published in more than thirty-five languages.

WILLIAM M. CHACE is professor of English and president emeritus of Emory University. He is the author of *100 Semesters: My Adventures as Student, Professor, and University President, and What I Learned along the*

Way (2006); *Lionel Trilling: Criticism and Politics* (1980); and *The Political Identities of Ezra Pound and T. S. Eliot* (1973); as well as numerous essays on twentieth-century British and American writers.

NORA CROOK is emerita professor of English at Anglia Ruskin University, Cambridge, England. She graduated from Newnham College, University of Cambridge, and has lived in the city since then. Her first book was *Shelley's Venomed Melody* (1986), coauthored with Derek Guiton. Her academic career has been largely spent as a critic and editor of the works of Percy Bysshe and Mary Shelley. She is the general editor of twelve volumes of Mary Shelley's writings and is currently the co–general editor, with Donald Reiman and Neil Fraistat, of the *Complete Poetry of Percy Bysshe Shelley* (in progress). She received the Keats-Shelley Association's Distinguished Scholar award in 2006. The quotation from *The Triumph of Life* is taken from *Shelley's Poetry and Prose* (2002), edited by Donald H. Reiman and Neil Fraistat. In order to interweave reality with romance she has drawn on not only the biographers and critics mentioned in the text but also the work of Helen Rossetti Angeli, Betty T. Bennett, Paula R. Feldman, Diana Scott-Kilvert, F. L. Jones, Donald H. Reiman, Charles E. Robinson, and Marion K. Stocking.

PAUL DELANY has written four biographies: of D. H. Lawrence during the Great War (1978), of Rupert Brooke (1987), of Bill Brandt (2004), and, most recently, of George Gissing (2008). He also is the author of *Literature, Money and the Market from Trollope to Amis* (2004). He is emeritus professor of English at Simon Fraser University and lives in Vancouver.

COLIN DEXTER spent all of his working life in education, both as a teacher of classics and as an administrator of school examinations, but he is far better known as the creator of the fictional investigator Inspector Morse. Already the coauthor of three sixth-form textbooks, he began writing crime novels in the early 1970s; the TV series based on his work became a success worldwide. Over the years he has been honored with many awards, including Officer of the Most Excellent Order of the British Empire (OBE) and the rarely conferred Freedom of the City of Oxford. On several occasions he was a national crossword champion; and indeed crossword puzzles, together with Wagner and the reading of the poets, have been the greatest love of his leisure hours.

MARGARET DRABBLE was born in Sheffield in 1939 and educated at York and Cambridge. Her first novel, *A Summer Bird-Cage*, was published in 1963. Since then she has published seventeen novels, most recently *The Sea Lady* (2006). Among her nonfiction works are biographies of Arnold Bennett (1974) and Angus Wilson (1995), and she edited the fifth and sixth editions of *The Oxford Companion to English Literature* (1985, 2000). Her memoir *The Pattern in the Carpet* was published in 2009. Drabble has three children by her first marriage and is married to the biographer Michael Holroyd. They live in London and Somerset.

The late PETER FIRCHOW (1937–2008) was professor of English at the University of Minnesota. His many books include *Aldous Huxley, Satirist and Novelist* (1972), *The Writer's Place: Interviews on the Literary Situation in Contemporary Britain* (1974), *W. H. Auden: Contexts for Poetry* (2002), *Modern Utopian Fiction from H. G. Wells to Iris Murdoch* (2007), and *Strange Meetings: Anglo-German Literary Encounters from 1910 to 1960* (2008). He is also the translator of Friedrich Schlegel's *Lucinde and the Fragments* (1971). Nearly all the details referring to the various characters in his play are based on documental facts, even including the rum that Orwell drank (and hid) and the cigarettes that he smoked while in hospital. Orwell's primary physician, Dr. Andrew Morland, had also treated D. H. Lawrence for tuberculosis in 1929–1930. Alexander Litvinenko did in fact die of Polonium 210 poisoning at the University College Hospital in late 2006. Aside from the two nurses and students, the only purely fictional character in the play is Dr. Smythies.

ALAN W. FRIEDMAN is Thaman Professor of English and Comparative Literature at the University of Texas at Austin, specializing in twentieth-century British and American literature while regularly teaching a Shakespeare seminar; coordinating a residency program, Actors from the London Stage; and working with a student performance organization, Spirit of Shakespeare. He has also taught at universities in England, Ireland, and France. Among his five authored books are *Party Pieces: Oral Storytelling and Social Performance in Joyce and Beckett* (2007) and *Fic-*

tional Death and the Modernist Enterprise (1995, reprinted 2008). His six edited books include *Beckett in Black and Red: The Translations for Nancy Cunard's Negro* (2000). He recently coedited four special issues of journals on Joyce and Beckett. To imagine his encounter with Samuel Beckett, he has drawn on the work of Walter D. Asmus, Anne Atik, Deirdre Bair, Enoch Brater, Robert Brustein, John Fletcher, Lois Gordon, Mel Gussow, Jonathan Kalb, James Knowlson, Alan Schneider, and Israel Shenker, as well as the centenary edition of Beckett's work (edited by Paul Auster) and Beckett's correspondence with Alan Schneider (edited by Maurice Harmon).

EUGENE GOODHEART is Edytha Macy Gross Professor of Humanities Emeritus at Brandeis University. He is the author of eleven works of literary and cultural criticism, including *The Utopian Vision of D. H. Lawrence* (1963), *Desire and Its Discontents* (1991), and *The Reign of Ideology* (1996). His latest book is *Darwinian Misadventures in the Humanities* (2008). In recent years, he has become addicted to the writing of personal essays, a number of which went into the writing of a memoir, *Confessions of a Secular Jew* (2001). "Whistling in the Dark," reflections on aging and mortality, appeared in *Best American Essays of 2006*.

JOHN HALPERIN's books include *Trollope and Politics* (1977), *Gissing: A Life in Books* (1982), *C. P. Snow: An Oral Biography* (1983), *The Life of Jane Austen* (1984), *Jane Austen's Lovers* (essays, 1988), *Novelists in Their Youth* (1990), and *Eminent Georgians* (1995). He is a fellow of the Royal Society of Literature and has twice held Guggenheim Fellowships. He is research professor of English at the Claremont Graduate University.

FRANCIS KING, novelist, biographer, and critic, was born to British parents in Switzerland in 1923. Having graduated from Oxford, he joined the British Council in the immediate aftermath of World War II and served in a number of countries—Italy, Greece, Finland, Egypt, and Japan—that were to provide backgrounds for many of his novels. He was drama critic of the *Sunday Telegraph* for eight years and now reviews regularly for the *Spectator* and the *Literary Review*. His most recently published novel (his fiftieth) is *Cold Snap* (2009). He is a former international president of International PEN and has been decorated by the queen as Commander of the Most Excellent Order of the British Empire (CBE).

JEFFREY MEYERS, a distinguished biographer, has published forty-nine books and more than seven hundred articles on literature, film, and art. He has had thirty works translated into fourteen languages and published on six continents and is one of ten Americans who are fellows of the Royal Society of Literature. In 2005 he received an Award in Literature from the American Academy of Arts and Letters "to honor exceptional achievement." His recent books include *Samuel Johnson: The Struggle* (2008), *The Genius and the Goddess: Arthur Miller and Marilyn Monroe* (2009), *Orwell: Life and Art* (2010), and *John Huston: Courage and Art* (2011).

LAURA NAGY is an educator, editor, writer, and ecologist enjoying the challenge of interdisciplinarity among the academic halls and forested hillsides of northern New England. She holds advanced degrees in English, journalism, and environmental science and is currently doing research for a doctorate in natural resources. She has worked in newspaper, magazine, and book publishing and has taught writing, literature, communications, journalism, and environmental science at several American colleges and universities. Her publications include an eclectic array of journalistic pieces, scholarly essays, short stories, and poetry.

CYNTHIA OZICK is the author of more than a dozen award-winning works of fiction and nonfiction. Her essay collection *Quarrel & Quandary* won the 2001 National Book Critics Circle Award, and her collection *Fame & Folly* was a finalist for the 1996 Pulitzer Prize. Her most recent novel, *Heir to the Glimmery World* (2004), was a New York Times Notable Book and a Book Sense pick and was chosen by NBC's *Today* Book Club.

JAY PARINI, a poet and novelist, teaches at Middlebury College. His most recent volume of poems was *The Art of Subtraction: New and Selected Poems* (2005). He has also written many novels, including *The Last Station* (1990), *Benjamin's Crossing* (1997), and *The Apprentice Lover* (2002). His biographies include the lives of John Steinbeck, Robert Frost, and William Faulkner. He has also written various books of essays and criticism, including *Why Poetry Matters* (2008) and *Promised Land: Thirteen Books that Changed America* (2008). His reviews often appear in journals, including the *Guardian* and the *Chronicle of Higher Education*.

CARL ROLLYSON is a professor of journalism at Baruch College, the City University of New York. He has published biographies of Marilyn Monroe, Lillian Hellman, Martha Gellhorn, Norman Mailer, Rebecca West, and Susan Sontag. He writes frequently about biography and has also published *A Higher Form of Cannibalism? Adventures in the Art and Politics of Biography* (2005) and *Biography: A User's Guide* (2008). He is currently at work on biographies of Amy Lowell and Dana Andrews.

The late ALAN SILLITOE (1928–2010) was one of the most important British writers of the postwar era. His novels include *Saturday Night and Sunday Morning* (1958), *The Loneliness of the Long Distance Runner* (1959), *The Lost Flying Boat* (1985), *The Broken Chariot* (1998), *Birthday* (2001), and *A Man of His Time* (2004). His autobiography, *Life without Armour*, was published in 1996.

ANN THWAITE published many children's books before writing her first biography, *Waiting for the Party: The Life of Frances Hodgson Burnett* (1974). *Edmund Gosse* (1984) and *A. A. Milne* (1990) both won prizes and were published on both sides of the Atlantic. She received a D. Litt. from Oxford University and is a fellow of the Royal Society of Literature. Her two most recent biographies, *Emily Tennyson: The Poet's Wife* (1996) and *Glimpses of the Wonderful: The Life of Philip Henry Gosse* (2002), have been published in the United Kingdom. She and her husband, the poet Anthony Thwaite, live in Norfolk, England; their lives are interrupted from time to time by ten grandchildren. She normally has little time for fantasy. Most of her essay is closely based on fact, though there was obviously no shared railway journey. Gosse and Burnett wrote nearly every one of the words attributed to them as speech.

INDEX